THE SUBMERGED SITE OF LA MARMOTTA (ROME, ITALY)

THE SUBMERGED SITE OF LA MARMOTTA (ROME, ITALY)

DECRYPTING A NEOLITHIC SOCIETY

Edited by

MARIO MINEO, JUAN F. GIBAJA AND NICCOLÒ MAZZUCCO

With contributions from
Eva Andersson, Daniele Arobba, Amaia Arranz, Vittorio Brizzi, Rosanna Caramiello, Laura Caruso-Fermé, Miriam Cubas, Vanessa Forte, Bernard Gassin, Denis Guilbeau, Caroline Hamon, Christina Margariti, Alba Masclans, Lionello F. Morandi, Millán Mozota, Cristiana Petrinelli Pannocchia, Marta Portillo, Gerard Remolins, Mauro Rottoli and Alice Vassanelli

OXBOW | books
Oxford & Philadelphia

Published in the United Kingdom in 2023 by
OXBOW BOOKS
The Old Music Hall, 106–108 Cowley Road, Oxford, OX4 1JE

and in the United States by
OXBOW BOOKS
1950 Lawrence Road, Havertown, PA 19083

Paperback Edition: ISBN 978-1-78925-871-4
Digital Edition: ISBN 978-1-78925-872-1 (epub)

A CIP record for this book is available from the British Library

Library of Congress Control Number: 2023933523

Printed in the United Kingdom by Short Run Press

Typeset in India by Lapiz Digital Services, Chennai.

For a complete list of Oxbow titles, please contact:

UNITED KINGDOM
Oxbow Books
Telephone (0)1226 734350
Email: oxbow@oxbowbooks.com
www.oxbowbooks.com

UNITED STATES OF AMERICA
Oxbow Books
Telephone (610) 853-9131, Fax (610) 853-9146
Email: queries@casemateacademic.com
www.casemateacademic.com/oxbow

Oxbow Books is part of the Casemate Group

Front cover and back cover: © Courtesy of the Museo delle Civiltà – Roma

Contents

Authors

Mario Mineo Museo delle Civiltà – Roma, Piazza Guglielmo Marconi 14, 00144 Rome (Italy), mario.mineo@cultura.gov.it

Juan F. Gibaja Escuela Española de Historia y Arqueología en Roma (EEHAR-CSIC). Via di Sant'Eufemia 13, 00187, Rome (Italy), juan.gibaja@eehar.csic.es

Niccolò Mazzucco Università di Pisa, Dipartimento di Civiltà e Forme del Sapere. Via dei Mille 19, 56126, Pisa (Italy), niccolo.mazzucco@unipi.it

Eva Birgitta Andersson SAXO-Institute – Archaeology, Ethnology, Greek & Latin, History. Karen Blixens Plads 8, 2300 København S, 11B Bygning 11B (Afsnit 2), Building: 11B-1-18 (Denmark), evaandersson@hum.ku.dk

Daniele Arobba Archeologico del Finale, Istituto Internazionale di Studi Liguri, Laboratorio di Archeobotanica, Chiostri di Santa Caterina, 17024 Finale Ligure SV (Italy), arobba@museoarcheofinale.it

Amaia Arranz Ikerbasque Research Associate. Dept. of Geography, Prehistory and Archeology, C/ Tomás y Valiente s/n, 01006 Vitoria-Gasteiz (Spain), amaiaarranz@hotmail.com

Vittorio Brizzi Università di Ferrara, Via M.L.King 29, 40132 Bologna (Italy), vittorio.brizzi@unife.it

Rosanna Caramiello DBios Università di Torino, Viale P.A. Mattioli 25, 10126 Torino (Italy). rosanna.caramiello@unito.it

Laura Caruso-Fermé Instituto Patagónico de Ciencias Sociales y Humanas (IPCSH-CONICET). Boulevard Alte. Brown 2915, 9120, Puerto Madryn, Prov. de Chubut (Argentina), lcarusoferme@gmail.com

Miriam Cubas Universidad de Alcalá, C/Colegios, 2, 28801 Alcalá de Henares, Madrid (Spain), miriam.cubas@uah.es

Vanessa Forte Dipartimento dei Beni Culturali: Archeologia, Storia dell'Arte, del Cinema e della Musica. Università di Padova, Piazza Capitaniato 7, 35139 Padova (Italy), vanz.forte@gmail.com

Bernard Gassin Chercheur associé, Travaux et recherches archéologiques sur les cultures, les espaces et les sociétés (TRACES, UMR 5608), Université Toulouse Jean Jaurès Maison de la Recherche, 5, allées Antonio Machado, 31058 Toulouse cedex 9 (France), bernardgassin7@gmail.com

Denis Guilbeau Ministère de la culture, UMR5140 Archéologie des Sociétés Méditerranéennes. Université Paul Valéry, site de Saint-Charles 2, rue du Professeur Henri Serre, 34090 Montpellier (France), denis.guilbeau@culture.gouv.fr

Caroline Hamon CNRS Permanent Researcher, UMR 8215 Trajectoires 9 rue Mahler, 75004 Paris (France), caroline.hamon@cnrs.fr

Christina Margariti Applied Research Department, Directorate of Conservation of Ancient and Modern Monuments, Hellenic Ministry of Culture, 81 Pan. Tsaldari (Pireos) Avenue, 10553 Athens (Greece), chmargariti@culture.gr

Alba Masclans Indi Group. Department of Archaeology and Anthropology. Milà i Fontanals Institution. Spanish National Research Council, C/ Egipcíaques 15, 08001 Barcelona (Spain), alba.masc@gmail.com

Lionello F. Morandi Competence Center Archaeometry Baden-Württemberg, Eberhard-Karls-Universität Tübingen,

Wilhelm Str. 56, 72074 Tübingen (Germany), lionello.morandi@uni-tuebingen.de

Millán Mozota Indi Group. Department of Archaeology and Anthropology. Milà i Fontanals Institution. Spanish National Research Council, C/ Egipcíaques 15, 08001 Barcelona (Spain), millanmozota@gmail.com

Cristiana Petrinelli Pannocchia Università di Pisa, Dipartimento di Civiltà e Forme del Sapere. Via dei Mille 19, 56126, Pisa (Italy), cristiana.petrinelli@unipi.it

Marta Portillo Archaeology of Social Dynamics Research Group. Department of Archaeology and Anthropology. Milà i Fontanals Institution. Spanish National Research Council, C/ Egipcíaques 15, 08001 Barcelona (Spain), mportillo@imf.csic.es

Gerard Remolins Regirarocs, S.L. Plaza de les Homilies 6, 25794 Organyà, Lleida (Spain), menairo@hotmail.com

Mauro Rottoli Laboratorio di Archeobiologia dei Musei Civici di Como. Piazza Medaglie d'Oro 1, 22100 Como (Italy), archeobotanica@gmail.com

Alice Vassanelli Università di Pisa, Dipartimento di Civiltà e Forme del Sapere. Via dei Mille 19, 56126, Pisa (Italy), alice.vassanelli@cfs.unipi.it

Acknowledgements

We feel obliged to dedicate this page to the many friends, researchers and colleagues who, since 1989, have to a greater or lesser extent participated in and/or collaborated with the excavation campaigns, documentation, restoration, study, determination, dating, etc. of the materials from the submerged Neolithic village of 'La Marmotta', all special people in their own way (Fig. 0.1).

We are especially grateful to the Director of the Museo delle Civiltà F.M. Gambari who honoured us with his friendship and trust in this research; to Dr Maria A. Fugazzola, organiser and director of the excavations from 1989 to 2009 and the creator of this exceptional discovery and collection of archaeological material; to dear Fabio Faccenna, volcanic archaeologist; to Euro Cerioni, a brilliant site manager who was always ready to solve any problem that arose during the work; to all the exceptional underwater technicians who took turns in the various excavation campaigns; and to the wonderful restorers in the Museo delle Civiltà (formerly Museo Nazionale Preistorico Etnografico 'L. Pigorini'), who have restored the immense number of ceramic and wooden remains etc. from the excavation.

A heartfelt thank you also goes to all the most recent collaborators of the research staff built together since 2018 by the Museo delle Civiltà, CSIC (Milà i Fontanals Institut, IMF-CSIC; and Spanish School of History and Archaeology of Rome, the EEHAR-CSIC), Pisa University and all the team from different institutions that worked at La Marmotta. Several projects funded by the Ministry of Science and Innovation of Spain, Agencia Estatal de Investigación of Spain, CSIC, Marie-Skłodowska Curie European Program and Ministry for University and Research of Italy have resulted from this collaboration: PID2020-112513RB-I00, HAR2016-75201-P, PIAR-201818008, PIAR-201918010, QUANT-792544 and Rita Levi Montalcini project-AGER. The photographs of La Marmotta and the archaeological artefacts were kindly ceded by the Museo delle Civiltà.

Sincere thanks go, in particular, to those colleagues who had started to study some of these materials but then could not continue because their careers took other paths. But special thanks also go to the perseverance and constancy in not abandoning the research that brought us to this result.

Finally, we would like to thank Peter Smith for the translation of some chapters of this book and Eva Martínez Bajo for her work with the databases and photo editing.

Figure 0.1. We would like to thank all our colleagues who worked at La Marmotta. Thanks to them, today we can continue studying the remains from this magnificent site and have been able to publish this book. We are aware that not everyone who took part is here, but this photographic montage stands for them all.

Prologue, Director General of Museums of Italy

This volume, which I have the pleasure of introducing, deals with the archaeological materials from the submerged Neolithic site of 'La Marmotta' (Anguillara Sabazia, Rome), one of the most relevant archaeological discoveries of the last decades.

The publication of the La Marmotta materials is an important event, part of a broader framework involving the re-organization and promotion of the prehistoric collections in the Museo delle Civiltà (MuCiv, Rome), recently carried out under the guidance of the Directorate General of Museums in the Ministry of Culture of Italy. The materials recovered from the excavation of 'La Marmotta' are at the core of the new exhibition in the Museo and offer an essential testimony of the life of the first farming communities in the Neolithic period, almost 8000 years ago.

The site of La Marmotta, located on the southern shore of Lake Bracciano, was first excavated in 1989 under the coordination of the then Superintendence of the 'L. Pigorini' National Museum of Prehistory and Ethnography, which merged into the current Museo delle Civiltà in 2016.

Even if during the last decades several articles about the site have been published, a unitary and monographic publication on the site and its materials was missing. The amazing state of preservation of the inorganic and organic remains makes La Marmotta an exceptional site, a sort of 'prehistoric Pompeii'. This volume therefore presents, for the first time, an updated view of research on this lakeshore site, including the most recent results obtained within the framework of a collaboration agreement between the Museo delle Civiltà (Italy) and the Consejo Superior de Investigaciones Científicas CSIC (Spain), which since 2017 have been conducting a new series of studies on the materials recovered from the site and conserved in Rome, at the Museo delle Civiltà. The various chapters of this book offer a first interpretation of the site and of its numerous and varied archaeological features, especially focusing on the study of the wooden and stone tools related to agriculture, navigation, basketry and textile production. The number of archaeological artefacts found at La Marmotta is enormous if compared with other Mediterranean Early Neolithic sites, and this volume provides a careful revision and digitalization of the available evidence, including plans and photographic documentation. Through the various contributions, the reader will explore the wealth of La Marmotta, discovering the huge variety of finds that can be recovered from wetland sites but that usually disappear in dry contexts. Among the most amazing materials that are included in this volume, we cannot forget the five large monoxylon canoes. These finds represent the most complete and exceptional testimony of Neolithic navigation, a unique discovery that sheds light on the navigation techniques and knowledge of the first river- and sea-faring farming communities in Europe.

In conclusion, this volume provides the necessary basis for a better understanding of the Neolithic phenomenon and its arrival into Italy. Much work is still to be done on this site and many aspects need to be discussed further. Pottery, faunal and plant macro-remains, and dendochronological data all need to be included in future research. However, the publication of these first results represents a necessary step towards the valorisation and diffusion of La Marmotta site and of its exceptional heritage. This volume also reflects the important role played by the Superintendences, the National Museums and the Ministry of Culture in conserving, promoting and increasing national heritage.

Massimo Osanna
Direttore Generale Musei
Ministero della Cultura

Prologue, Director of the Museo delle Civiltà

This volume testifies to the importance of studying the changes that have occurred in the relationships between human beings and the natural environment in the course of history. This topic is at the core of the Museo delle Civiltà prehistoric exhibition, which has been recently rearranged to put human-environment relationships at its centre. And La Marmotta holds a special place in this narrative.

Thanks to the research conducted by an international team established in 2017, born from the collaboration between the Museo delle Civiltà and the Consejo Superior de Investigaciones Científicas (CSIC), this volume documents how human communities became engaged in food production; breeding livestock and cultivating a wide range of plants. The archaeological materials recovered from the excavation of the Neolithic village of 'La Marmotta', submerged in the waters of Lake Bracciano, provide invaluable evidence of how prehistoric people developed new ways of exploiting the ecosystem, moving from hunter-gathering to farming. A transition that led to a definitive change in the human way of life and that, in this volume, is reconstructed from the viewpoint of a plurality of multidisciplinary analyses. Through the chapters of this book, Neolithic La Marmotta is reconstructed by the study of a huge diversity of artefacts made from organic raw materials, such as wood and bone, or from inorganic ones, such as stone, but also dwelling and housing structures, faunal remains, etc.

The lakeshore site of 'La Marmotta', sealed by three metres of sterile silt and submerged under nine metres of water, is characterised by an exceptional state of conservation of the archaeological remains. In normal, dry, conditions, materials such as leaves, fruits, seeds and non-charred wood would decay rapidly. This does not happen when the organic materials are submerged in water or deposited in wetland contexts where the low oxygen content considerably slows down the decomposition process. Furthermore, in plant cells, the decomposed material is replaced by water, allowing the original shape to be preserved and identified even after thousands of years. Consequently La Marmotta, with its richness of organic remains, represents a unique archive for reconstructing the prehistoric landscape and the beginning of its anthropic exploitation.

Thanks to the palaeobotanical study of these remains – uncharred remains of wood, leaves, parts of fruits (wild and cultivated), including nuts and seeds – it has been possible to recreate the techniques used to make textiles and ropes, prepare medicinal plants for curative purposes and food for both the human and animal diet. La Marmotta offers the opportunity of gaining precious insights into Neolithic food practices. Numerous food remains were recovered from the excavation: aggregates of cereals mixed with meat or unleavened 'bread-like' products, prepared with wheat and barley flours mixed with water. Some of these ancient 'loaves' even conserve the impression of the vegetal mat on which they were prepared, before being baked on hot stones.

The authors also investigated the use of plants in the phytotherapeutic field, through the presence of poppy seeds and capsules that attest the first domestication of *Papaver setigerum* and the consequent evolution of *Papaver somniferum*. The plant was presumably harvested and/or cultivated as food, but its use for its psychotropic properties should not be ruled out. Ten fragments of mushrooms belonging to the genus *Daedalopsis Tricolor*, used for the control of hypothermia, have been also recovered in the La Marmotta excavations, in addition to the large number of seeds of wild saffron (*Carthamus lanatus*) and Madonna thistle (*Silybum marianum*), that are still used today for these same purposes.

This volume offers an amazing overview on the early tools used for cultivating and transforming the products obtained from agriculture and livestock. For example, tools used for agricultural activities (sickles), for cutting wood (axes and adzes), for the manufacture of pottery (spatulas) and for working leather (awls). Exceptional finds are also ropes and woven baskets. Many remains are also the architectural elements of the wooden houses, which testify how the inhabitants of La Marmotta were skilled craftsmen. About 3,400 wooden posts, which constituted the bare structure for roofs and walls, most of them still standing in the waterlogged soil, were recovered and analysed.

Building educational narratives from all this fascinating evidence is one of the main goals of the Museo delle Civiltà, whose aim is to bring a remote past into life and to share a multiplicity of perspectives on past human civilizations, their mutual relationships and their relation with our planet.

Andrea Viliani
Direttore
Museo delle Civiltà, Roma

1

Introduction to the volume: La Marmotta, an exceptional Neolithic site

Mario Mineo, Juan F. Gibaja and Niccolò Mazzucco

The objective of this volume is to present some of the most important aspects of the life, material culture and knowledge of the first Neolithic farming groups that settled in the modern region of Lazio in the centre of the Italian Peninsula and, more precisely, of the population that lived at the site of La Marmotta, Anguillara, Sabazia on the southern shore of Lake Bracciano (Figs 1.1 and 1.2).

The timeframe being studied covers much of the second half of the sixth millennium cal BC, which corresponds to the Tyrrhenian cardial phase of the Italian Neolithic and to the populations that gradually travelled westwards until they reached the Atlantic seaboard of Portugal (Guilaine 2000–2001; Gronenborn 2009; Maninnen 2014; Shennan 2018). The heritage carried by those communities as they left their homes in search of new territories explains why the first Neolithic sites in south-east France and the east and south of the Iberian Peninsula still display reminiscences of that Tyrrhenian and cardial past in their ceramics.

Probably sailing by pilotage means navigation with shoreline in sight with the shore permanently in sight, those first Neolithic populations travelled around the Mediterranean Sea in their dugout canoes. They also crossed open sea, from island to island, and settled in the most favourable places for their crops of wheat, barley and pulses, where they could look after their livestock, make their pottery and stone tools, fabricate their ornaments and, in short, establish their way of life. These first Neolithic settlers must have been sailors in order to travel those long distances but they were mainly farmers in their economic system and subsistence strategies.

One of the peculiarities defining these communities is the way they decorated their pottery with impressed motifs made with the edge of *Cardium edulis* shells, or with their fingers and nails, or by incision with different kinds of implements. Perhaps with that decoration they aimed to show their link to the sea and their identity, in an expansion process that was culturally unified in the territories they occupied in the western Mediterranean. Although the pottery of those populations shared the impressed-cardial decoration, the motifs and forms of the recipients obviously changed over time to reflect regional differences as the groups adapted to different

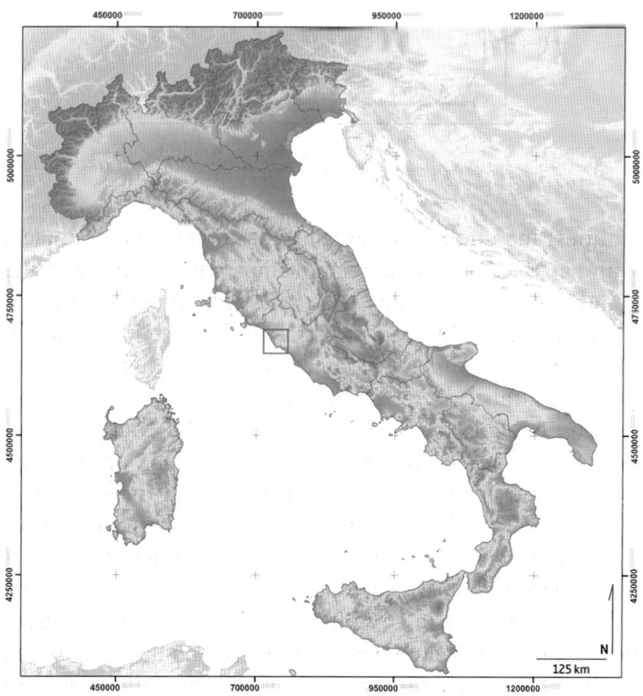

Figure 1.1. Location of the La Marmotta site in the centre of the Italian Peninsula.

Figure 1.2. Location map of Lake Bracciano where the site of La Marmotta was found.

realities: the quality of the land, the forest cover, contacts with native populations, relationships with other Neolithic communities, etc. In any case, the decorations on cardial wares now allow archaeologists to follow the long journey of those communities from one shore to another across the whole central-western Mediterranean.

This book is devoted to the site of La Marmotta, an outstanding site occupied by the first farming groups that lived in the centre of the Italian Peninsula for 430 years (from *c.* 5690 to 5260 cal BC). While the number of archaeological remains that have been found is huge, the site is really exceptional because many of those remains can be considered unique in a Neolithic setting and, even more so, because new archaeological analytical techniques have been applied to many of the remains which has allowed us to approach the way of life of the community at La Marmotta and some aspects of their social organisation. That organisation is not always easy to interpret from archaeological remains but our understanding is gradually improving. The re-appraisal of remains excavated over 15 years ago and the development of a full programme of studies will enable a fuller comprehension of the people who lived there and whose experiences we are discovering (Fig.1.3).

In this way, the new inter-disciplinary approach and the refinement of methodologies applied to the study of prehistoric remains will provide more precise knowledge about the most concrete aspects: the archaeological artefacts that have been found, the technology they used, and the age of the site and the objects, and also more general traits: social, economic and political organisation, as well as the symbolic and ideological realm. Thus, the multi-disciplinary character of the research, which combines skills in human and experimental sciences (archaeology, anthropology, palaeobotany, palaeoclimatology, bioanthropology, archaeozoology, etc.) will allow increasingly reliable and solid historical interpretations to be drafted and proposed.

Figure 1.3. (Left) view of Lake Bracciano; (right) underwater excavation at the La Marmotta site.

This book presents a general, but still preliminary, overview of the information obtained about the extraordinary artefacts, many of them organic, that were found in the excavations at La Marmotta: canoes, sickles, bows, textiles, baskets and many more. However, it does not omit other implements, like those of stone that were used to create the objects made of wood and plant fibre. Therefore, a short chapter is devoted to those lithic tools because of their use with the organic objects. However, as we focus on the utensils, recipients and ornaments made from wood, other kinds of artefacts, like the pottery, receive less attention here. The ceramic assemblage consists of thousands of remains; many of them complete vessels thanks to the rapid sedimentation that buried the site. They have provided an amazing picture of the array of sizes, shapes and decoration that existed (Fugazzola 2002; Delpino 2020).

However, if there was one thing that completely changed our image of Neolithic societies, it was the discovery of five large dugout canoes. These boats demonstrate the great technical skill acquired by Neolithic artisans in working with wood and also in sailing. They were veritable shipbuilders who, with those monoxylons, were able to travel across the sea or simply on Lake Bracciano itself. The canoes also testify to the relationships and exchanges maintained with other communities on the islands and shores of the Mediterranean. They were solid boats of a considerable size, nearly 11 m long, which, as will be explained later, may have been equipped with poles attached to a stabilising board or even a second canoe, like a catamaran. In any case, their characteristics allowed stable maritime travel and the transport of people, animals and materials over several nautical miles.

The large size of at least two of the five canoes at La Marmotta (Number I: 10.43 m long by 1.15 m wide at the stern and 0.85 m at the bow; Number V: 9.50 m long by a maximum width of 60 cm at the stern: this canoe is in the process of being restored) seems excessive for a use solely on Lake Bracciano. It is possible that at the time when those monoxylons were made, the Mediterranean coastline was not as far away as it is now, and it might have been possible to sail there along the River Arrone. The river would have been a route from the settlement to the sea, which would have allowed a means of exchange, social relations with other communities and ease of travel to other territories.

The seasonal or permanent occupation of a territory or an island would be a complex operation that would have to be planned. It implied the transport of large loads of people, animals and supplies, and success depended on technical and organisational ability in order to sail in large and safe boats. It was not only a matter of the technical skills involved in making the dugouts but also of knowledge of navigation on the open sea and the best routes to follow. Sailors do not usually go to sea without knowing what lies ahead and the problems they might find. This information must have been handed down from generation to generation. If these premises are correct, we should accept the idea that the art of navigation and the exploitation of marine resources was a very early activity that pre-dated the Neolithic. The Mesolithic might have been the key time for the development of navigation and the use of all that the sea had to offer. This would explain, for example, the canoes that have been found belonging to that time, the numerous fishing utensils, the location of settlements near the coast and estuaries, and the consumption of food from the sea as detected in studies of human remains (Meiklejohn *et al.* 2009; Fontanals-Coll *et al.* 2014; Gibaja *et al.* 2015; Lo Vetro and Martini 2016).

Clearly, many other aspects of the Neolithic are being addressed through the numerous studies that are now being carried out: chronology, the routes of expansion and the territories occupied, the ways in which the communities acquired and produced food, changes in the diet, the range of productive activities, the division of labour and social roles based on the gender and age of the individuals, social organisation, rituals and funerary and cultural practices, the symbolic sphere, contacts and exchange networks on and between islands in the central Mediterranean, and so on. We are sure that La Marmotta will play a significant role in all these fields of study and it will become a point of reference for the scientific community studying that period in human history.

La Marmotta is one of those sites that are radically altering our conception of prehistory and human communities in the past. In this book, readers will discover an astonishing site that has preserved implements and objects never seen before or that are little known at other settlements. We aim to make these scarcely published artefacts known to the scientific community. Turning these pages is, in short, like opening a door to the past.

2

La Marmotta site in the framework of the Mediterranean Early Neolithic

Niccolò Mazzucco, Juan Gibaja and Mario Mineo

The Near-Eastern roots of the Mediterranean Neolithic

The establishment of a village on the shores of the Lake Bracciano, *c.* 5690 years cal BC, was part of a much larger process of expansion of farming populations that started approximately 1000 years before. Until the end of the seventh millennium cal BC, Neolithic farming remained limited to a large 'core zone' located in south-western Asia, to which the wild progenitors of the different domesticated plant and animal species were native. This area comprises territories located in the Fertile Crescent, south western Anatolia, the Central Zagros, and Cyprus. The so-called Neolithisation process, tied to the domestication of plants and animals, the emergence of sedentism and village life, craft specialisation, monumentality, new forms of symbolic expression and burial practices, and exchange and trade networks, had taken place gradually (but perhaps discontinuously) in this core zone since the Upper Palaeolithic (Verhoeven 2011; Ibáñez *et al.* 2018).

How, when, and why farmer communities started moving from these regions towards Europe, Africa and the rest of Asia has been a huge topic of debate among scholars. It is generally agreed that population expansion began between the end of the Pre-Pottery Neolithic (PPNB) and the emergence of the first ceramic cultures, the Pottery Neolithic (PN). Indeed, this phase of expansion coincided with the disruption of the cultural unit of the PPNB world and has been variously interpreted as the outcome of different processes: environmental changes pushing farmers towards new exploitable territories; increasing population pressure and conflicts and the consequent social and territorial restructuration; and acculturation of neighbouring indigenous hunter-gathering populations (Asouti 2006; Watkins 2008).

Towards 6700 cal BC, the Neolithic reached the westernmost coasts of Anatolia and the Aegean Sea. Sites such as Çukuriçi Höyük and Ulucak Höyük, located at the centre of the western Anatolian coast, or the early layers found under the palace of Knossos, at Crete, represent the first Neolithic farming villagers outside the Neolithic core zone (Bar-Yosef 2019). Sites like Paliambella, Revenia, Mavropigi-Fillotsairi (Greek Macedonia) Sesklo, Argissa, Prodromos II (Thessaly), and Franchthi Cave (Peloponnese) represent the earliest Neolithic occupations on the European mainland (Reingruber *et al.* 2017; Horejs 2019; Maniatis and Adaktylou 2021). Neolithic settlers brought with them a complex set of innovations, including domesticated cultivars and animal species, mud-brick architecture, sickles, polished and ground stone technology and, probably from the earliest phases, pottery. Despite that, several transformations are observable in the first European Neolithic cultures compared with south-western Asia. Several components of the Near-Eastern archaeological cultures disappeared, while other, original, elements were introduced. This can be documented in all spheres of society: subsistence, technology, architecture, village organisation and symbolic and aesthetic expression (Perlès 2005; Özdogan 2008). Whether such changes were due to spontaneous transformations of the migrant groups, possibly because of the changing social and environmental conditions encountered in the newly occupied territories, or because of the influence of the indigenous, hunter-gatherer populations already inhabiting the area of Neolithic expansion, is a complex subject of discussion. Most likely, both scenarios occurred and interacted.

The successive expansion towards the west and north occurred a few centuries after the first arrival of migrant farmers in south-eastern Europe, around 6000 cal BC.

After 700–500 years from their first arrival in south-eastern Europe, just as abruptly, Neolithic communities started moving again towards new territories, such as the Adriatic and the central Balkans. That slowdown in the expansion process would correspond to a further phase of recomposition and adaptation of the Neolithic package to all those above-mentioned changing conditions: climate, environmental, demographic and social factors (Guilaine 2017; Ivanova *et al.* 2018; Krauß *et al.* 2018). New cultural entities have been defined by archaeologists to describe these transformations of the Neolithic material culture (i.e. Karanovo, Starčevo–Körös–Criş, Impresso-Cardial, LBK, etc.), highlighting differences at a regional scale, with special attention to changes in pottery production and decorative styles. However, in all newly colonised areas, despite local variations, a fully developed farming economy based on a broad variety of domesticated plants (emmer, einkorn, barley and pulses) and animals (sheep, goat, cattle and pigs), is attested from its first arrival. Exogenous species were introduced, new habitats were created. Waterways, both rivers and the sea, probably played a fundamental role in these successive expansions, with a very rapid advance along the Danube–Rhine corridor and the Mediterranean coastline, for example.

During the last decades, scholars have tried to model the speed and rate of diffusion through mathematical modelling, obtaining varying results (Fort 2022), from 1 km/yr up to 10 km/yr. What we know for sure is that in ~ 600–800 years the Neolithic reached the Atlantic shores of the Iberian Peninsula and the lowlands of Central Europe. However, although the Neolithic expansion into Europe seems to have been a continuous, unidirectional, westward progression, on a closer look it better resembles a mosaic of different paths and rhythms of spread, with less directionality than is perceived by observing it at the continental scale. It should not be forgotten that the Neolithisation of Europe occurred on a very short time scale, a few centuries, and the resolution of radiocarbon chronology, and the archaeological record itself, does not allow us to detect processes of change that might occur at speeds and scales out of reach of our current methods and capabilities (Vierra and Carvalho 2019).

The Central Mediterranean Neolithic

During their spread towards the west, in the Central Mediterranean Neolithic cultures assume specific features that clearly differentiate them from the northern (i.e. Central Europe) and southern societies (i.e. north Africa). As stated above, a recomposition and re-assessment of the Neolithic material culture is observable. The larger and more densely inhabited mudbrick and stone villages of the Eastern Mediterranean gave way to smaller, ditched, villages, with sparse rectangular houses made of stone, wood and daub. Several examples of Neolithic houses have been excavated, as in the recent case of Lugo di Romagna in central Italy (Degasperi and Steffè 2019).

As the result of maritime expansion, the new pioneer settlements were dominantly established along the Mediterranean coasts, at least in the early phases. However, not only were open-air villages founded, but caves and rock-shelters were also used by groups of farmers and herders as dwelling spaces (Angelucci *et al.* 2009; Mazzucco *et al.* 2015). Contrary to what might be thought, during the Early Neolithic caves were not only used as specialised spaces for specific activities, for example for animal penning or as hunting shelters, but they often bear evidence of domestic everyday activities (e.g., food consumption and preparation, artefact manufacture and maintenance, symbolic behaviour). This pattern of land occupation is quite different from the Eastern Mediterranean Neolithic, where caves or rock-shelters were only marginally used, at least until the later phases of the Neolithic (Halstead 2000). Another important difference is that, at first sight, artefactual abundancy and complexity at most of the sites in the Central and Western Mediterranean appear to be much reduced compared with the Eastern Mediterranean Neolithic. However, conservation issues and excavation strategies are possibly biasing our perception of the Mediterranean Neolithic. At most of those sites, occupational surfaces are not preserved, and most of the information comes from negative features such as pits, postholes and ditches. The expansion and the extension of large-scale mechanised agriculture in Europe have surely impacted the preservation of the open-air sites located on agricultural soils.

The earliest Neolithic of the Mediterranean area is found, almost contemporaneously, in south Italy and on the Adriatic shores of Greece, Albania and Croatia, towards 6100–5900 cal BC (Binder *et al.* 2017). Sites are characterised by pottery sherds with rows and sequences of impressions made by means of different tools, such as shells, bones, wooden sticks or by hand (i.e. Impressed Ware) (Fig. 2.1). One of the areas where Impressed Ware sites were first documented and show a greater density is the Tavoliere area (Apulia, Italy). Here, ditched Neolithic villages were first discovered from the air during the Second World War, in the 1940s, when Sir John Bradford recognised them from vegetation marks visible on aerial photos taken by the Royal Air Force and United States Army Air Forces (Whitehouse 2014), with almost 800 documented and georeferenced sites. Even though many of those sites bear occupational layers of later chronology (i.e. Middle and Late Neolithic), still the number of Early Neolithic sites in the region is remarkable.

From here, after a brief phase of local evolution (from Archaic to Evolved Impressed Ware), the Neolithic spread rapidly northward and westward. Approximately around 5800–5700 cal BC Neolithic groups bearing Impressed Ware settled in Abruzzo (Central Italy), ~ 200 km from the Tavoliere, but also reached Liguria, at the Arene Candide

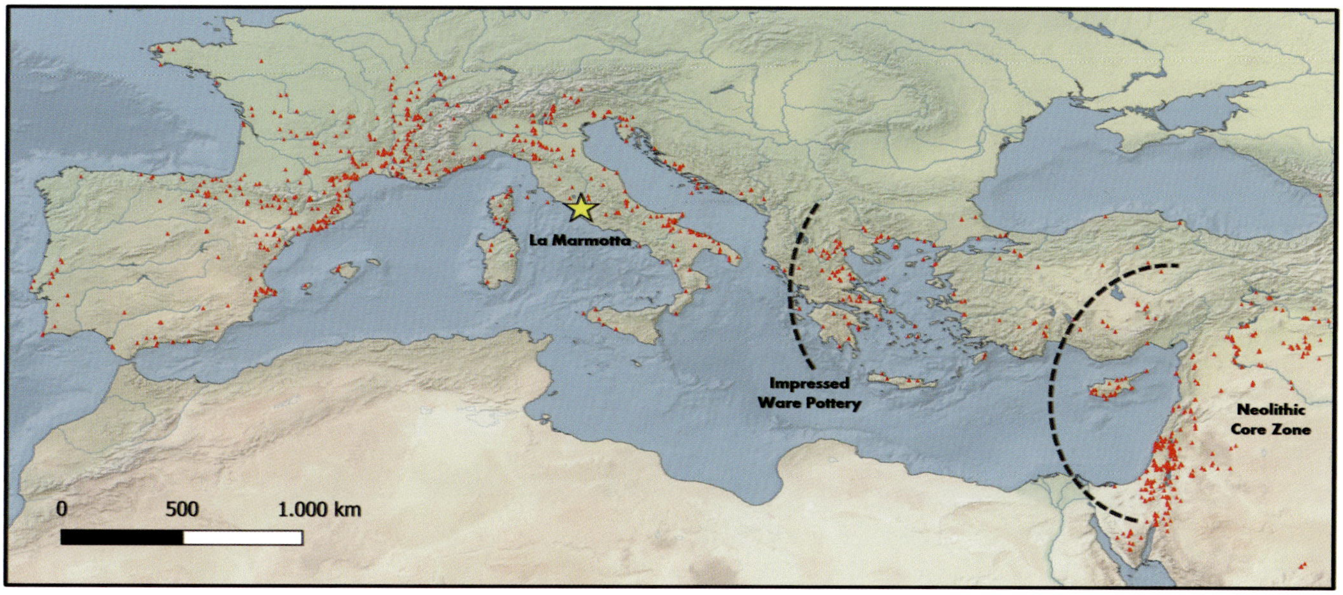

Figure 2.1. Map of the Mediterranean and south-west Asian Neolithic, between c. *14,000 and 5000 BP. Sites has been taken from NeoNet (Huet* et al. *2022) and Nerd datasets (Palmisano* et al. *2022). The western limit of the Neolithic Core Zone and the eastern limit of the Impressed Ware distribution are indicated. (Map realised with QGis v.3.26.3 using Natural Earth data).*

and San Sebastiano di Perti, or Peiro Signado and Pont de Roque-Haute in the Gulf of Lyon. Long-distance maritime travel was probably responsible for such rapid diffusion (Gabriele *et al.* 2019), with archaeological materials that were tracked up to 1000 km from their sources. However, Neolithic groups gradually spread also by inland routes, most likely using both rivers and terrestrial paths, as documented by the numerous sites in the inner areas, and settled in the valley bottoms but also at mid-altitudes and in mountain areas (Radi and Pannocchia 2018).

La Marmotta, located on the shores of Lake Bracciano, probably belongs to this phase of expansion, between 5690 and 5260 cal BC, in which Peninsular Italy was permeated in a more capillary way by Neolithic groups (Fig. 2.2). Nevertheless, La Marmotta might be used simultaneously as both a good and a poor example of a Mediterranean Neolithic site. On the one hand, it perfectly exemplifies the arrival of a community of farmers in inland territories. Lakes represented attractive ecosystems for Neolithic communities, and it is not by chance that several Neolithic occupations are known near both large and small lakes from the early phases of the period: Lake of San Lorenzo, Lake Paterno, Lake Trasimeno and Lake Varese. On the other hand, the extraordinary conditions of preservation, the abundancy of recovered materials and the considerable extent of the excavated surface, make it hard to compare La Marmotta with the surrounding Neolithic sites in dry environments. The comparison between sites excavated in wetlands and on dry land is always compelling because of the diversity of the two archaeological records. In general terms, we should be able to assume that all those aspects that are unique to wetland sites (i.e. preservation of organic matter, organic components of abiotic artefacts, a less fragmentary record, etc.) should have been originally present also at dry land sites and they are missing only because of the different preservation conditions. Alternatively, some sites might have been more important or richer than others and so certain classes of materials might be missing because of the different role played by a site within the local exchange network, or because of its territorial and/or political prominence. What we know regarding La Marmotta is that it was fully embedded in the exchange network of the Mediterranean Early Neolithic, a sort of point of juncture between the Tyrrhenian and Adriatic sides and between the Alpine and Mediterranean worlds. Although most of the data come from preliminary or pilot studies, it is acknowledged that a diversity of exogenous raw materials arrived at La Marmotta and that the inhabitants of the site shared technical knowledge with different neighbouring groups.

Obsidian from Lipari and Palmarola islands (Tyrrhenian Sea) arrived at La Marmotta in abundant quantities (De Francesco *et al.* 2012). A few axes of HP-metaophiolites of probable Alpine provenance (north Italy) have been recovered from the underwater excavations (D'Amico *et al* 2004). Preliminary data also suggest that chert from Gargano outcrops (south Italy) also reached the site. Figulina pottery, widespread along the Adriatic coastline, where it appeared around the middle of the sixth millennium cal BC, has also been recovered at La Marmotta (Spataro 2002).

This evidence, despite being fragmentary, suggests that La Marmotta was part of local, regional and supra-regional

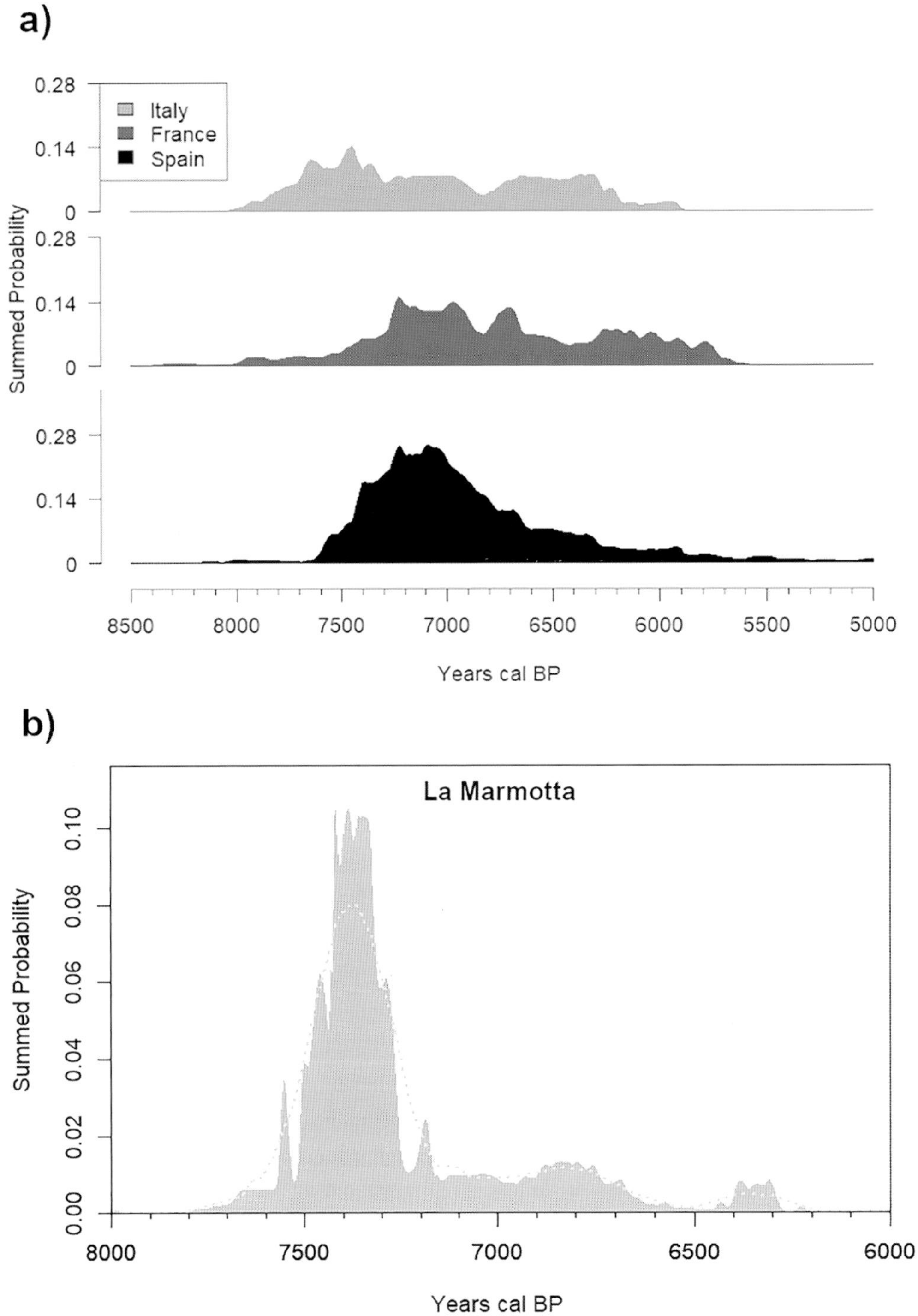

Figure 2.2. a) Summed Probability Distributions (SPD) for France, Italy and Spain obtained from 747 dates from the NeoNet dataset (Huet et al. *2022). Only short-lived samples (*i.e., *plant seed, animal bone, human bone) with SD<90 have been selected; b) SPD of La Marmotta dating. All SPDs have been realised with Rcarbon package (Crema and Bevan 2021).*

networks of exchange of materials and know-how that connected Mediterranean Neolithic communities and people over large territories. In the future, a more detailed study of pottery and polished and flaked stone tool assemblages, as well as other categories of materials such as beads and other ornaments, wooden artefacts, etc., will enable a better understanding of the role of the site within these cultural and economic networks. As, for example, demonstrated by the study of the carpological remains, we know that La Marmotta not only received 'stimuli', but was also a centre of innovation.

Recent research has proved that La Marmotta is the earliest site in Europe with direct evidence of the domesticated poppy (Salavert *et al.* 2020). Poppy is one of the few proven cases of domestication occurring outside the Neolithic core zone, providing further proof of the multiple processes of innovation and cultural recomposition that farming communities experienced during their spread from south-western Asia. The extent to which those processes of change were stimulated by the encounter and mixing with local hunter-gatherer populations or from spontaneous adaptations is still to be determined. This is, of course, complicated because of the scarce knowledge that we have of the Late Mesolithic communities and of the ephemeral character of this kind of process, but recently genetic studies have provided evidence for Mesolithic–Neolithic admixtures (Rivollat *et al.* 2020), suggesting that the emergence of certain technical traditions may be associated with farmer–hunter-gatherer interactions. Ongoing research, as currently being carried out at La Marmotta, is adding fresh and stimulating evidence to this debate and the paths of the Mediterranean Neolithic will certainly be revealed in the coming decades.

3

La Marmotta: location, history, stratigraphy and cultural sequence, chronology

Mario Mineo, Juan F. Gibaja, Niccolò Mazzucco and Gerard Remolins

La Marmotta is a *Pompeii-type* of site. That is to say, it can be regarded as unique and exceptional because of the quantity, quality and characteristics of the many thousands of archaeological remains that have been found. Many of them, made of organic substances, are rarely encountered on Neolithic sites or have never been seen before: canoes, bows, sickles, baskets, ropes, textiles, etc. The review of the remains has not been able to determine the exact number of finds. This is because the archive includes bags containing just one object and reference number and others containing several items identified with a single number for all. This occurs especially with the potsherds and lithic artefacts. However, in the last fieldwork season in 2009, the last reference number issued was 51,608. In any case, we can be sure that study of these remains will imply rewriting many aspects of the life of the first Neolithic communities that occupied the central-western Mediterranean as they spread from the Near East several centuries before. La Marmotta represents a sea change in archaeological research and will become a point of reference in both the academic world and outside it.

In April 1989, in the locality of La Marmotta, works were carried out on the bottom of the lake on behalf of the Azienda Comunale Elettricità ed Acque di Roma, for the positioning in water of the pipelines of a new aqueduct. About 360 m from the shore and at a depth of about 9 m, under 2.5 m of silt on the bottom of the lake, the excavator dredge encountered an archaeological deposit, rich both in wooden poles and planks and ceramic materials attributable to Neolithic times. The Superintendence to the National Prehistoric Ethnographic Museum L. Pigorini (henceforth SMNPE L. Pigorini) immediately began a short fieldwork season, directed by Dr Maria Antonietta Fugazzola Delpino, aimed both at the recovery of the materials disturbed by the dredger and at the rescue excavation of the trench sector, still intact, which would have been affected by the laying of the water pipes.

Subsequently, from 1992 to 2009, the SMNPE L. Pigorini conducted annual research fieldwork and excavations of the settlement, in the area to the right of the pipe laying. During the fieldwork in summer 1994, in an area of the submerged settlement close to the ancient shoreline, the first of five large wooden dugout pirogues was discovered, surveyed and recovered (Fig. 3.1).

The Neolithic settlement was a large 'shore village', on the south-eastern shore of Lake Bacciano, within a protected cove to the west of the high promontory where the town of Anguillara Sabazia stands today, and to the north of the headland now called Pizzo Prato. The southern part of the settlement was bordered to the south by the River Arrone, an emissary of the lake, which after 35 km flows directly into the Tyrrhenian Sea allowing the lake community to come into contact with the transmarine trade routes.

At 164 m above sea level, with a perimeter of 31.5 km, the lake is the largest of the lacustrine basins in the Sabatino volcanic complex. It is today supplied with water partly from short streams but, above all, from underground strata. Owing also to the presence of other small lakes, at the time of Neolithic habitation the area enjoyed a mild climate and the neighbouring fertile and water-rich soils offered many food resources such as fish, waterfowl and berries, in addition to land ideal for the cultivation of cereals, legumes, flax and opium poppy.

The 'scrub' surrounding the village, typical of the Mediterranean area in warm and humid periods, consisting predominantly of oaks, laurels, ash trees and alders, supplied the village with the precious wood essential for the reclamation work and for the construction of houses and other structures, boats and most of the tools, as well as the firewood necessary for heating, lighting, firing pottery and cooking food, and processing boats and the tools. The village can be traced back to one of the oldest Neolithic phases in central Italy.

The appearance of the first Neolithic communities is mostly attributed to an action of 'colonisation' carried out by small pioneer groups and, to a lesser extent, a process of 'acculturation' of the pre-existing local, Mesolithic populations.

For La Marmotta, we can assume the arrival, from the Tyrrhenian coast, of groups of farmers looking for new territories. The large expanse of lake water, which would be extremely tempting at a time of hot and dry climatic conditions, its mild climate, the fertile soils, the presence of a perennial stream and a spring were probably the factors the stimulated the construction of a stable village on the shores of Lake Bracciano.

We currently possess but a partial image of the site because, according to Dr Fugazzola, only 25% of the total area of the settlement, which would have covered about 2 hectares, was excavated. This means that incredible prehistoric 'treasures' are still waiting under the waters of the lake. Fortunately, the fact that they are at a depth of 11 m ensures that they are preserved naturally with hardly any risk of being altered by meteorological, geological or

Figure 3.1. Basic site plan of the submerged site 'La Marmotta' (after Fugazzola et al. *2002) showing the wooden structures and canoes.*

human impact. They are protected in a natural 'safe' that has allowed them survive to the present day in outstanding condition.

Neolithic occupations at La Marmotta

The excavations of La Marmotta revealed a stratigraphic sequence formed by three levels (Fugazzola *et al.* 1993; Fugazzola 1996).

- Level II corresponds to the foundational time and is linked to the presence of pottery with impressed, cardial and, sporadically, incised decoration (Delpino 2020).
- Level I is associated with painted and incised ware in the *Sasso-Fiorano* style. It is characterised mostly by 'negative' decoration with linear and geometric motifs, linear painted designs and occasionally cardial decoration (Delpino 2020). (Fig. 3.2)

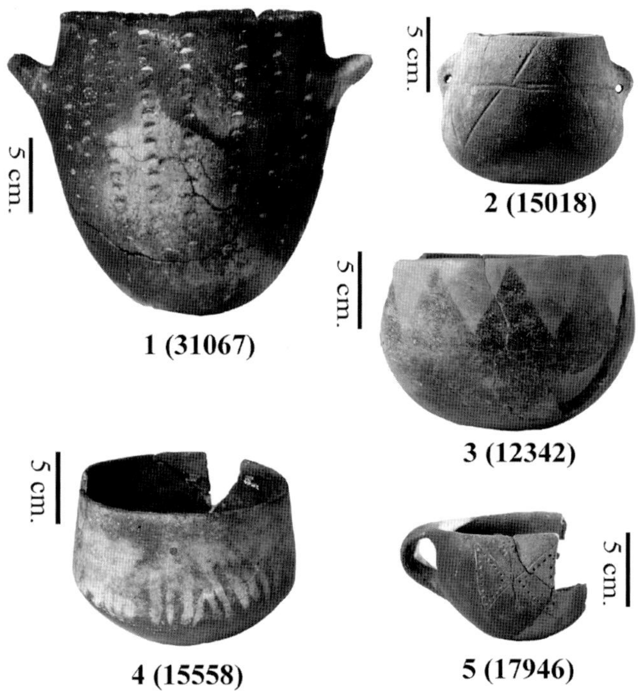

Figure 3.2. Ceramic vessels from La Marmotta: 1 impressed decoration; 2 and 5 incised decoration; 3 and 4 painted.

- Finally, the level known as the *Chiocciolaio* layer is at the top of the sequence and reflects the abandonment of the site. It is formed by dark silt, produced by numerous plant remains and the ruined structures of the houses. It is called *Chiocciolaio* because it is characterised by large quantities of dead lake snail shells.

The radiometric dating of the village of La Marmotta was mainly carried out on wood samples taken from poles deeply embedded in the lake bed. The sequence of dates obtained by radiocarbon of these samples greatly enriches the picture of absolute chronology that has been emerging for Italian Neolithic complexes in both the Tyrrhenian and Adriatic areas in recent years.

The dates obtained so far are distributed over a time interval between 5690 BC (Pole 214, Square A2) and 5260 BC (Pole 21, Square B29). Two main chronological groupings seem evident: an older one, around 5450 BC, and a more recent one around 5260 BC; a third grouping, older than the previous ones, can be hypothesised around 5690 BC (Fugazzola and Tinazzi 2010). Thus the dates cover an uninterrupted period of 430 years. A new dating programme has recently been started, concentrating on the analysis of short-life samples (cereal grains from the different levels; Mazzucco *et al.* 2022a). The objective is to define the time of the occupation more precisely, especially Levels I and II. In the framework of the current research, six samples of charred caryopsides of *Triticum dicoccum* were dated (Table 3.1). The results confirm the chronology previously obtained; charred seeds from Layer II are dated between 5611 and 5327 cal BC, while Layer I is dated between 5616 and 5220 cal BC. Both contiguous and overlapping phase Bayesian models have been used to test hypotheses regarding the site chronological sequence (Bronk Ramsey 2009). The contiguous phase model shows a low overall agreement (Amodel=28.2; Aoverall=53.8), while the overlapping phase model shows higher values (Amodel=106.4; Aoverall=105.7), suggesting that no chronological hiatus exists between the two phases. It may be wondered whether two of the dated samples (CNA-5289.1.2 and CNA-5291.1.1) were intrusive in their respective layers but only with a larger series of dates will it be possible to define better the chronology of the two main layers.

Table 3.1. Radiocarbon dates obtained from charred Triticum dicoccum *caryopses. Calibrations have been made with OxCal online 4.4.4 (Bronk Ramsey 2021) using IntCal20 atmospheric data (Reimer* et al. *2020). Dates have been calibrated at 95.4% probability (2σ).*

Lab. code	*Sample no.*	*Layer*	*Square*	*Determination (BP)*	*$\delta^{13}C$ (‰)*	*Date cal BC*
CNA-5754.1.2	24837	I	A281	6367±34	−23.92482	5471–5220
CNA-5288.1.1	19985	I	A25	6393±40	−27.30331	5470–5313
CNA-5289.1.2	18769	I	A120	6577±43	−21.39406	5616–5477
CNA-5290.1.1	28564	II	A274	6534±43	−21.28299	5611–5380
CNA-5291.1.1	28627	II	A268	6431±42	−21.84272	5475–5327
CNA-5755.1.1	26126	II	A235	6558±31	−18.30000	5611–5475

Similarly, samples are being collected to determine the age of such wooden objects as the canoes, sickles, bows, spindles, etc. This information is important to establish the time when these implements were used and to distinguish between the different types. The results of this dating project, which started in 2022, will be made known in the coming years.

One of the questions that always arise as regards the occupation of La Marmotta is whether the settlers encountered indigenous Mesolithic populations when they came to Lake Bracciano or if the area was uninhabited. In fact, evidence of occupations or contacts with Mesolithic communities is still scarce. In 1998, in the neighbouring area of Mola Vecchia, a little over 900 m from La Marmotta, a small, dryland, rescue excavation was performed on the occasion of canalisation (Mantero 1993; Mineo 2018). According to Diego Mantero, then entrusted by the Superintendency of Southern Etruria with the supervision of the earthworks that ACEA was carrying out, two levels were found. The lower one was formed by small pebbles associated with lithic implements and faunal remains, possibly of Palaeolithic–Mesolithic age, while the upper level consisted of dark sand with abundant woody organic material, including several wooden piles, lithic tools and potsherds in the *Sasso-Fiorano* style. This type of pottery is similar to the kind found in Level I at La Marmotta. The archaeological remains at Mola Vecchia were found at a depth of 5 m. It is possible that in this part of Italy, many open-air Mesolithic sites might lie beneath metres of sediment and, for that reason, are little known.

However, apart from these possible Mesolithic occupations, some elements are suggestive of contacts and the transfer of knowledge between Mesolithic hunter-gatherer groups and the new Neolithic farming communities. The most significant are the morphology of certain geometric microliths, the methods with which the geometric artefacts were made, sometimes employing the microburin technique, and the first use of some plant species, such as opium poppy and grapes (Fugazzola 2002).

To date at La Marmotta, 12 houses have been documented, of which eight have been excavated completely (3, 4–8, 5, 6, 7, 11, 13, 16), while a further six are still unstudied (2, 9, 10, 14, 15, 17) (Fugazzola and Tinazzi 2010). Although several types of wood were used to build them, *Quercus robur* (penduncalate/English oak) and *Quercus suber* (cork oak) were the most frequently used species. Other trees were sometime used: *Alnus glutinosa* (alder), *Quercus ilex* (holm oak), *Fraxinus excelsior* (ash) and *Fagus silvatica* (beech). The distribution of the piles that supported the houses shows that they were rectangular buildings with internal compartments and a central hearth. About 8 m or 10 m long and 6 m or 8 m wide, they were arranged parallel to one another, which is one of the first indications for the Neolithic in the central-western Mediterranean that the settlements were perfectly organised. The only five Neolithic canoes currently known in the Mediterranean basin were found next to some of these houses (Fugazzola 2002). Further details about the construction of the houses and about the canoes is given in Chapters 5.1 and 5.2.

The Neolithic domestic economy and the settlers knowledge of the territory

The environment that the Neolithic settlers found at La Marmotta was exceptional: a very similar climate to the present one, terrain of great ecological diversity, ideal for their farming activities, a lake for a permanent supply of freshwater and forests in the surroundings where they could obtain numerous species of fungi, plants and wild fruits, in addition to a wide range of wild terrestrial and aquatic animals. In the same area they could also procure raw materials, especially timber, plants and clay, with which they made their houses, containers and implements. A route to the sea along the River Arrone connected them with different exchange networks, through which they accessed raw materials such as obsidian and salt.

The abundant remains of animals, plants and fungi that have been preserved show that the domestic economy was perfectly consolidated. Livestock, which makes up 75% of the MNI (Minimum Number of Individuals) of recorded animal species, included goats (*Capra hircus*) and sheep (*Ovis aries*), which are the most frequent animals, as well as cattle (*Bos taurus*), swine (domestic *Sus scrofa*) and dog (*Canis familiaris*), of which a medium-sized specimen and a small one have been documented.

The age at death of the animals that have been found indicates that the management of livestock varied depending on species. Thus, while some goats, sheep and pigs were consumed as young animals, at less than 6 or 7 months, some cattle lived to an adult age (5–8 years). This may be related to their use (Tagliacozzo 2005). While oxen are ideal as draught animals for farming work, the ovicaprids would have been kept not only as a source of meat but also for their milk. This is an important point, because of the important role that secondary products may have played in the development and expansion of Neolithic societies (Sherratt 1981; Debono Spiteri *et al.* 2016).

Although comparative studies have been carried out for the different levels at La Marmotta, specialists affirm that the results should be taken with precaution until an overall study is concluded. Thus, in 2005, it was published that whereas the number of wild species decreased in the more recent levels (Levels I and *Chiocciolaio*), some bird and fish species only appear in Level I (Tagliacozzo 2005). The lake and woodlands were places for fishing and hunting different mammal species such as *Cervus elaphus* (red deer), *Capreolus capreolus* (roe deer), *Bos primigenius* (aurochs), *Vulpes vulpes* (fox), *Sus scrofa, Mustela putorius* (weasel), *Felis silvestris* (wild cat), *Lutra lutra* (otter), *Meles meles (badger)*, *Lepus europaeus* (European hare) and *Erinaceus europaeus* (European hedgehog) for meat and/or pelts; birds (*Podiceps nigrivollis* (little grebe), *Podiceps cristatus* (great crested grebe); *Fulica atra* (coot), and *Phalacrocorax carbo* (cormorant); and various ducks; as well as reptiles, tortoises, molluscs and fish (*Cyprinidae*) (Cassoli and Tagliacozzo 1993; Fugazzola *et al.* 2002; Tagliacozzo 2005).The scarcity of fish remains and the absence of implements clearly employed in fishing, such as hooks and traps, which have been found at other Neolithic lacustrine sites such as Veksa in Russia (Piezonka *et al.* 2020), has prompted the suggestion that fish might not have been consumed habitually. However, this needs further research as it cannot be ruled that many of the ceramic weights found at La Marmotta (see Chapter 6) are really parts of nets.

About 65% of the plant remains correspond to cereals. Of these *Triticum dicoccum* L. is the most abundant, followed by other wheat and barley species: *T. monococcum S., Hordeum distichum, H. vulgare* L. and *T. aestivum compactum* and *T. durum*. The other percentage is formed by pulses (*Pisum sativum* (pea), *Lens culinaris* (lentil), *Lathyrus cicera/sativus* (Indian/red pea), *Vicia cfr. Sativa* (common vetch); types of fruit and nuts: *Prunus spinosa* (sloe), *Ficus carica* (fig), *Sambucus* sp. (elderberry), *Fragaria vesca* (wild strawberry), *Rubus fruticosus* (blackberry), *Corylus avellana* (hazelnut), *Quercus* sp. (oak apples), etc; *Linum usatissimum* flax; as well as *Papaver somniferum* (poppy) and such plants as *Carthamus lanatus* (saffron thistle) and *Silybum marianum* (milk thistle) that might have been used to obtain oil and dye or for their therapeutic properties (Rottoli 1993; 2002; 2006). Some containers full of cereal grains and legumes were found during the excavation. This storage might have involved three different forms: storing the full ears to process them later; keeping the spikelets without extracting the glume; or storing the completely clean grains for their processing and consumption. This is indicated by the remains that have been documented (Fig. 3.3).

The abundance of grape pips (*Vitis vinifera*, sub-species *selvatica*) and seeds of opium poppy, of which the capsules have also been found, has suggested that both plants may have been managed and domesticated by the Neolithic community at La Marmotta (Fugazzola 2002). A recent study has determined that La Marmotta is the oldest European site with evidence of the use of opium (Salavert *et al.* 2020). Four small pipes, one decorated with impressed motifs (no. 15969, Level I, Square D188), a painted example (no. 30547, Level II, Square A38) and two that are undecorated (34659, Level I, Square A328; 34693, Level I, Square A328), may have been used for smoking. They are about 75 mm long (of which 15–20 mm correspond to the mouthpiece), 60 mm wide and 50 mm thick (Fig. 3.4). These pipes are currently being studied to look for remains of phytoliths or other substances that would confirm our hypothesis that they were used for the consumption of opium.

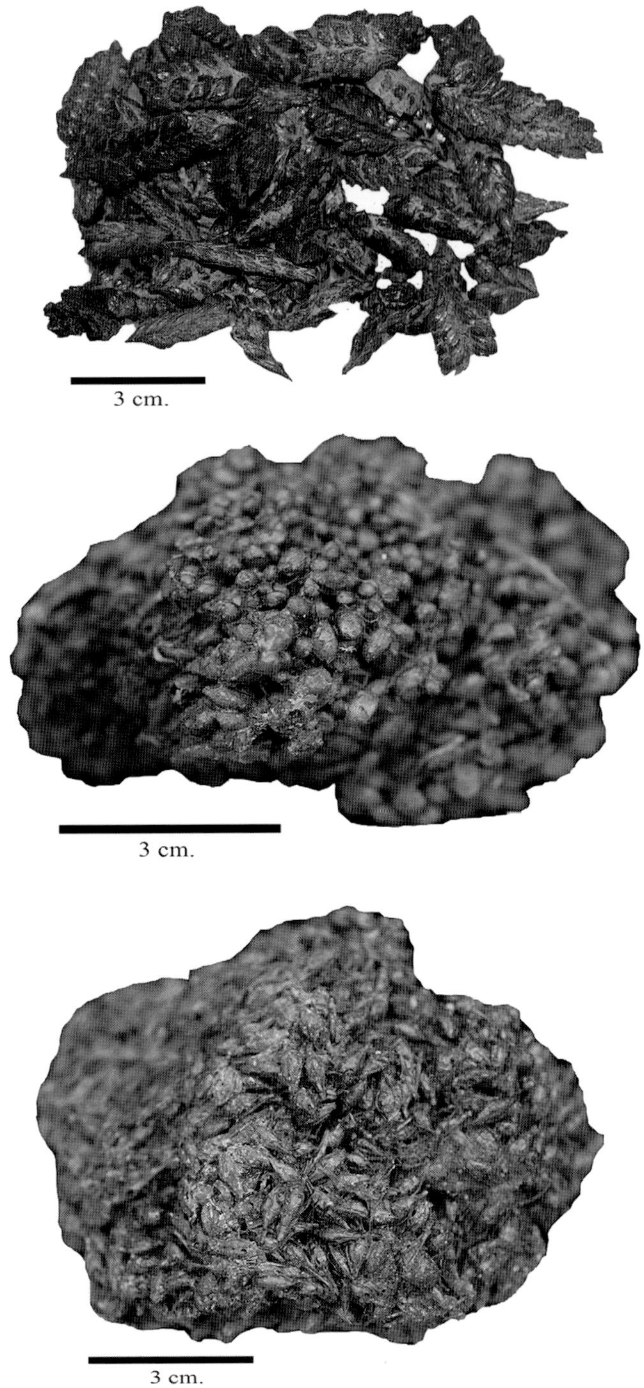

Figure 3.3. Remains of seeds from La Marmotta. They have been documented in different states of processing: spikelets, without the glume and with the glume.

The number of remains of basketry, cordage and occasional finds of textiles made with plant matter or perhaps animal materials (they still have to be analysed) is equally significant. Although they are described specifically in Chapter 6, their quantity, variety and quality already indicate the wide technical know-how of the Neolithic communities.

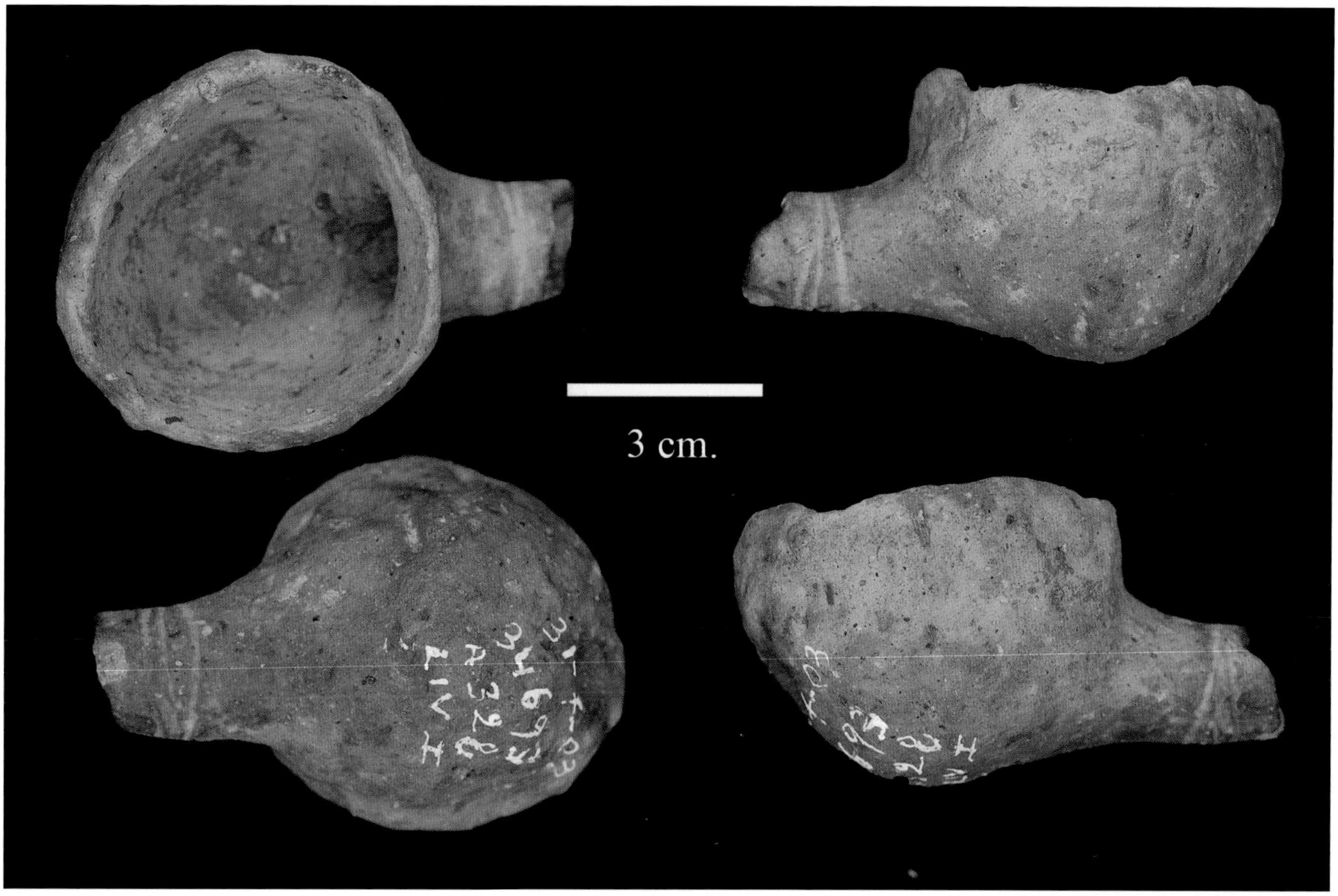

Figure 3.4. Ceramic pipe (Object No. 34693).

Indeed, many of the ways in which they were made are still used today by artisans who make the same kinds of objects. The manufacture of these objects requires a series of implements that may be highly specialised: spindles, whorls and loom weights, flint blades and bone tools used for working with plant fibres and other wooden utensils such as weaving swords, 'spadoni' and 'draghetti' (see Chapter 5, Figs 5.3.19–20), possibly utilised to process vegetal substances.

Similarly, fungi may have formed part of the kit used to light fires (*Fomes fomentarius*) and for psychotropic or medicinal purposes (Fugazzola 2004a; Bernicchia *et al.* 2006). In this regard, the exceptionally high concentration of *Oenanthe* t. pollen on one of the sickles (No. 23001, Level II, Square A179) is unusual and unexpected. The genus *Oenanthe* includes hydro-hygrophilous plants inhabiting humid meadows, swamps and lakeshores, and it is still present in the Tyrrhenian area of central Italy. Due to the content of oenanthotoxins in the fruits and roots, several species of *Oenanthe* genus possess pharmacological properties. These substances have active principles similar to the cicutoxin of *Cicuta virosa* (hemlock), with a neuro-enterotoxic effect. Some species, when consumed fresh and even in small quantities, seem to be able to induce a mental state similar to drunkenness, but can also cause nausea, vomiting and convulsions.

La Marmotta also offers the opportunity of understanding the culinary preferences and ability in the processing of food of the setlement's inhabitants. Numerous fragments of bread have been found among the preserved remains, some of which still display the imprint of the basket that contained the bread but which has now disappeared. Nonetheless, some ceramic pots and baskets contain the residues of food and several studies have recently been started to determine the nature of this food waste. The information we expect to obtain would never have been imagined for such a distant period as the Neolithic.

Containers, implements and ornaments

If there is anything that defines La Marmotta and its classification as a *Pompeii-like* site, it is the conservation of the biotic remains. The numerous and varied objects and implements made of wood, basketry and textiles, presented in this book, reflect their importance for the Neolithic communities and the technical skill reached in manufacturing them. This technological know-how can undoubtedly be explained by a socio-economic organisation based on the specialisation of particular artisans. Only people with specialised knowledge would be capable of building the large dwellings but also many of the artefacts described below: bows, sickles, spindles, wooden vessels and, above all, the canoes.

In the same way, the thousands of pottery remains have revealed the enormous diversity of the vessels that they made. This variety is shown in the shapes, sizes and decoration. Level II is represented especially by pots of great technical quality with cardial and Tyrrhenian (known in Italy as the *Basi-Pienza* style) impressed decoration (Fig. 3.2: 1–2). The motifs were made with different means and tools: fingernails or fingers themselves, awls, shells, branches or straw, etc. These types of forms and decorations are very similar to those found at contemporarneous sites in the Lazio region, as well as in Tuscany, Sardinia, coastal areas of Corsica and on the smaller islands in the Tyrrhenian Sea.

The quality of the containers in Level I continued to be very high but, in this case, painted decoration is more significant. The applications and decorations are very diverse. The latter include geometric motifs, such as triangles, lines, zigzags, etc., but also human forms, animals and plants: cross-shaped human figures, suns, possible goats, cereal ears and a very special motif representing a butterfly (Fig. 3.2: 5). During the last phase of occupation of the site, the pottery becomes gradually less carefully made and is practically undecorated (Fugazzola *et al.* 1993; Fugazzola 2002; Delpino 2020). This pottery type is known in Italy as the linear *Sasso-Fiorano* style.

Different colours of paint were used, like black, grey, white, red and beige. These tones were obtained by using charcoal and other minerals or by the *negative* technique that employed a double slip to obtain black and grey colours (Fig. 3.2: 3–4).

The contaners appear in a wide range of sizes. The smallest, some of them paired, must have been used to hold some type of special liquid, such as oil. The medium-sized vessels would be linked with the usual activities of cooking, preparing and consuming food and beverages. Finally, the largest would have been storage recipients. It has been calculated that some of them might hold as much as 72 kg of cereal or 85 litres of liquid (Fugazzola 2002; 2019).

Some white sherds belong to the type known as *figulina* ware in Italy. This is of an extraordinary quality. The fine walls are another indication of the degree of technical knowledge those populations possessed, since otherwise its manufacture would be impossible. This type of white ware is reminiscent of the pottery found in the eastern Mediterranean (Nilhamn *et al.* 2009). The remains will be analysed further in the near future to determine their provenance because they may come from a very distant source.

Similarly, some of the most characteristic recipients at La Marmotta, because of their resemblance to the dugout canoes, are known as 'barquettas'. This shape, which is very unusual in Italy, is also found at Hellenic sites like Dispilio, another lacustrine site on the shore of Lake Orestiada (Hourmouziadis 1996; 2002) and Tsangli, both in Greece (Marangou 2001). Christina Marangou (1991) also speaks about clay boats at other sites in Albania and North Macedonia. This similarity is evocative of the solid connections that may have existed in the past between populations on each side of the Adriatic Sea, or the heritage that Neolithic populations brought with them as they travelled from east to west in the Mediterranean.

Figure 3.5. Canoe-shaped ceramic containers: (top): Object No. 691; (bottom): Object No. 17901 in situ *as found during the excavation.*

It has been proposed that these canoe-shaped vessels may have held liquids or solids but they may also have been used as lamps or possessed a symbolic value (Fugazzola 2002; 2019). The first analyses of the organic residue conserved in the clay fabric have shown that some of them were used to process dairy products and the meat of ruminant and non-ruminant animals.

These pottery canoes differ somewhat in their shape, handles and size. Thus, in their cross-section some have a convex base and others a flat bottom. At the ends there may be vertical handles or holes that would help to hold or carry them or hang them from a fixed surface. In contrast, others display no kind of application or modification so they must have stood on a surface or been held in the hands. They vary considerably in size; from the smallest of about 100× 40 × 35 mm in size, to the largest, measuring 280 × 100 ×40 mm (Fugazzola 2019) (Fig. 3.5).

It is quite clear that the shapes and decorations of the ceramic record at La Marmotta are related to technical traditions documented both in the Italian Peninsula and in the Balkans and Aegean. However, the diversity of the pottery at La Marmotta is also seen in the manufacture and decoration of recipients that are unknown or very scarce in the central-western Mediterranean. This is the case, for example, of the canoe-shaped containers, the pipes, the *figulina* ware and the vessels decorated with both paint and cardial impressions (Fig. 3.6).

Together with the wooden implements, a large number of lithic tools were made mostly from different varieties of flint and, to a lesser extent, from obsidian and, very rarely, quartz. The different remains show that all the products created by lithic reduction are represented at La Marmotta: cores, percussors, flakes, blades, knapping waste, etc. This indicates that much of the production of flint and obsidian tools was carried out on-site.

At a morphological level, blades are especially abundant, knapped by pressure or indirect percussion; many of them were retouched. The morphotypes include blades with lateral retouch, geometrics and truncations. Scrapers, borers, denticulates and burins are less frequent. Microburins employed to shape the geometric artefacts have also been found (see Chapter 9.1).

Different flint varieties have been identified, most of them of excellent quality. Although provenance studies still have to be carried out, they must have come from different sources. Some were probably acquired locally or regionally, for example in the Apennines, whereas others came from distant locations such as the Defensola mines in the Foggia region on the east coast of Italy (Radi and Danese 2003; Pessina and Tiné 2010; Muntoni *et al.* 2021). The analysis of the obsidian artefacts has shown that most came from the islands of Palmarola and a smaller number from Lipari (Bigazzi *et al.* 2005; De Francesco *et al.* 2012). In this case, the obsidian was used especially to obtain blades by pressure knapping.

Additionally, a large number of polished axes and adzes were made from a variety of rock types and in very different sizes and weights. In total 119 finished examples of these tools were found. That they were often polished on-site is shown by the finds of preforms (Chapter 9.2), the abundant flakes generated during their preparation and the abrasive rocks with negative scars in the shape of the axes. The green and dark rocks may have come from the area of the Alps. Their hardness would endow the tools with a long working life. Moreover, the use of some of these axes and

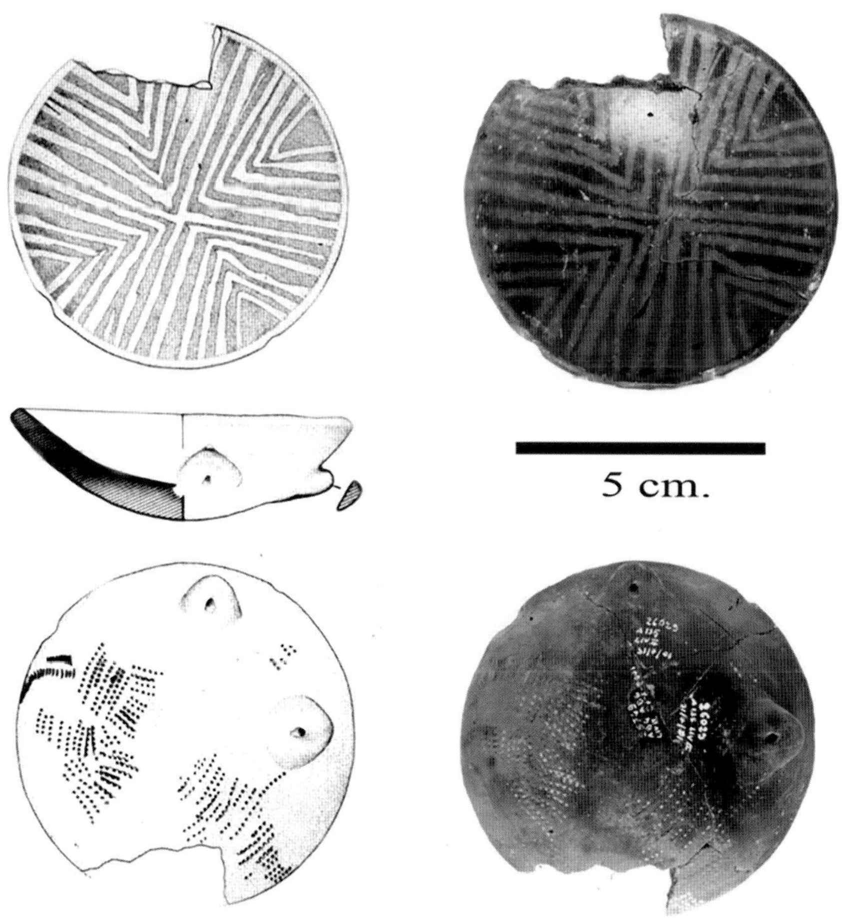

Figure 3.6. Ceramic vessel decorated with both paint and cardial impressions. Reconstruction made from several fragments found during the excavation.

adzes is observed in the marks of such varied objects as the canoes and smaller items like the sickle handles and bows. However, recent studies have noted that these kinds of tools were used in other types of activities, such as butchery tasks, working with hides, etc. (Masclans *et al.* 2017).

The macrolithic assemblage also includes numerous querns made from a variety of raw materials. The review of the objects deposited in the Museo delle Civiltà has documented a total of 784 macrolithic artefacts in a wide range of sizes and weights. The functional study and phytolith analyses being carried out will determine their use and the plant resources processed with them (Chapter 9.3).

The osseous assemblage comprises especially awls and spatulas, most made from the bones of ovicaprids, and wild boar tusks. Use-wear study on the tusks has shown that, whereas some were used to work with artefacts of different hardness, others were elements of ornamentation (Fiore *et al.* 2006).

It is evident that the shapes and decorations of the pottery, and the provenance of some raw materials, indicate that the community at La Marmotta formed part of extensive and complex exchange networks together with populations in several parts of Europe. That is the only way to explain the presence of flint from the Apennines or the Defensola mines in the Foggia region, obsidian from the islands of Palmarola and Lipari, or some of the rocks used to make axes and adzes from the Alps (D'Amico 2000; Bigazzi *et al.* 2005; De Francesco *et al.* 2012).

Osseous human remains

One of the deficiencies of the site of La Marmotta is the practical absence of osseous human remains. This means that we do not know what the funerary practices of the habitants were. The existence of a single partial burial, three isolated teeth (two representing two children between 4 and 7 years of age and one child between 7 and 10 years) and two human femurs made into spatulas are all that have been recorded (Fugazzola 2002). The most complete individual was a 14 year old youth found near dwellings S5 and S6. However, there is no direct evidence linking the individual with either of the houses. It seems that the body was found on its side, with the head pointing towards the south, on a layer of bark. One of the sticks found next to the head, P933, was dated to obtain an indirect chronology. The result was 6445±57 BP (5484–5307 cal BC at 92.9% probability: OxCal 4.4). We have recently sent a human bone sample to the National Accelerator Center (CNA). The result has been negative because the sample does not have collagen.

Bearing in mind that La Marmotta was occupied for approximately 430 years, the scarcity of human remains may be due to two main factors: 1) there was a place reserved for the deceased that has not yet been discovered; or 2) the funerary practices have not left any evidence in the archaeological record (abandonment of the bodies, cremation and deposition of the ashes in the lake or other place where they have not been preserved, etc.). This lack of human remains is a problem that remains to be solved.

The symbolic world and artistic representations

One of the most curious archaeological objects documented in House 3 (Level II, Square A129) at La Marmotta was a small Palaeolithic female sculpture (Fig. 3.7). Although its interpretation is difficult, it seems clear that this sculpture was re-used because of its singularity, beauty or symbolic

Figure 3.7. Palaeolithic female sculpture documented in House 3 (Object No. 23058).

significance. Made of steatite, it is 48 mm high, 21 mm wide and 22 mm thick, and weighs 22.44 g (Fugazzola 2000–2001). A further two objects, which are currently in an unknown location, may have also possessed a symbolic significance that we cannot comprehend: a fragment of long bone diaphysis probably of an elephant, possibly collected when it was already a fossil, and a shark's tooth (Tagliacozzo 2005).

Other artefacts associated with the realm of ornamentation and symbolism are the wild boar tusks and beads. The former are characterised by perforations through their roots while the occlusal zones are unmodified. In general, their appearance is quite fragile. This type of object is very common at other Neolithic sites in the Mediterranean area (Chiquet *et al.* 1997; Martí *et al.* 1997).

About 200 beads and adornments made from stone, wood, clay, teeth, shells and some type of seed have been found. They were pierced very carefully from both sides so they could be threaded on a fine string (Chapter 8).

Finally, the subject of symbolic elements and graphic representations encompasses not only many of the ceramic vessels described above with human, animal and plant motifs but also the geometric patterns documented on some wooden and bone implements. Moreover, the fact that a human femur was made into a utensil possibly reflects a symbolic significance unknown to us.

Conclusion

La Marmotta is undoubtedly a unique site in the world. However, its importance runs parallel to the numerous enigmas that are still to be solved. The new project headed by Mario Mineo, Juan F. Gibaja and Niccolò Mazzucco is making a huge effort to form an inter-disciplinary and international working group to tackle the study of such exceptional remains through cutting-edge methodologies.

We still need to know much more precisely how the inhabitants of La Marmotta lived, what techniques they used, what they ate, how they obtained animal and plant resources, what relationships they maintained with other groups and how they organised themselves. These questions will help us to understand the particularities of those communities living on the shore of Lake Bracciano for about 430 years.

Why did they abandon such an idyllic site, the place where they lived for so long? While we have begun to study this question from a geological and environmental perspective, the fact is that the inhabitants left very suddenly, abandoning their homes and their past. It is likely that a rapid rise in the level of lake made them move to higher land further away. Yet, it seems clear that this abandonment might also have been associated with a fire in the settlement, as demonstrated by the numerous constructive elements and tools that are burnt. This would have occurred in one or several episodes that took place unexpectedly and for that reason they left vessels with food, containers full of seeds, implements in perfect condition and the canoes next to their houses.

They abandoned all those things but also their ancestors. People who, if they were buried, we do not know where their bodies are. This is another aspect that requires further investigation, to find the places reserved for the deceased. Because, while La Marmotta is teaching us about the way of life of the first Neolithic societies in Italy, we hardly know anything about their treatment of the dead.

4

First palynological contribution towards a palaeoenvironmental reconstruction of the Neolithic site La Marmotta

Daniele Arobba, Rosanna Caramiello and Lionello F. Morandi

Over the last 30 years, several palynological studies have analysed borehole sequences collected in central Italian lake basins, accomplishing the identification of the main variations in the vegetation cover and their relationship with Holocene climate change and human activities. To date, such investigations never included Lake Bracciano, for which the only archaeobotanical data were acquired through the excavation of the submerged site of La Marmotta (Early Neolithic Impresso-Cardial Culture, *c.* 5690–5260 cal. BC), which brought to light wooden artefacts and carpological remains (Fugazzola *et al.* 1993; 2002; Martinelli 1993; Rottoli 1993; 2002; Fugazzola and Mineo 1995; Fugazzola and Tinazzi 2010; Rottoli and Pessina 2007; Caruso Fermé *et al.* 2021).

Our pollen analysis focused on a few sediment samples collected in dwelling unit 7 during the 2004 fieldwork, although originally not for palynological purposes, that were subsequently stored at the Museum delle Civiltà of Rome. The samples were taken from a short stratigraphic sequence deposited inside a ceramic vessel (inventory no. 40128) which was found in Layer II, corresponding to the first settlement phase, found placed vertically and filled with sediment. To assess whether significant differences occurred in the pollen content, three samples from this sequence were taken from within the vase.

Two further samples were obtained from sediment lumps adhering to harvesting sickles: the lowest one (inventory no. 39112) from Layer I-peaty horizon, and a shallower one from Layer I-grey horizon (inventory no. 38056) (Fig. 4.1).

These five samples represent the only material available so far for pollen analysis, which therefore have to be considered preliminary, whilst awaiting undisturbed boreholes necessary for a more detailed palaeoenvironmental reconstruction. The samples were treated according to the standard extraction procedure involving heavy liquid separation (Stockmar 1971; Riding 2021) and observed by optical microscopy at 400×–630× magnifications. All samples were in an excellent state of preservation and they all showed high absolute pollen frequencies (20,843–71,028 grains/gram).

The diagram in Figure 4.2: a–b shows the percentages of the tree-shrub (AP) and herbaceous (NAP) taxa along the chronological sequence reconstructed using the sediment samples from the vessel and from the surface of the sickles. No significant differences occur in the three samples from the ceramic vessel, which seem to point to the presence of a moderate tree canopy (AP between 61.1% and 65.7%) corresponding to a mixed oak wood formed by *Quercus* deciduous-type, *Acer*, *Tilia*, *Carpinus*, *Ostrya*/*Carpinus orientalis*, *Ulmus*, *Laurus*, *Fraxinus*-type and *Corylus*. Thermophilous formations with *Quercus ilex*-type, *Olea* type, *Viburnum tinus*-type, *Ephedra fragilis*-type and *Eric arborea* also occur, along with elements of riparian areas such as *Alnus glutinosa*-type, *Populus* and *Salix* (Fig. 4.3). Elements of mountain environments are also present, although in lower percentages, including *Fagus* and sporadic records of *Picea* and *Abies*. Lacustrine habitats are represented by a number of herbaceous hydrophytes, particularly *Typha*, *Sparganium*, *Hottonia*, *Callitriche* and *Myriophyllum alterniflorum*-type. Traces of anthropic impact are revealed by plants of grass pastures (15%), together with synanthropic taxa like Urticaceae, Cheno-Amaranthaceae, *Rumex*, *Polygonum*, *Plantago* and *Papaver argemone*-type. In this regard, the constant and abundant occurrence of pollen of *Avena-Triticum* type and *Hordeum* type (2–3.3%) is particularly worthy of note.

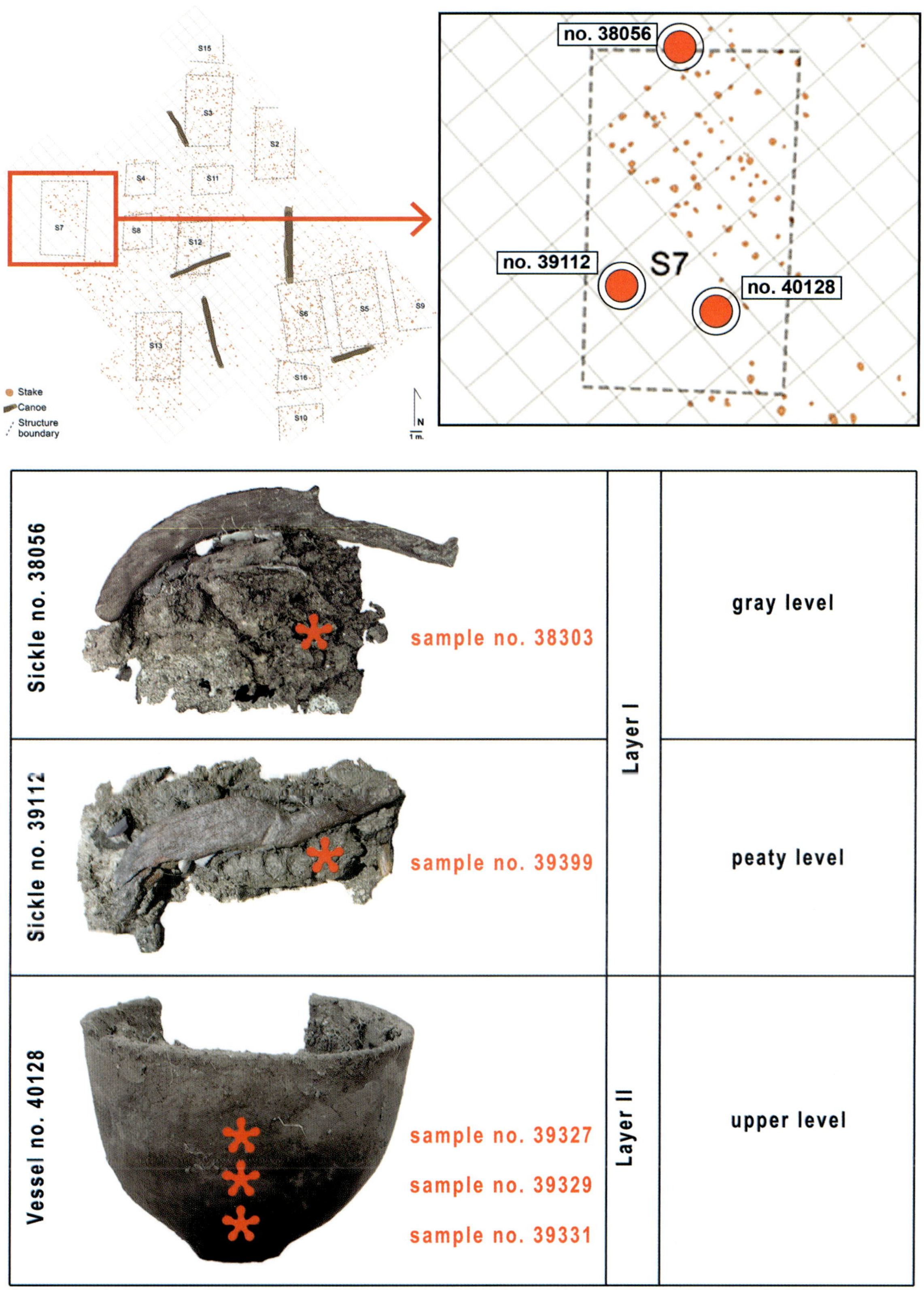

Figure 4.1. (Top): site plan and location of the three archaeological finds from dwelling unit S7 which provided the sediment samples; (bottom): codes of the five samples analysed and their position within the stratigraphic sequence.

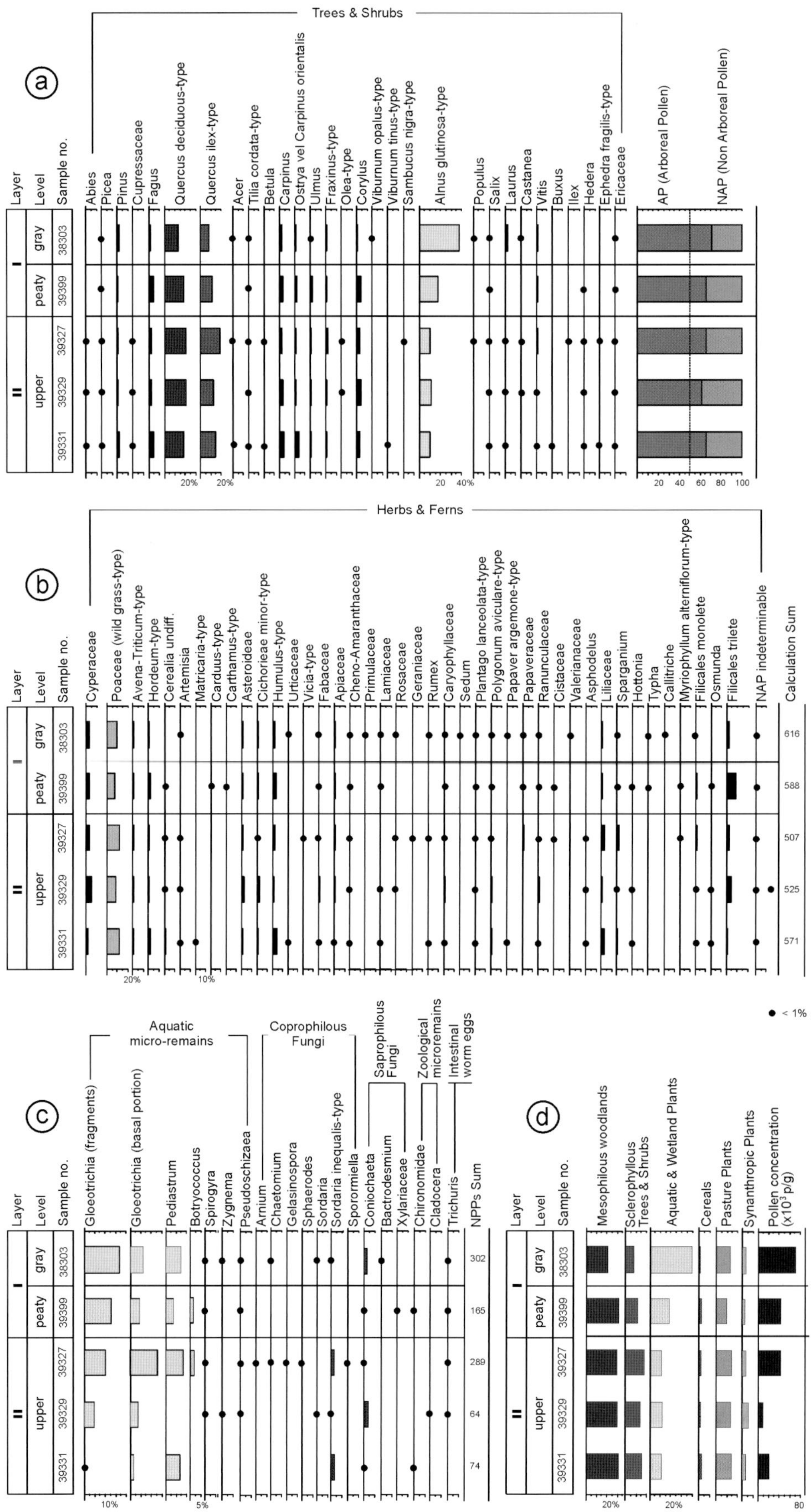

Figure 4.2. Pollen diagrams from the sickle sediment samples: a–b: pollen percentage diagram of AP (Arboreal Pollen) and NAP (Non-Arboreal Pollen) taxa; c. percentage diagram of NPPs (Non-Pollen Palynomorphs); d. cumulative pollen percentage diagram of selected groups of taxa.

The analysis of the sediment samples from the sickles found above, in Layer I, shows a certain degree of variation in the landscape and a stronger influence of anthropogenic factors. While the total arboreal cover increases (AP from 65.4% to 71.2%), the contribution of deciduous and evergreen oak decreases and, in contrast, *Alnus glutinosa*-type, a heliophilous, fast-growing species suitable to hydromorphic soil, becomes more abundant (up to 38%). The same types of Cerealia were identified, although in lower percentages (from 2.2% to 1%), as in the case of synanthropic herbaceous taxa (up to 3.4%).

The sediments are also rich in aquatic micro-remains like unicellular algae, algal spores and algal colonies (*Gloeotrichia*, *Pediastrum*, *Botryococcus*, *Spirogyra*, *Pseudoschizaea*), and coprophilous (*Chaetomium*, *Sordaria*, etc.) and saprophyte (*Coniochaeta* and *Xylariaceae*) fungi also occur, along with whipworm eggs of the genus *Trichuris* (Fig. 4.2: c; Fig. 4.3: k–n).

The reduction in pollen of *Quercus* deciduous-type within the mesophilous oak wood, matched by a contemporary rise in *Alnus glutinosa*-type, points to massive oak felling to set up the first pile structure of the village upon which the dwellings were built. This evidence agrees with dendrochronological analyses of the trunks (Martinelli 1993; Fugazzola and Tinazzi 2010), which have shown that the use of deciduous oak prevailed (76.4%), while alder only reaches 0.3%. Only a few other woody species were considered suitable for this purpose: *Laurus nobilis* (14.4%) and *Fraxinus excelsior*-type (8.9%). These two latter taxa are also documented in the pollen record, providing a rough estimate of their presence in the lakeshore area around the village, even though some arboreal species might be under-represented within their coenosis, such as the case of *Laurus nobilis* in particular. Furthermore, deciduous oak was already likely well known in antiquity as a notable species for its excellent technological characteristics, among which

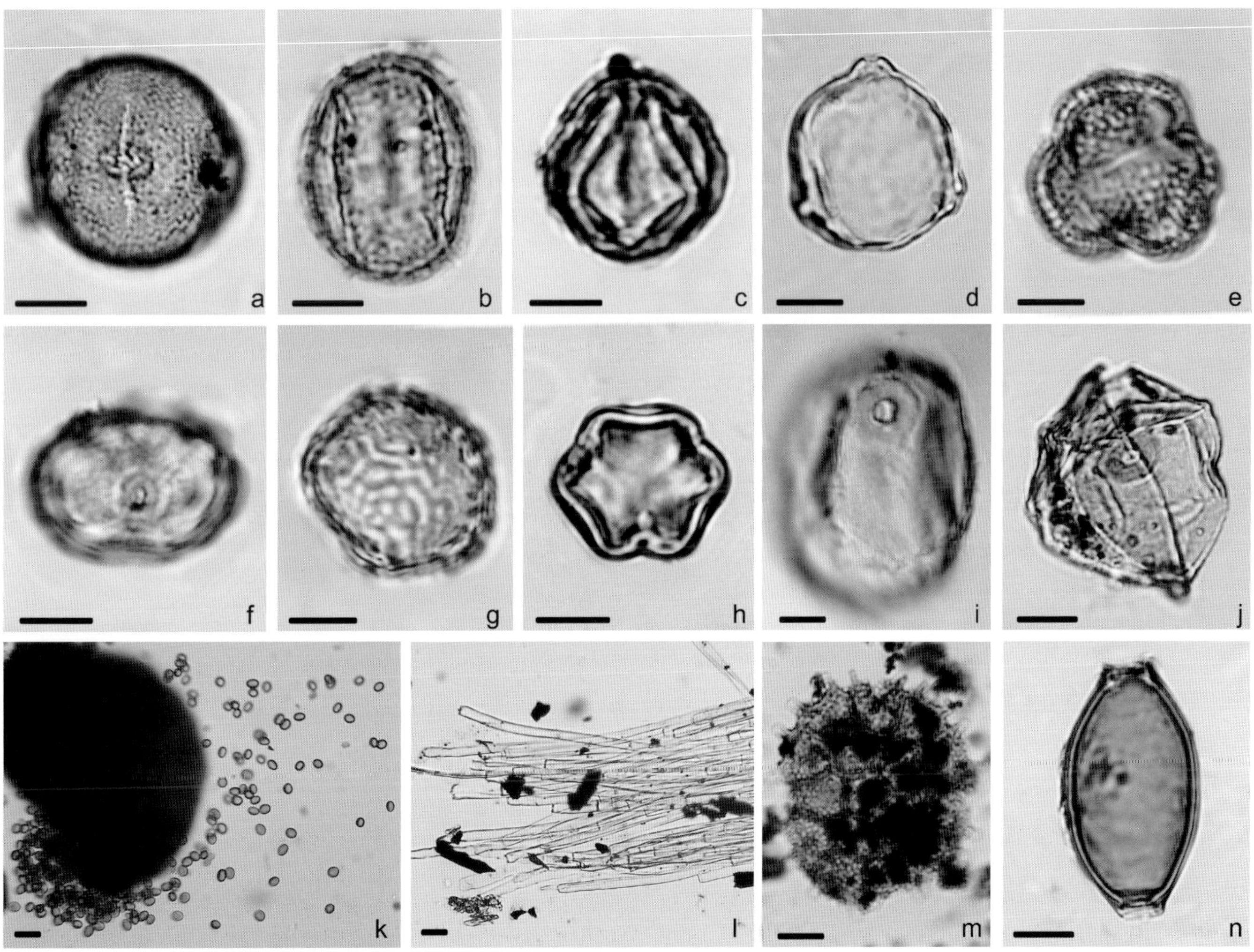

Figure 4.3. Light micrographs of some significant pollen and NPPs from La Marmotta (scale bar = 10 µm:. a. Fagus*; b.* Quercus deciduous-*type; c.* Quercus ilex-*type; d.* Ostrya vel Carpinus orientalis*; e.* Olea-*type; f.* Alnus glutinosa-*type; g.* Ulmus*; h.* Vitis*; i.* Avena-Triticum-*type; j.* Hordeum-*type; k. ascocarp and spores of Chaetomiaceae; l. colony of cyanobacteria of the genus Gloeotrichia;* m. Pediastrum cf. P. boryanum*; n. egg of the intestinal whipworm* Trichuris *(probably* T. trichiura*).*

its resistance to immersion was so remarkable as to make it the first building choice.

As pointed out by Fugazzola and Tinazzi (2010), 85% of the piles were put in place during the first century of occupation of the village. Therefore, from the very beginning of the settlement the inhabitants made a marked impact on the original vegetation communities, quickly downsizing the main component of the mixed oak wood. The clearings created by tree felling probably favoured the expansion of a fast-growing heliophilous species like *Alnus glutinosa*, which can successfully tolerate a high water table (Fig. 4.2: d).

Plant macrofossil data from previous studies (Rottoli 1993; 2002; Rottoli and Pessina 2007) have identified some taxa which were also detected in the pollen record, although it should be born in mind that palynological determinations reach a lower level of accuracy: first, pollen grains of cereals (*Avena-Triticum*-type and *Hordeum*-type), but also spontaneous arboreal taxa (*Corylus avellana*, *Vitis vinifera*, *Sambucus nigra*-type) and a range of herbs such as *Carthamus*-type, *Vicia*-type and *Papaver argemone*-type.

Everyday life activities in the village certainly contributed to water eutrophication in the surroundings, through the input of nitrogenous and phosphatic organic compounds, partly responsible for the bloom of nitrogen-fixing organisms such as the cyanobacterium *Gloeotrichia* and the green alga *Pediastrum* cf. *P. boryanum*, particularly common during the Holocene climatic optimum. Spores of dung fungi, some belonging to the Sordariaceae family, may be correlated with herding activities.

A further element showing the extent of anthropogenic impact is the finding of eggs of *Trichuris* (cf. *T. trichiura*), a whipworm species which may have infected the inhabitants of the site with trichuriasis, usually caused by poor hygiene in food preparation and consumption (Morandi 2018).

These first results appear to fit quite well with the data from lake sediment records in Tyrrhenian central Italy (Kelly and Huntley 1991; Lowe *et al.* 1996; Magri 1999; Magri and Sadori 1999; Allen *et al.* 2002; Mercuri *et al.* 2002; Drescher-Schneider *et al.* 2007; Sadori *et al.* 2011; Sadori 2018; Stoddart *et al.* 2019). In particular, the sequence from Lake Martignano, *c.* 4 km from Lake Bracciano, shows the presence of oak-dominated deciduous forest with other mesophilous species from 9000 years uncal. BC. Around 5000 years uncal. BC, *Quercus ilex*-type, *Olea*-type and *Phillyrea*-type start to increase. In this case the mesophilous deciduous oak wood is well represented and more xeric formations are characterised by *Quercus ilex*-type, while *Olea*-type only occurs sporadically. However, at Lake Martignano a progressively increasing human impact only occurs from 3500 years uncal. BC, as indicated by cereal pollen and synanthropic species; therefore later than at Lake Bracciano.

Pollen of *Castanea sativa*, a component of the deciduous oak wood that had already spread in the central Apennines in the middle Holocene, occurs sporadically and in very low values also at La Marmotta, while grains of *Juglans regia*, a rather unusual finding documented earlier at Lake Martignano, were not detected.

Overall, this study has provided a preliminary palaeoenvironmental assessment of the area during the Early Neolithic, complementary to previous plant macrofossil data from the same site.

5

Woodworking: Introduction to wood working and artefact crafting

5.1. Village organisation and domestic structures

Mario Mineo, Gerard Remolins, Juan F. Gibaja and Niccolò Mazzucco

The area where La Marmotta was located is about 300 m from the current lake shore and lies, submerged, at a depth of 12 m (3 m of sediment and 9 m of water). The remains of the village are on a slightly sloping bed, inclined towards the north; in fact, the further the archaeological surfaces are from the current beach, the greater the depth.

The organisation of the village and the type of dwelling structures identified during the excavation was published by the director of the project, M.A. Fugazzola, in 2003 and 2010 (Fugazzola 2002; Fugazzola *et al.* 2003; Fugazzola and Tinazzi 2010). Data was obtained during 29 excavation seasons, from 1992 to 2009, when an area of approximately 49.5 × 33 m^2 was excavated. The evidence that was retrieved supported hypotheses about village organisation, use and design of domestic space, and construction methods (Fig. 5.1.1).

According to published data (Fugazzola 2002), the first action that Neolithic people took before settling in the area was probably land drainage. It would have been necessary both to isolate the occupied land from the damp ground and to regularise it with clay and planks. Almost 3400 wooden posts (Fig. 5.1.2) that have been found bedded into the basal clay were probably placed to stabilise the ground and also to support the structures. Of them, 2044 posts were analysed by the Italian Institute of Dendrochronology at the Civic Museum of Natural History in Verona (Fugazzola and Tinazzi 2010).

The piles were of considerable size and in some cases exceeded 3.5 m in height (when the entire pile was preserved), with a diameter varying between 150 mm and 300 mm. They were often bedded into the ground in groups of two or three, probably in order to sustain greater weights and to provide maximum stability. In addition, the embedded piles were often re-inforced by adding ceramic fragments or pressed clay as wedges. The clay that was put into the cavity produced by the insertion of the pile was also occasionally fired in order to further stabilise it and fix it firmly into the ground.

Most of the logs used for the houses were of oak (1562 of *Quercus robur* and *Q. suber*), but also of laurel (294 of *Laurus nobilis* or Lauracea) and, in smaller numbers, of ash (181 of *Fraxinus excelsior*) and alder (7 of *Alnus glutinosa*). Most of these species were locally available in the surrounding forests. The two predominant species, oak and laurel, are well-known for their durability and resistance to deterioration processes and for that reason they were not only predominantly used for the construction of houses but also for crafting other equipment and tools.

The spatial distribution of the posts, together with the radiocarbon dates calibrated by dendrochronology, made it possible to reconstruct a general plan of the village, allowing the identification of the posts belonging to the same structures and their chronological phases. Once the wood species had been determined, the dendrochronological analyses were carried out by observing the cross-section of the tree-ring samples, but only for oak and ash since laurel wood does not allow dendrochronological analysis. The identified alder samples were too few, and ash has almost the same characteristics as oak. The measurements of the amplitudes of the rings were performed using the CCTRMD instrument (Computer Controller Tree Ring Measurement Device; Aniol 1987) and were archived using the specific Catras software (Aniol 1983). The analysis allowed the construction of several average curves that can be attributed to different construction and occupation phases by identifying groups of posts with similar radiocarbon dates (Fig. 5.1.3). Ongoing analysis of radiocarbon dates seems to suggest that not all the piles of each house were cut in the same period. This suggests that earlier structures were not abandoned but maintained by adding and substituting older posts with newer ones (Fugazzola and Tinazzi 2010).

Figure 5.1.1. Hypothetical reconstruction of the shape and internal organisation of La Marmotta domestic unit.

Structure S13 has been dated by dendrochronology much more than any other structure. To minimise any distortion to the geostatistical analysis, Structure S5, with the smallest number of dated piles, has not been taken into account.

Owing to these limitations, only an exploratory approach to the data has been made (description and basic interpolation of the distribution). At first glance, it can be seen that no structure is formed by piles in the same chronological interval. This has been interpreted in terms of the continual re-use of dwelling structures through the complete replacement of piles that had deteriorated over time. For this reason, it is difficult to determine which structure is the oldest and which is the most recent. However, some of them possess more piles dated in early phases whereas others have a larger number of later ones. To facilitate their discrimination, a preliminary deterministic interpolation (IDW) of the data was performed, while a geostatistical interpolation will be made after the data have been revised.

The results show that Structure S7, although it is incomplete, possesses the largest number of piles belonging to an early date. S13 may also form part of this group of old structures. However, this is not certain, as it was repaired many times and the piles display a wide chronological range. The more recent structures are easier to identify. The prediction map obtained by interpolation shows that S6 and S3 are the dwellings with the most recent piles. Structure S10 may also be included in this group although it was not completely excavated.

Following the proposal of M.A. Fugazzola, the general plan of the village remained fairly stable during all the occupation phases (Fugazzola and Tinazzi 2010, 1):

> *dalla lettura della pianta generale sembrerebbe risultare evidente la capacità degli abitanti del villaggio di creare – pur se condizionati dalla presenza del corso del fiume Arrone (e forse ad oriente anche dalle acque di un piccolo breve fosso affluente nel lago) e della distesa lacustre verso settentrione – un impianto razionale, con un 'tracciato' maggiore orientato in direzione Nord–Sud e largo circa 2 metri e con diverse 'vie' minori, larghe da 1 metro ad 1 metro e mezzo circa, con gli assi orientati Est–Ovest.*

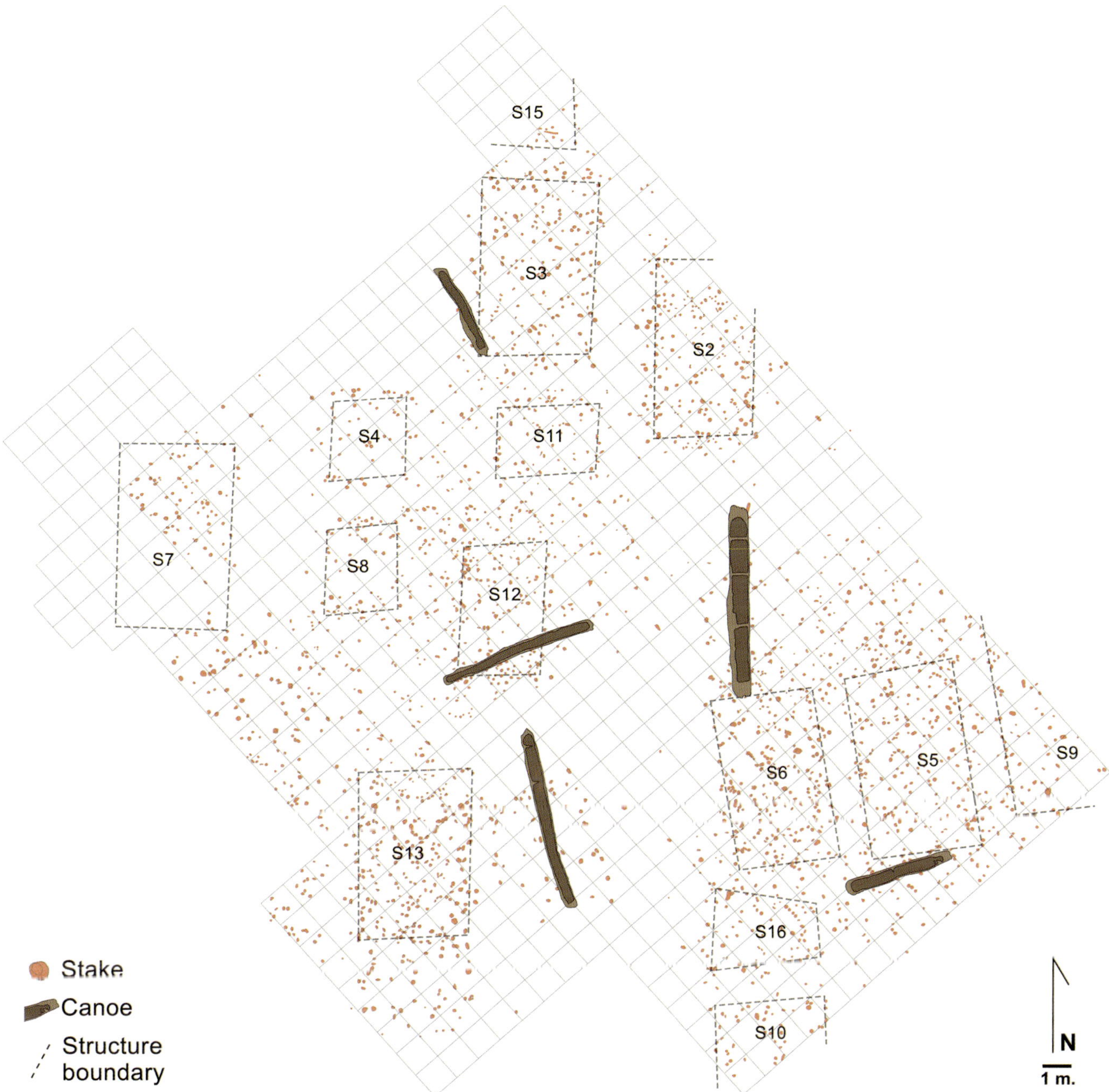

Figure 5.1.2. Distribution of wooden piles and the hypothetical boundaries of the different structures documented at La Marmotta.

Viewing the general plan it would seem evident that the inhabitants of the village were able to create – even if constrained by the presence of the course of the River Arrone (and perhaps to the east by the waters of a small short ditch flowing into the lake) and of the lake's northern expansion – a rational layout, with a major 'axis' oriented in a north–south direction, approximately 2 metres wide, and with various minor 'alleys', approximately 1 to 1.5 metres wide, with an east–west orientation.

The village was formed by several quadrangular wooden structures of different, but similar, sizes. They are rectangular and display regular proportions (the largest is up to 6 × 9 m), aligned along the lake shore in a relatively orderly manner and accordingly to the natural relief of the area (Fig. 5.1.2).

The space between the various dwellings was dedicated to production activities. In between the 'houses', several archaeological features were identified, such as floors made of various raw materials (wood paving, clay paving, and clay paving containing clay conglomerates), and walls with diversified and articulated wooden elements, also covered with clay and connected to vegetal roofs (Fig. 5.1.4). Accessory structures have also been identified, such as roofing

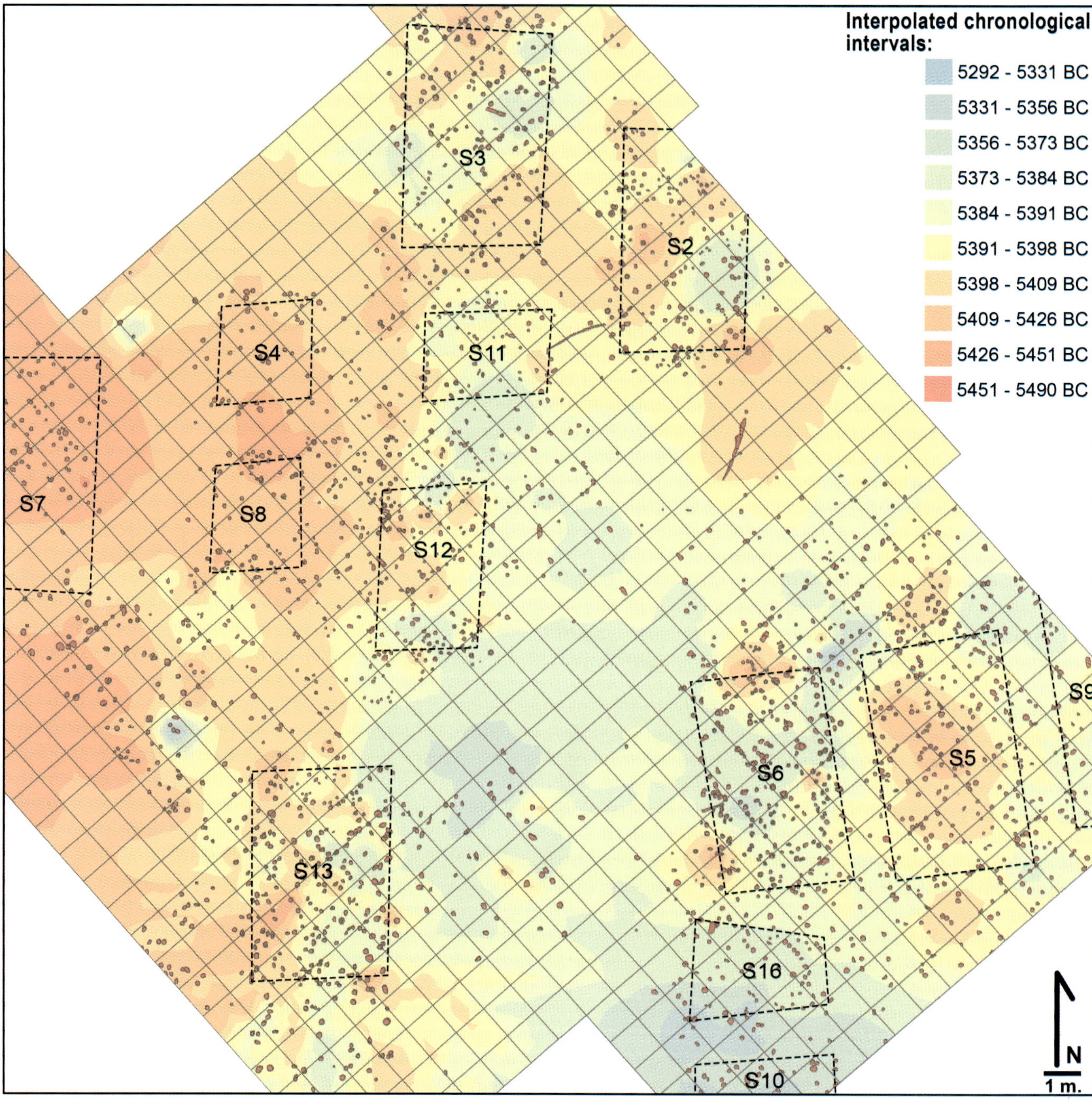

Figure 5.1.3. Plan produced by interpolation of the dendrochronological data obtained from wooden piles. Map made with ArcMap v.10.8.1.

of specific areas, cobbled pavements, large flask-shaped silo with a cylindrical necks and ovoid bodies, large pits probably used for food preparation or clay extraction, etc. Storage pits were often plastered and sealed with clay to drain and isolate them.

Recently, by means of ongoing spatial analysis of different categories of remains, it has been observed that significant patterns exist in the distribution of pottery and lithic tools. As regards the density of ceramic remains, the largest volume of sherds was found inside the boundaries of Structures S13, S12, S3 and S6, in decreasing order (Fig. 5.1.5). In contrast, lithic assemblages are concentrated in Structures S11, S3, S6 and S12, in decreasing order (Fig. 5.1.6). Finally, wooden artefacts are grouped mostly in Structures S6, S5, S12 and S3, in decreasing order (Fig. 5.1.7). The results of this density analysis

Figure 5.1.4. Photographs taken during the excavation: 1–2 wooden posts, fragments of wood from the house structures and the remains of floors; 3–4) excavation of one of the silos with remains of the clay used to plaster its mouth.

should, however, be taken with caution as they might be influenced by post-depositional processes creating locations with greater fragmentation of the remains.

Pavements

The floors were prepared once the plan of the structure and elevation had been defined. After levelling the underlying ground, a layer of clay was spread, including also pottery and osteological remains in order to create a first drainage layer. Successively, a layer of leaves and straws was placed and then, again, a layer of pressed clay. Remains of these vegetal layers, placed to dry the house floor, have been recovered during the excavation process. In some cases, even wooden panels were put on the floors (Fig. 5.1.8).

Hearths

The hearth was placed directly on the pavement. Larger hearths can measure up to 1.50 × 1.50 m. For their construction, vegetal bundles, stones, large fragments of terracotta and clay were used.

Elevation

Once the flooring had been prepared, the walls were raised using posts and logs of various sizes, creating wattle-and-daub walls with reeds, straw and clay (Fig. 5.1.9). Very similar, and detailed, information on Neolithic wattle has recently been provided by the nearby site of Lugo di Ravenna (Tasca 2019). More detailed analysis of the materials from La Marmotta will allow a better understanding of the specific techniques employed in order to establish comparisons with neighbouring sites (Tinè 2009). At La Marmotta, stone footings were also occasionally used at the bottom of the wall and around the wooden posts that held up the structure.

Fragments of vegetal roofs have been also discovered (Fig. 5.1.10), together with some wooden implements that were probably part of the roofing structures (Fig. 5.1.11). Most of these materials are still unstudied.

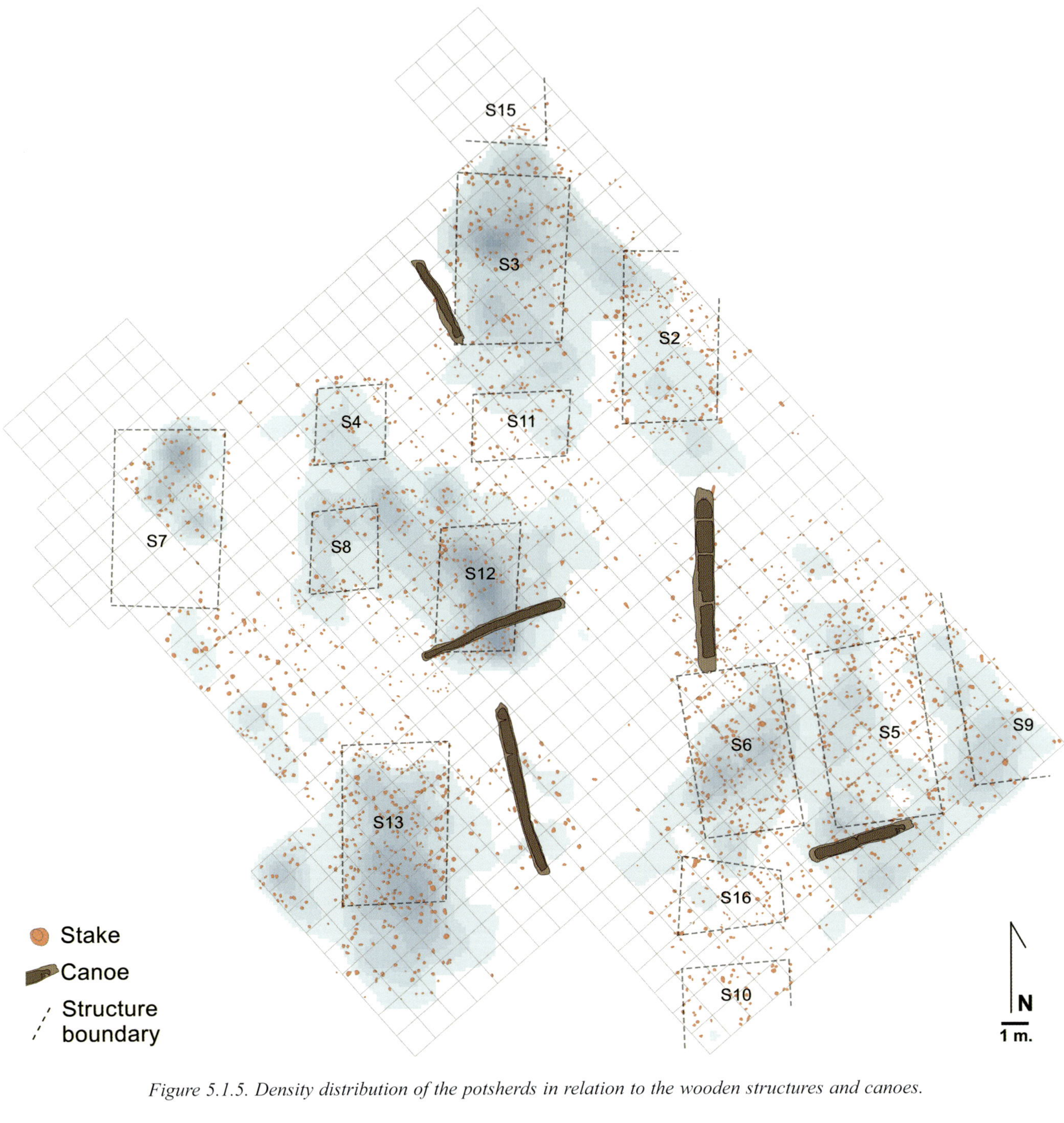

Figure 5.1.5. Density distribution of the potsherds in relation to the wooden structures and canoes.

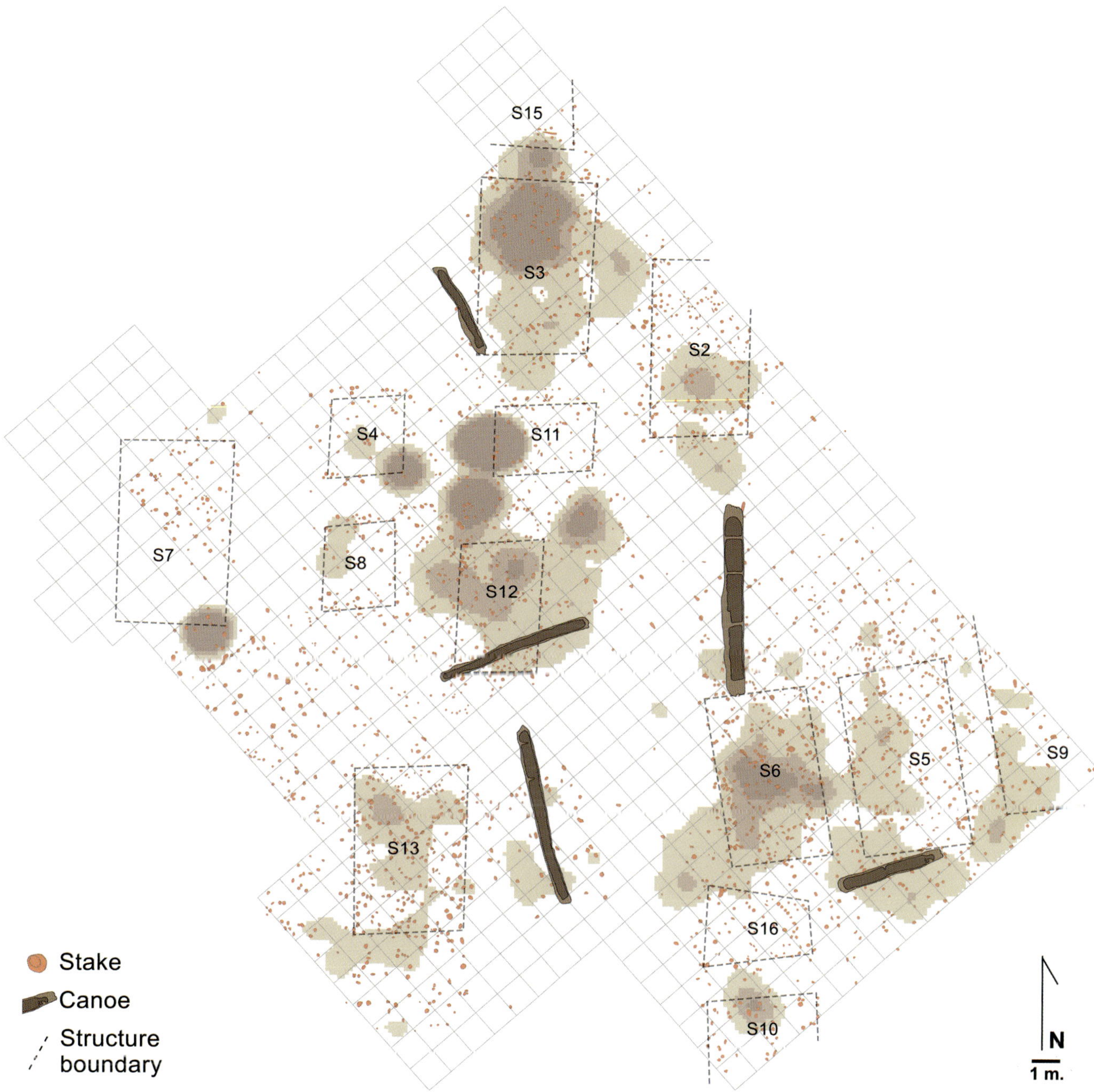

Figure 5.1.6. Density distribution of chipped lithic remains in relation to the wooden structures and canoes.

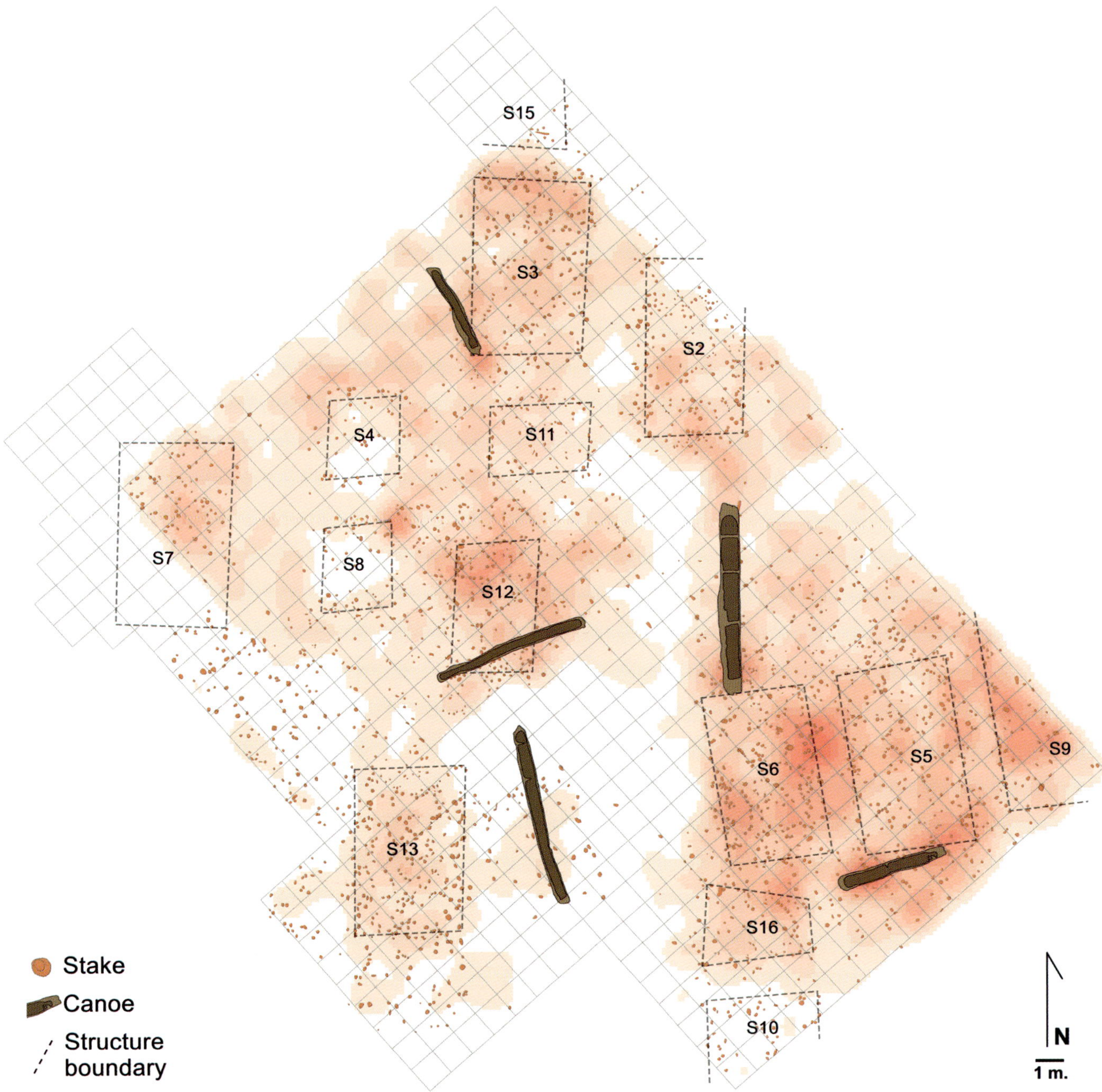

Figure 5.1.7. Density distribution of wooden artefacts in relation to the wooden structures and canoes.

INFORMATION

33137

OBJECT:	Wooden panel probably made with bark
YEAR:	2002
LEVEL:	II
SQUARE:	A318
NUMBER:	33137
SIZE:	577 x 288 x 12 mm

Figure 5.1.8. Wooden panel probably made with bark and used to isolate the house floor from ground moisture (Object No. 33137).

Figure 5.1.9. Wattle and daub remains. Negatives of plant remains can be observed on the surface of the dry clay (Object No. 14815).

Internal and external spaces

Some of the wooden implements recovered seem to suggest the presence of both internal and external spaces in the dwellings. The main access to the dwellings faced south. In some cases, it seems that external roofing was present. It is also probable that external covering was present on the side of the houses.

This section has briefly explained the general features of the houses and other structures, such as storage pits and hearths, how they were distributed spatially and what materials were used to build them. Thanks to the excellent excavation and recovery of these materials, as well as the gigantic effort to define the chronology of each structure through dendrochronological analysis, today, 20 years after the excavations, we can work on the remains recovered and continue researching La Marmotta village life. Many analyses are still to be done and the potential of this site is not exhausted. On the basis of current data, we can note that the organisation of the site into freestanding domestic units of uniform sizes, with axial spaces in between, is reminiscent of roughly contemporary Neolithic villages in the Balkan and Aegean area (Furholt 2016). This places La Marmotta within the cultural tradition of Neolithic Mediterranean villages, reflecting a specific organisation form and type of village life.

5.2. Navigation. Dugout canoes and artefacts related to navigation

Mario Mineo, Juan F. Gibaja, Niccolò Mazzucco and Laura Caruso-Fermé

Mesolithic and Neolithic boats in Europe

Some of the great ancient Mediterranean civilisations were largely seafaring people. Phoenicians, Greeks and Romans, for example, sailed around the Mediterranean Sea to occupy new territories, transport goods and people, and exchange raw materials. A practically enclosed sea, the proximity of the European and African coasts, and the existence of numerous islands, some of considerable size, made it an excellent way to travel rapidly and safely.

However, to discuss the earliest evidence of boats in Europe we need to turn back the clock of history to prehistoric times. Because the first canoes documented to date were made by hunter-gatherer groups in the Mesolithic and the first Neolithic farmers (Cornaggia and Calegari 1978; Lanting 2000). Mesolithic boats have been found at archaeological sites in the north of Europe, where anaerobic conditions of the place in which they were deposited has enabled their preservation. However, Mesolithic groups in the Mediterranean must also have used boats because they were able to reach islands like Cyprus, Corsica, Sicily, Icaria, Lemnos and Melos (Vigne and Desse-Berset 1995; Vigne 1998; Guilaine and Briois 2005; Knapp 2010; Cesari *et al.* 2012; Sampson *et al.* 2012; Efstratiou 2014; Efstratiou *et al.* 2014; Sampson 2014; Simmons 2014; Vigne *et al.* 2013; Moutsiou *et al.* 2021). Melos is precisely one of the places most widely referenced in archaeological literature since it was the source of much of the obsidian documented at Mesolithic sites and especially at Neolithic settlements in the whole Hellenic territory, from Crete to Macedonia (Wagstaff and Cherry 1982; Perlès 1995; 2001).

The last hunter-gatherer societies in the Mesolithic were probably the great originators of knowledge about boat-building, navigation on the sea, lakes and rivers, and the fabrication of numerous implements for fishing and capturing different kinds of aquatic resources. This is shown not only by their canoes but also by nets, hooks and harpoons (Attenbrow *et al.* 1998; Pickard and Bonsall 2007; Lozovski and Lozovskaya 2016; Cristiani and Boric 2020; Zhilin and Savchenko 2020).

Mesolithic canoes have been found at archaeological sites in several countries: at Noyen-sur-Seine and Le-Codray-Montceaux-Nandy, in France; Dümmerlohausen and Stralsund-Mischwasserspeicher, in Germany; Pesse, in Holland; Tybrind Vig, Lystrup and Praestelyng II-Baden in Denmark, and Hotiza, in Slovenia (Andersen 1986; 1994; Arnold 1995; 2014; Guerrero 2006; Klooss and Lübke 2009; Erič and Kavur 2012), among others. Although pine (*Pinus sylvestris*) was most commonly used to make them, the boat-builders occasionally resorted to other trees, like poplar (*Populus tremula*) in the case of the Lystrup canoes, holm oak (*Quercus* sp.) and alder (*Alnus* sp.) for those at Dümmerlohausen, and lime (*Tilia* sp.) for the ones at Tybrind Vig and Stralsund-Mischwasserspeicher. One special case is the canoe from Dabki 9 in Poland, made from the bark of pine or spruce (Kabaciński and Terberger 2015). The choice of wood surely depended on the species in the surrounding areas. Mesolithic communities were perfectly aware of the properties of the

INFORMATION

24973

OBJECT:	Remains of roof
YEAR:	2001
LEVEL:	I
SQUARE:	A133
NUMBER:	24973
SIZE:	437 x 136 x 50 mm

Figure 5.1.10. Remains of roof made with different plant materials (Object No. 24973).

INFORMATION

16957

OBJECT:	Part of the roofing structure
YEAR:	1999
LEVEL:	I
SQUARE:	D45
NUMBER:	16957
SIZE:	720 x 127 x 82 mm

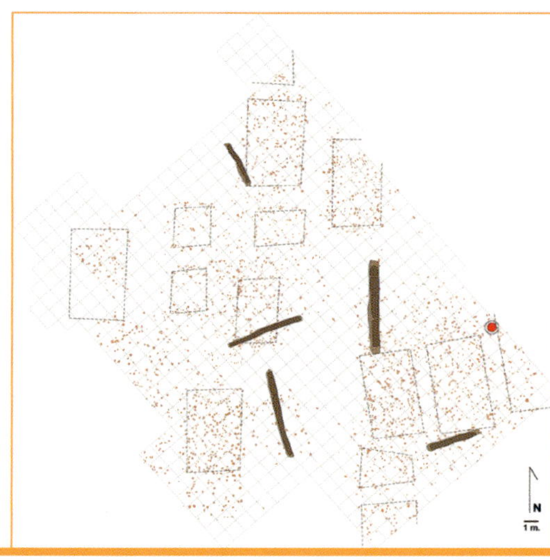

Figure 5.1.11. Wooden implement, probably part of the roofing structure (Object no. 16957).

different species and chose the most appropriate trees to make their boats.

These were all monoxylons, that is to say, dugout canoes, or pirogues, made from a single trunk. They vary greatly in size. Some of the smallest, practical for a single person only, are the Pesse canoe (7920–6470 BC), at only 3 m long, and the one from Noyen-sur-Seine (7190–6540 BC), 4.5 m long. Longer examples are the Lystrup I and II canoes (5200–5000 BC), at 6–7 m, that from Le-Codray-Montceaux (7240–6720 BC) and boat no. 2 at Stralsund-Mischwasserspeicher (4800–4700 BC), both 8 m in length, and those from Tybrind Vig (4300–4100 BC), 10 m long. At a few sites, like Tybrind Vig, Holmegård and Ulkestrup Lyng, some other nautical elements have occasionally been found in association, such as oars (Andersen 1986; 1994; Rieck and Crumlin-Pedersen 1988). Indications of burning inside some of these canoes shows that fire was used in their construction.

It is likely that information transmitted from generation to generation is the explanation for the wide knowledge of sailing possessed by the first farming communities who, in their expansion across the Mediterranean, started from the Near East in about 10,000 cal BC and reached the shores of Portugal in about 5400–5200 cal BC (Guilaine 2000–2001; Gronenborn 2003; Perrin and Manen 2021; Huet *et al.* 2022). In the course of those centuries, technical progress must have improved the boats and increased their size and seaworthiness.

Like the Mesolithic boat-builders, Neolithic farming communities selected different types of wood depending on the place where they lived. Thus, whereas the canoes at Seeland, Denmark (3640 and 2920 BC) were made of alder (*Alnus* sp.), the one at Bevaix, Switzerland (3500–3030 BC) was made of pine (*Pinus* sp.), Canoe 1 at Stralsund-Mischwasserspeicher, Germany, (3858 BC) was made of lime (*Tilia sp.*) and those at Paris-Bercy (2890–2510 BC) and Charente, in France (3650–2900 BC), and the canoe at Šventoji 58, in Lithuania (2895–2640 BC), were made of oak (*Quercus sp.*).

The size of Neolithic canoes also varied considerably. While the one at Charente was 5.56 m long, those at Paris-Bercy measured 6–8 m, the examples at Seeland about 7 m; the one from Bevaix, 8.27 m and the Stralsund-Mischwasserspeicher canoe up to 12 m (Gómez 1982; Rieck and Crumlin-Pedersen 1988; Arnold 1995; Klooss and Lübke 2009; Piličiauskas *et al.* 2020).

The Marmotta canoes: the first nautical engineers in history

Of the five monoxylons documented at La Marmotta so far, only two have been published more-or-less in detail (Fugazzola and Mineo 1995; Fugazzola and Mauro 2014; Mineo 2015). The other three are presented here for the first time.

Canoe Marmotta 1

Canoe 1 was found in Level II (Squares A62, A64, A106, A108–A113, A153, A154, A156 and A157). Excavated in 1994, it is a huge pirogue made from an oak trunk (deciduous *Quercus* sp.), 10.43 m long and 1.15 m wide at the stern and 0.86 m wide at its bow. Its depth varies between 0.65 m and 0.44 m. On the base of the canoe, four transversal trapezoidal re-inforcements made in the trunk would have increased the durability and protection of the hull and facilitated its steering (Fugazzola and Mineo 1995) (Fig. 5.2.1).

Some of the most surprising elements associated with this canoe are three T-shaped pieces on the starboard side. Their shape demonstrates the technical complexity reached by the Neolithic community. They are extremely advanced and hardly any parallels are known in prehistoric archaeology. They are objects whose lower part is ogive-shaped and the upper part is flat. Two, three or four holes were made in the flat part. These pieces were found inserted in the starboard side of the boat so that the holes were visible from the outside at a similar distance and at the same height. The first, with two holes, is 455 mm long at the top, 145 mm wide and 110 mm thick. The lower part measures 235 × 40 × 107.5 mm and the two holes are 25 mm in diameter. The second piece (No. 144363), with three holes 37.5–52.5 mm in diameter, measures 725 × 130 × 187.5 mm in the ogival part and 527.5 × 68 × 122.5 mm at the bottom (Fig. 5.2.2). Finally, the third object, with four holes, with diameters of 20–42.5 mm, measures 622.5 × 140 × 160 mm at the top and 545 × 43 × 113 mm at the bottom.

It is difficult to determine the function of these objects, of which no other archaeological or ethnographic cases are known. Only one relatively similar archaeological example was found at the Neolithic site of Stralsund-Mischwasserspeicher (Funnel Beaker culture) dated to 3618–3530 cal BC. It is a rectangular board, made of alder (*Alnus* sp.) 130 × 380 mm in size, with rounded edges. In the centre, an irregular oval handle made from a single piece of wood has two parallel holes. One side was carefully polished to create an oval form. Several hypotheses have been proposed for this object: that it was linked to some kind of container; formed part of a repaired element; or was used to hold a removable crosspiece at the stern of a canoe (Klooss and Lübke 2009).

In the case of La Marmotta 1, the characteristics and position of these objects on the starboard side suggest that they may have been used to tie ropes connected to a possible sail or other nautical elements, like a stabiliser of even another boat such as a catamaran or a double-hulled canoe. These boating strategies may have given greater safety and stability to the canoe and greater ability to transport people, animals or goods (Guerrero 2006). A wooden object 4 m long and 100 mm wide was found next to the canoe: possibly a kind of bargepole, part of a mast or other object associated with a sail (Fugazzola and Mineo 1995). However, this association

CANOE 1

INFORMATION

OBJECT: Canoe

YEAR: 1994

LEVEL: I-II

SQUARE: A62, A64, A106, A108, A109, A110, A111, A112, A113, A153, A154, A156, A157

NUMBER: Canoe "Marmotta 1"

SIZE: 10,43 x 1,15 x 0,86 m

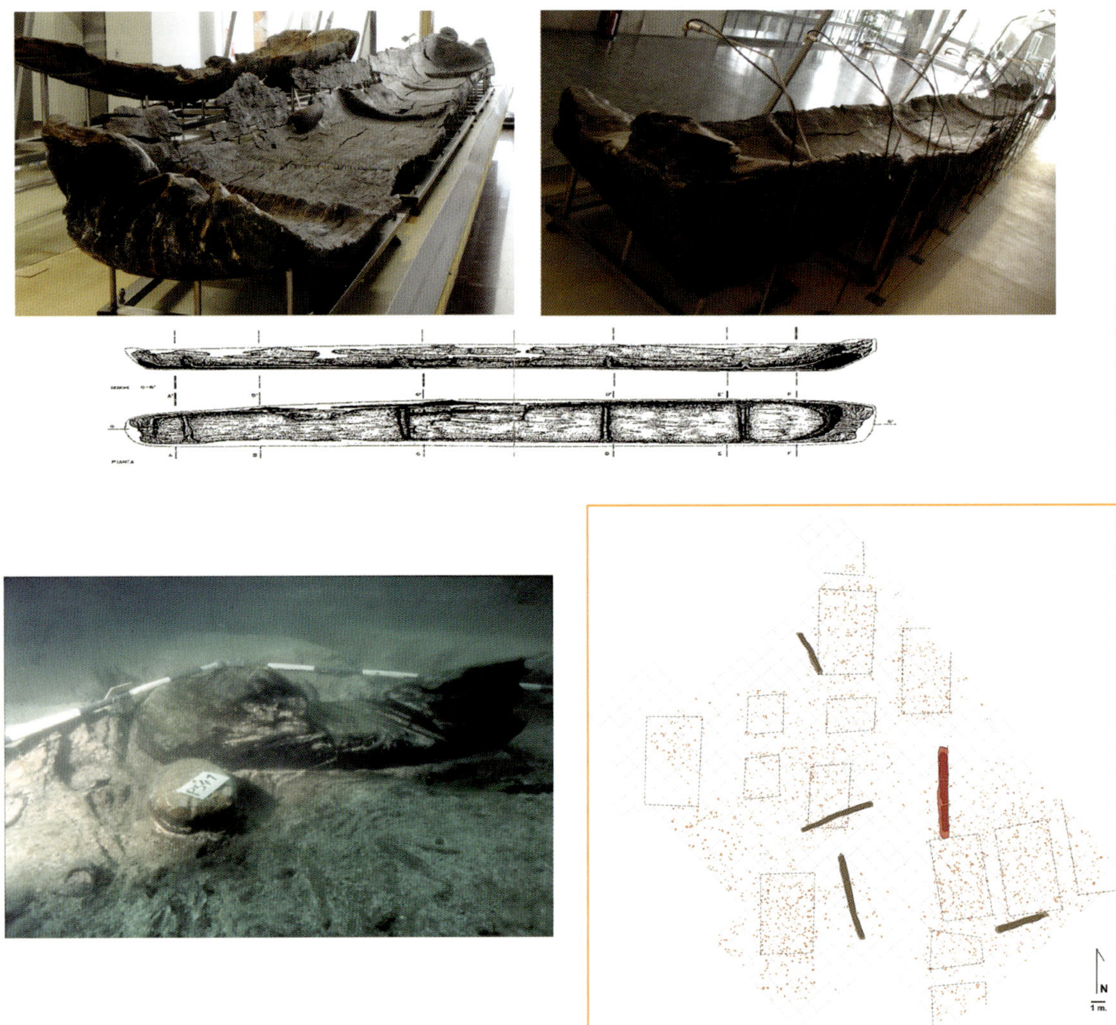

Figure 5.2.1. Canoe Marmotta 1, now on display in the Museo delle Civiltà – Rome (Fugazzola and Mineo 1995).

Figure 5.2.2. T-shaped object with three holes associated with Canoe Marmotta 1 (Object No. 144363).

and interpretation must be taken with caution. This kind of canoe with bargepoles and double hull are well known in ethnographic groups in the Indian and Pacific Oceans (Haddon 1937; Kapitän 1987). The fact that this canoe was found next to one of the huts, tied to seven vertical poles along its port side, suggests that it was being worked on or undergoing repairs (Mineo 2015).

Canoe Marmotta 2

The second pirogue was also found in Level II (Squares D186, D188, D237, D238 and D240). It was discovered in 1998 and excavated in 1999. Made from an alder trunk (*Alnus* sp.), it was fastened to the ground by two sticks in the middle of the port and starboard sides. It is 5.4 m long with widths of 0.4 m at the stern and 0.36 m at its bow. Based on its size and shape it is thought that this canoe was used for hunting and fishing, gathering plants or perhaps for transporting people and small animals on the lake or even in the sea (Fugazzola and Mauro 2014) (Fig. 5.2.3).

A wooden object, very different from those described above, was found next to this dugout. It has a single hole with a diameter of about 28 mm (Fig. 5.2.4). It is mushroom-shaped, 134 mm long and 83–91 mm wide. The characteristics of this object and its similarity to modern bollards found on docksides suggest that it might have functioned in the same way, to secure the canoe when the lake level rose.

Canoe Marmotta 3

The third dugout was discovered at the end of the 2000 fieldwork. The first evidence appeared in Square A263 and belonged to the area of the stern. In later years, 2001 and 2002, excavation continued in Squares A264–A266, A315, A316, A318 and A365–A368 (Levels I and II). At the end of the excavation the canoe was found to have a transversal fracture about 4 m from the stern and from that point the hull was broken longitudinally into two as far as the bow (Fig. 5.2.5).

Made from an alder trunk (*Alnus* sp.), it is 8.35 m long with widths of 0.58 m at the stern and 0.50 m at its bow. Three crosswise re-inforcements made from the trunk itself are seen on its bottom. They are placed at regular distances

INFORMATION

CANOE 2

OBJECT:	Canoe
YEAR:	1998-1999
LEVEL:	II
SQUARE:	D186, D186, D188, D237, D238, D240
NUMBER:	Canoe “Marmotta 2”
SIZE:	5,4 x 0,4 x 0,36 m

Figure 5.2.3. Canoe Marmotta 2, on display in the Museo delle Civiltà – Rome (Fugazzola and Mauro 2014).

INFORMATION

15958

OBJECT:	Possible bollard
YEAR:	1999
LEVEL:	I
SQUARE:	D183
NUMBER:	15958
SIZE:	13,4 x 9,1 x 8,3 cm

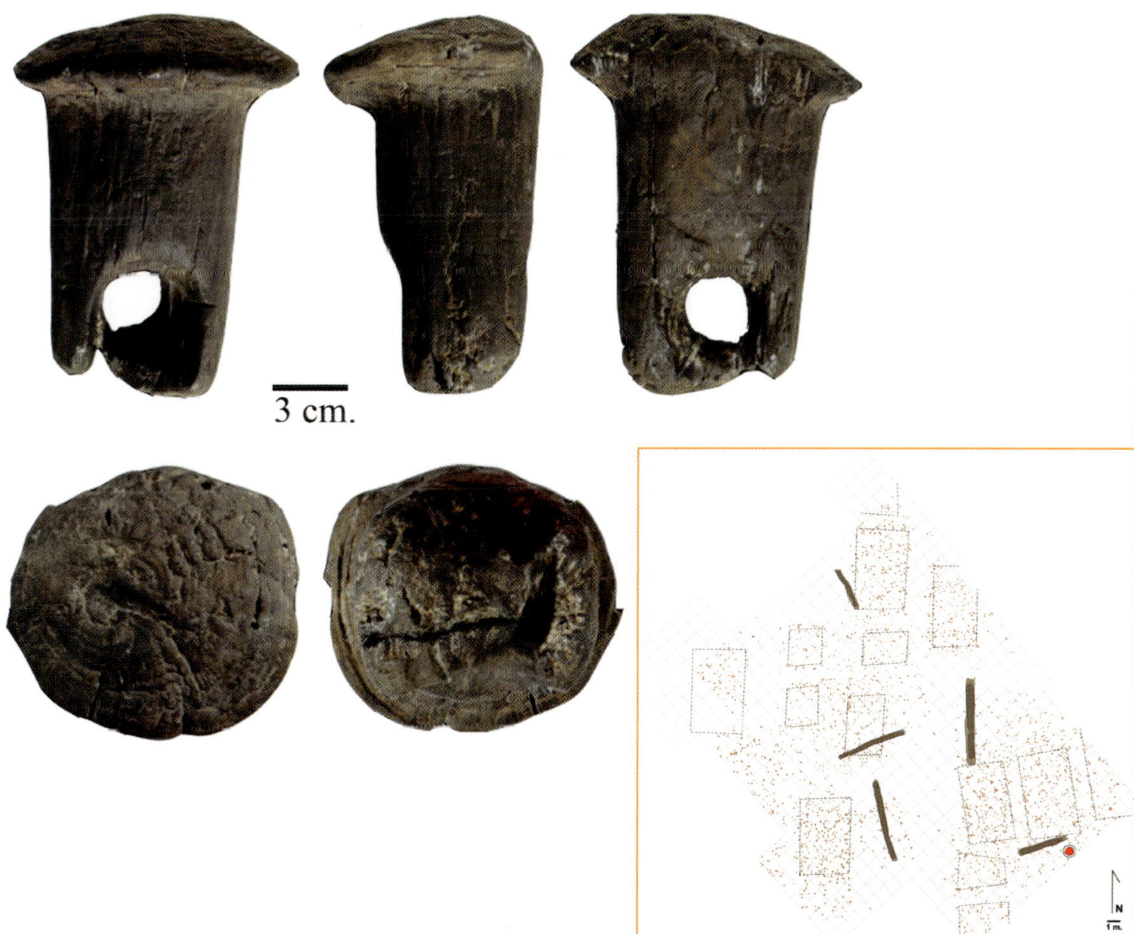

Figure 5.2.4. Possible bollard associate with Canoe Marmotta 2 (Object No. 15958).

and, like Marmotta 1, they are trapezoidal in shape. They are located at 1.90–1.95 m, 4.05–4.10 m and 6.39–6.44 m from the bow.

This pirogue was also fixed to the ground with three sticks: the first, about 2.10–2.20 m from the bow on the left, the second nearly in the middle, 2.90–3.00 m from the bow, and the third about 4.60 m from the bow. Although the canoe might have been undergoing repairs, it cannot be ruled out that it was being re-used to re-inforce the side of the beach, as a form of link between the dwelling area and the water.

Canoe Marmotta 4

After the fourth canoe was discovered in 2001, its excavation continued in 2002 and 2003. Found initially in Level I, during its recovery it was seen that this pirogue also occupied Level II, I and the *Chiocciolaio* level. It was located in Squares A134, A136, A138–A140, A183, A185, A187 and A189 (Fig. 5.2.6).

The canoe was affected by a transversal fracture 4 m from the stern, and the rest of the hull as far as the bow was missing. It was made from a poplar trunk (*Populus* sp.) and in the state in which it was recovered it can only be said that the fragments measured a maximum width of about 0.65 m, and 0.35–0.40 m in the area of the bow.

Canoe Marmotta 5

Canoe 5 was excavated in 2004 and 2005. Owing to its size, it occupied several excavation squares: A401, A 403, A 405, A354, A356, A 358–A362 and D449 (Fig. 5.2.7). Made from a beech trunk (*Fagus sylvatica*), it is currently 9.5 m long, with a maximum width of 0.60 m in the area of the stern. It must have been larger originally because it is fragmented. Two transversal re-inforcements made in the trunk itself are still preserved on the base of the dugout.

The restoration of Canoe 5 began in 2020, through a project promoted by the Museo delle Civiltà de Roma. Although it had been stored in a water tank since its discovery, the conditions were not ideal and it was slowly deteriorating.

Types of wood used

The taxonomical study revealed a heterogeneous use of tree species as raw material for the pirogues. Four species have been identified to make the five canoes and an artefact associated with one of them (the object with four holes).

Canoes Marmotta 2 and 3, and the artefact (No. 144364) were made from *Alnus* sp. whereas deciduous *Quercus* sp. was chosen from Marmotta 1, *Populus* sp. for Marmotta 4 and *Fagus sylvatica* for Marmotta 5. This is an important point, because the diversity of species used to make the dugouts is indicative of the knowledge that the craftsmen possessed of the properties of each species. They were perfectly aware of the types of trees that could be used to make the canoes. This is noteworthy because different types are not usually documented at other Neolithic sites with more than one boat. Thus, for instance, to make the ten canoes at Paris-Bercy (Arnold 1995) only trunks of oak (*Quercus* sp.) were used.

Methods and tools used to make the canoes

Studies carried out on the Marmotta monoxylons show that polished stone adzes and axes were used to create their shape (Fugazzola and Mineo 1995). The array of axes and adzes made from different rocks found at the site give an idea of the range of tools that the inhabitants of La Marmotta employed for woodwork. Some are very small, no more than 30 mm in size, while others are over 200 mm long (Chapter 9.2).

Another technique employed to make the canoes at La Marmotta, and which has been observed in many other European Neolithic boats, was the use of controlled interior burning (Fugazzola and Mineo 1995). Carbonisation speeded up the process of carving out the trunk as it made its removal easier. Nonetheless, this was a long and slow process that would have required hundreds of hours of work by the craftsmen.

Chronology

A programme of radiocarbon dating (using the AMS method) was initiated in 2020–2021 to determine the date at which the trees were cut down to make the five canoes as precisely as possible. The first study, which still needs to be confirmed, indicates that they were made between 5620/5480 and 5305–5045 cal BC. These results coincide with the dates that had been obtained for two of the sticks holding Canoes 1 and 2 to the ground. While the stick associated with the first canoe was dated to 5302–5057 cal BC, the second was dated by dendrochronology to 5384 cal BC (Fugazzola and Mineo 1995; Fugazzola and Mauro 2014).

Oars, paddles and rudders?

Several artefacts that might have been used as oars, paddles or even a rudder were documented during the excavation of the site. Even though they need to be studied further to be sure of their functionality, they are objects that again indicate the importance of sailing for the community and their technical skills.

Object No. 11618 (Level I, Squares D287–D288) is shaped like an oar or a rudder. Found close to Canoe Marmotta 2, it is a total length of 1.05 m, from the shaft to the blade. The latter is rectangular, 400 mm long, 89 × 113 mm thick in the middle and 60 × 15 mm where it merges with the shaft. This has a rounded cross-section in the proximal part and is oval in the middle. It is 650 mm long, with a maximum width of 28.7 mm and thickness of 27 mm in its middle (Fig. 5.2.8).

Object No. 4954 (Level II, Square A151), found near Canoe Marmotta 1, seems to be an oar or paddle. Although it is broken at the proximal end of the shaft, we can imagine

INFORMATION

CANOE 3

OBJECT:	Canoe
YEAR:	2000-2002
LEVEL:	I-II
SQUARE:	A264, A265, A266, A315, A316, A318, A365, A366, A367, A368
NUMBER:	Canoe "Marmotta 3"
SIZE:	8,35 x 0,58 x 0,50 m

Figure 5.2.5. Canoe Marmotta 3, on display in the Museo delle Civiltà – Rome.

INFORMATION

CANOE 4

OBJECT:	Canoe
YEAR:	2001-2003
LEVEL:	II-I-Chiocciolaio
SQUARE:	A134, A136, A138, A139, A140, A183, A185, A187, A189
NUMBER:	Canoe "Marmotta 4"
SIZE:	0,65 x 0,40 x - m

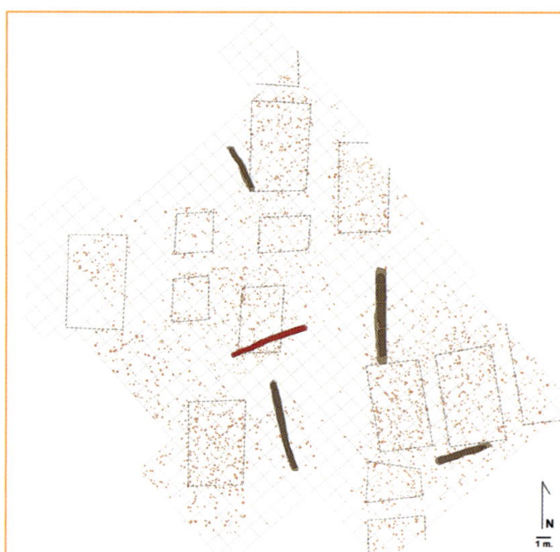

Figure 5.2.6. Canoe Marmotta 4, on display in the Museo delle Civiltà – Rome.

INFORMATION

CANOE 5

OBJECT:	Canoe
YEAR:	2004-2005
LEVEL:	I-II
SQUARE:	A401, A 403, A 405, A354, A356, A 358, A359, A360, A361, A362, D449
NUMBER:	Canoe "Marmotta 5"
SIZE:	9,5 x 0,60 x - m

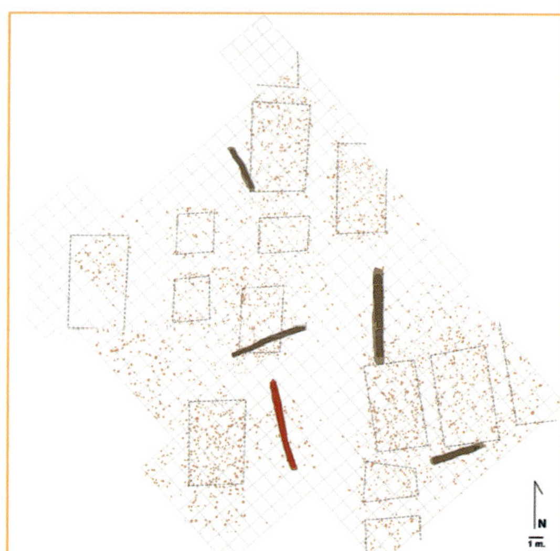

Figure 5.2.7. Canoe Marmotta 5, in storage in the town of Anguillara Sabazia and currently being restored and photograph in situ.

INFORMATION

11618

OBJECT:	Possible oar or rudder
YEAR:	1998
LEVEL:	I
SQUARE:	D287-D288
NUMBER:	11618
SIZE:	13,4 X 9,1 X 8,3 cm

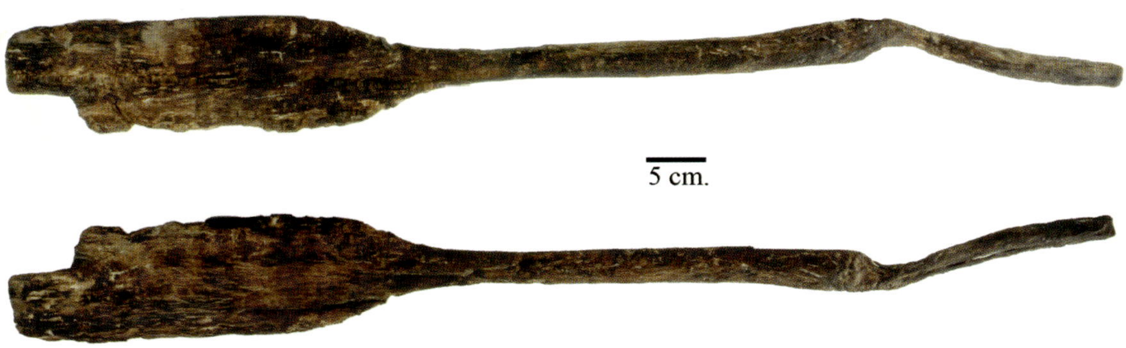

Figure 5.2.8. Possible oar or rudder (Object No. 11618).

INFORMATION

4954

OBJECT:	Possible oar or paddle
YEAR:	1995
LEVEL:	II
SQUARE:	A151
NUMBER:	4954
SIZE:	44 x 10 x 2,8 cm

Figure 5.2.9. Possible oar or paddle (Object No. 4954).

its approximate appearance. It is 440 mm long, of which 160 mm corresponds to the blade and 280 mm to the shaft. The blade, which is slightly trapezoidal in shape, is 100 mm wide and 28 mm thick. The shaft has a round cross-section with a diameter of 22–24 mm. Curiously, the axis of the shaft does not align with the middle of the blade but is displaced slightly to one side (Fig. 5.2.9). In this regard, it may be noted that it resembles some of the small paddles from the site of Fiavé-Carera, not because of a similar use as they are smaller (120 mm long) but because the axis of the blade is slightly displaced from that of the shaft (Perini 1987).

The third object is the blade of another possible oar. No. 12005 (Level I, Square D344) is rectangular, 280 mm long, 170–190 mm wide and 14–16 mm thick. This blade must have been fastened to the shaft by cords because six aligned holes can be seen in the area of the join, three on each side. Although two of the holes are barely preserved because that part of the blade has deteriorated, the others are very similar: oval in shape, with a long axis of 17–18 mm and short axis of 10 mm. This artefact was not found near any of the canoes, since it was recovered in a square between Marmotta 2 and Marmotta 5.

Conclusions

The dugouts from La Marmotta undoubtedly constitute outstanding evidence of boats and nautical systems in prehistory. Their size, the elements found with them and their number, variety and state of conservation make them a key point of reference in the neolithisation process in the Mediterranean and the beginnings of navigation. Although few dugout pirogues have been preserved, those found at La Marmotta and at other Mesolithic and Neolithic sites in Europe, and the fact that many islands in the eastern and central Mediterranean were occupied, attest to the extraordinary capacity of those societies for sea travel.

This capacity has even been demonstrated by experimental archaeology. In 1998, in the framework of the project *Sea Navigation in Early Neolithic Period. A Contribution of Experimental Archaeology to the Beginnings of Mediterranean Neolithization Monoxylon II,* Radomir Tichý made a replica of Canoe Marmotta 1 in which his crew sailed 800 km around the Mediterranean coast from Italy to the Atlantic beaches of Portugal (Tichý 2016). A new pirogue, similar to Marmotta 1, has now been launched as part of the Navis project (https://projektnavis.com). The crew of the *Monoxylon II*, sailors with no experience of navigation, consisted of 8–10 oarsmen and a helmsman. They usually sailed in three-hour shifts for most of the day. In that way they travelled an average of 50 km per day in good weather conditions. If we may suppose that Neolithic sailors were more experienced, they would surely have been able to travel further in less time, especially in the most suitable months.

La Marmotta has revolutionised our image of the first groups of Neolithic farmers. It has always been difficult to imagine how they were able to travel around the Mediterranean: the Marmotta canoes are not only outstanding evidence of how they achieved that but also of the complexity of those societies socially and technically. The dugouts and the other equipment found with them represent knowledge and experience accumulated over centuries and the ability of the craftsmen who made them. They were true specialists: prehistoric nautical engineers. In this way we can understand how they plied the Mediterranean Sea and, in few centuries, occupied the entire European and African coasts.

5.3. Wooden artefacts

Juan F. Gibaja, Mario Mineo, Vittorio Brizzi, Niccolò Mazzucco, Laura Caruso-Fermé, Miriam Cubas, Gerard Remolins, Daniele Arobba, Rosanna Caramiello and Lionello F. Morandi

The importance of vegetal and animal materials for making wood tools, textiles, baskets and cordage in prehistory is inversely proportional to their appearance at archaeological sites. Time and the problem of preservation have usually robbed us of those objects. But their study, with ethnographic information as a point of reference, can provide very valuable data about past societies: their ways of life, technology, knowledge of their environments, relationships with other communities and, in general, about the economic, social and symbolic value of those artefacts.

Environmental conditions very occasionally give archaeologists an opportunity to study them. In places of extreme cold or heat, or in aquatic or waterlogged sites, the reduction in oxygen and bacteria can allow their preservation. Their discovery is always surprising and radically changes our view of the prehistoric societies that made them.

Thus a few prehistoric sites have fortunately opened a door to the past wherever the conservation of vegetal and soft animal matter has allowed us to know their magnitude and importance. Paradigmatic cases include Ötzi the Iceman, discovered in the Alps in 1991 as a consequence of ice melting (Fowler 2000), and other lacustrine and maritime sites next to water or peat deposits in several countries in Europe. These are often dated between the Mesolithic and the Iron Age.

Although it is not possible to mention all the sites where wooden objects and utensils have been found, it is important to cite some particular cases belonging to the Neolithic, the period that La Marmotta corresponds to. They provide a very different picture of those farming societies from the one obtained at dry sites where, usually, only remains of pottery, bones, lithic implements and sometimes seeds and small fragments of charcoal are recovered. Among the examples nearest to La Marmotta, lacustrine sites in the area of Alps have been designated World Heritage sites by UNESCO since 2011 with the name of 'Prehistoric pile-dwellings around the Alps'. Belonging to Italy, Germany, Austria, Slovenia and France, they are dated between the middle of the Early Neolithic (*c.* 5300 cal BC) and the Late Bronze Age (last centuries of the second millennium cal BC). They include, for example, the settlements of Egolzwil, Muntelier/Fischergässli, Burgäschisee and Auvernier-Port, in Switzerland; Chalain and Clairvaux, in France; and Palù di Livenza, Bodio Lomnago and Fimon-Molino Casarotto in Italy, among others (Bagolini *et al.* 1973; Egloff 1987; Petrequin and Petrequin 1988; Wyss 1994; Ramseyer 2000; Schlichtherle *et al.* 2013; Gibaja *et al.* 2016; Micheli *et al.* 2018; Hafner *et al.* 2020).

Far fewer sites are known in the Mediterranean area. Of varying chronologies, the following may be cited: La Draga, in Spain (early Neolithic), Anarghiri IXb and Dispilio, in Greece (with occupations during the different stages of the Neolithic), Dunavec and Maliq, in Albania (Middle and Late Neolithic, respectively) and Ohrid in North Macedonia (Middle–Late Neolithic) (Hourmouziadis 1996; Bosch *et al.* 2000; Sofronidou 2008; Palomo *et al.* 2011; Prendi 2018; Giagkoulis 2020; Naumov 2020). La Marmotta would therefore be the oldest lacustrine Neolithic site in the Mediterranean area as demonstrated by the ages obtained for wood and seeds by rediocarbon dating and dendrochronology (see Chapter 3).

The construction of the houses, boats and a large number of objects and tools demonstrate the importance of wood for those communities. If access to freshwater and fertile land were two basic needs for their farming activity, the proximity to areas of mature woodland must have been another criterion they took into account when settling in a new territory and starting a new life.

This section will describe some of these wooden objects and implements made and used by the human groups that lived at La Marmotta. They are so numerous that the most representative and particular objects have been selected for description here. Through them, it is possible to envisage the wealth of archaeological remains that have been found and imagine what daily life would have been like in a Neolithic settlement. Building materials, boats and some tools probably used to make textiles, ropes and baskets will be studied in other chapters.

While it is a gaze over the past, we might almost say that it is also a look at the present, as many of the tools and techniques that our ancestors employed to make these artefacts have hardly changed with time. Apart from the replacement of stone tools by metal ones and the introduction of glass, the observation of La Marmotta is almost like viewing a medieval village or even some small contemporary rural villages in Italy, Greece or Spain.

The following descriptions will refer to objects whose form can be recognised because they are whole or practically whole. However, a large number of fragments have been recovered for which it is not possible to determine what kind of artefact they belonged to. They were obviously fabricated, but their small size or shapelessness does not allow their identification.

One problem that is often encountered when studying wooden remains is that when they are taken out of the water they inexorably undergo modifications. This makes it very difficult to assess all the technical processes involved in their manufacture because many of the technological traces are lost during their extraction and restoration. However, in the present case, it can be noted that the restoration process has achieved excellent results and succeeded in preserving the objects fully. They can now be handled, exhibited and stored without any risk of their destruction.

Containers

A total of five wooden contaners have been documented. As in the case of the pottery vessels, they vary in size although it is not always easy to assess their volume and shape. The problem is that some of them were burnt and are incomplete. This is the case of three examples of which only bases have been recovered (SR019, Level I, Indeterminate Square; 14027 (Fig. 5.3.1), Level I, Square D140; 5174, Level I, Square A251). Although the volume of these containers cannot be calculated, the sizes of the bases indicate that the first one must have been small because it measures about 120 mm, while the second and third were quite large because, even though not all the base was preserved, their diameters would be about 200 mm and 370 mm, respectively.

Regarding the two containers whose shape can be defined, No. 11272 (Level I, Square D342) is a cylindrical bowl that has lost much of its upper part. As a result, only a small portion of the rim has been preserved. This was a small vessel whose measurements are 135 mm in diameter and 40–75 mm in height, with walls that are 5–7 mm thick.

The third wooden recipient is also cylindrical (34424, Level II, Square A438). It is practically whole as it has only lost a small part of the rim. It would be a relatively small bowl, 165 mm in diameter and 75 mm high, with walls varying between 4 mm and 10 mm in thickness (Fig. 5.3.2).

All the bases are flat or slightly convex and therefore they could have been placed on a flat surface without any danger of spilling the contents. They are well-finished. The walls must have been worked with small chisels to hollow out the interior and shape the walls and base. It is very likely, that in the final phase of work, a flint implement or other kind of abrasive rock was used to scrape the walls and rims. This can be clearly seen in some areas of the vessels, where the walls and interior of the base are marked by numerous striations and abrasions. Similarly, striations can be seen on the rims of some contaners, made by cutting tools used to extract small pieces of wood and obtain a symmetric shape (Fig. 5.3.2).

INFORMATION

14027

OBJECT:	Base of a large wooden container
YEAR:	1998
LEVEL:	I
SQUARE:	D140
NUMBER:	14027
SIZE:	170 x 140 x 12 mm

Figure 5.3.1. Base of a large wooden container, badly affected fire (Object No. 14027).

INFORMATION

34424

OBJECT:	Wooden container
YEAR:	2003
LEVEL:	II
SQUARE:	A438
NUMBER:	34424
SIZE:	165 x 75 x 10 mm

3 cm.

1,5 cm.

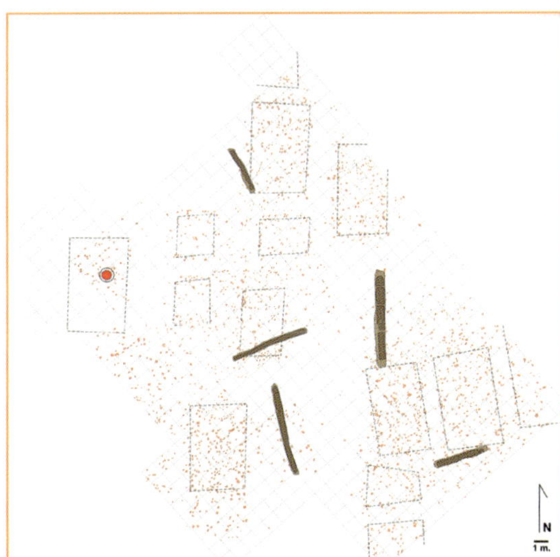

Figure 5.3.2. Almost complete wooden container (Object No. 34424).

Unlike the pottery, these containers do not appear to have been decorated. However, we cannot be totally sure because of the small number of them and they are not all complete. Furthermore, the use of paint that has not survived cannot be ruled out. However, to the naked eye, their walls are completely smooth, without impressed and incised decoration or holes.

Spatulas

These are among the most abundant utensils at La Marmotta. In general terms they are objects with a thin and usually very long handle and a flat end of very different shapes. A total of 12 full or partial specimens have been recovered. A further six artefacts might be part of the handles but without the working end. Although they resemble the handles of whole spatulas, they might also be part of other utensils, like spindles, or hafts.

While many examples have lost part of the handle, which makes it difficult to estimate their length, the complete specimens range from relatively small spatulas, 270 mm long, to others over 455 mm long. They are well finished with completely straight long profiles, which reflects the precision of the artisan's work.

The heads of the spatulas take different forms. Although round ones stand out (Fig. 5.3.3), others are semi-circular, hexagonal or rhomboidal. They are usually between 50 mm and 80 mm long, 45–65 mm wide and 3–8 mm thick. The handles have a round or slightly oval cross-section with a diameter of 5.5–9.2 mm (Fig. 5.3.4 and 5.3.5).

Like the spatulas in our own kitchen, their flat cross-section shows that they were used mainly to stir liquids or food that was not too thick; otherwise the long thin handles would have broken. These spatulas are so numerous that they must have been commonly used utensils for the inhabitants of La Marmotta.

Mixer

One of the artefacts resembles the mixers used to make cheese or butter (6272, Level I, Square A55). Its 'paddle' end is a triangular shape that is open in the middle. Although the handle is a little broken, it is 230 mm long in total, or which 130 mm correspond to the 'paddle', which has a maximum width of 50 mm and thickness of 9 mm or 11 mm. The handle has a maximum width of 23 mm (where it joins the 'paddle') and is 7 mm thick (Fig. 5.3.6).

Ladles

Unlike the spatulas, the ladles possess a very long handle, which is sometimes curved, and a small semi-spherical bowl. Of all the specimens recovered, two are complete, which allows an assessment of their appearance (45995, Level II, Square A510; 17200, Level I, Square D39). Unfortunately, only the ends of the other three have been preserved, often deteriorated by the action of fire (10136, Level II, Square D298; 17271, Level II, Square A510; 17582, Level I, Square D38) (Fig. 5.3.7).

One of the complete ladles (No. 45995) has a handle that is curved in the part next to the bowl. Although it is 365 mm long, the bowl-shaped part is only 70 mm in diameter. The handle is 8–19 mm wide and 8–11 mm thick. The bowl is 40 mm high with walls from 4–9 mm thick (Fig. 5.3.8).

The second of the complete ladles, No. 17200, is similar to the previous one: a curved handle finishing in a small bowl. 515 mm in length; the bowl has a diameter of 94 mm, walls 6 mm thick and a height of 67 mm. Of the three that only preserve the end, they possess a bowl 77–107 mm long, 68–107 mm wide, and 36–57 mm high. However, their measurements are difficult to calculate because of their degree of deterioration. Their handles are much more robust than in the case of the spatulas because, obviously, they needed to support a heavier weight. They are between 17 mm and 20 mm in diameter.

Number 17271 only consists of the bowl, which is cylindrical with an oblique upper part. The place where the bowl would connect with the handle has been preserved. Slightly oval, it is 98–107 mm in diameter, from 57 mm to 92 mm high and its walls are about 6 mm thick.

Sickles

Sickles are among the most representative tools at the site. This is probably connected to the importance of cultivation for the community. This is shown not only by the number of complete and fragmented wooden sickles, of varying sizes and state of preservation (Table 5.3.1) but also by the 500 lithic artefacts with cereal gloss among the 12,139 chipped lithic objects that have been studied (Chapter 9.1).

Two large groups of sickles can be discriminated based on their shape, although they have in common a slightly concave working edge in which flint pieces were inserted. These are normally blade fragments that were placed diagonally in the form of teeth. The number of teeth varied a little depending on the size of the flints and the sickle and the length of the part in which they are inserted. However, the complete sickles usually contain between six and nine flint pieces.

The fundamental difference between the two groups of sickles is that the handles in one group are closed into a loop and in the other they are open. However, within each group there are variations that allow an assessment of the technical complexity involved in their manufacture and the link between their use and the handle of the sickle (Fig. 5.3.9).

In Types 1a and 1b, the handle is closed at the end of the sickle, following the same axis. In contrast, Types 1c, 1d and 1e are slightly different because the end of the handle does not follow that axis and coincides with the start of the serrated blade and the first flint pieces. In both cases, the handle is semi-circular with a round or oval cross-section and, in the case of Type 1c, has an appendix to which a cord may have been tied to help hold the sickle. Flint

INFORMATION

17903

OBJECT:	Circular spatula
YEAR:	1999
LEVEL:	I
SQUARE:	D83
NUMBER:	17903
SIZE:	400 x 55 x 9 mm

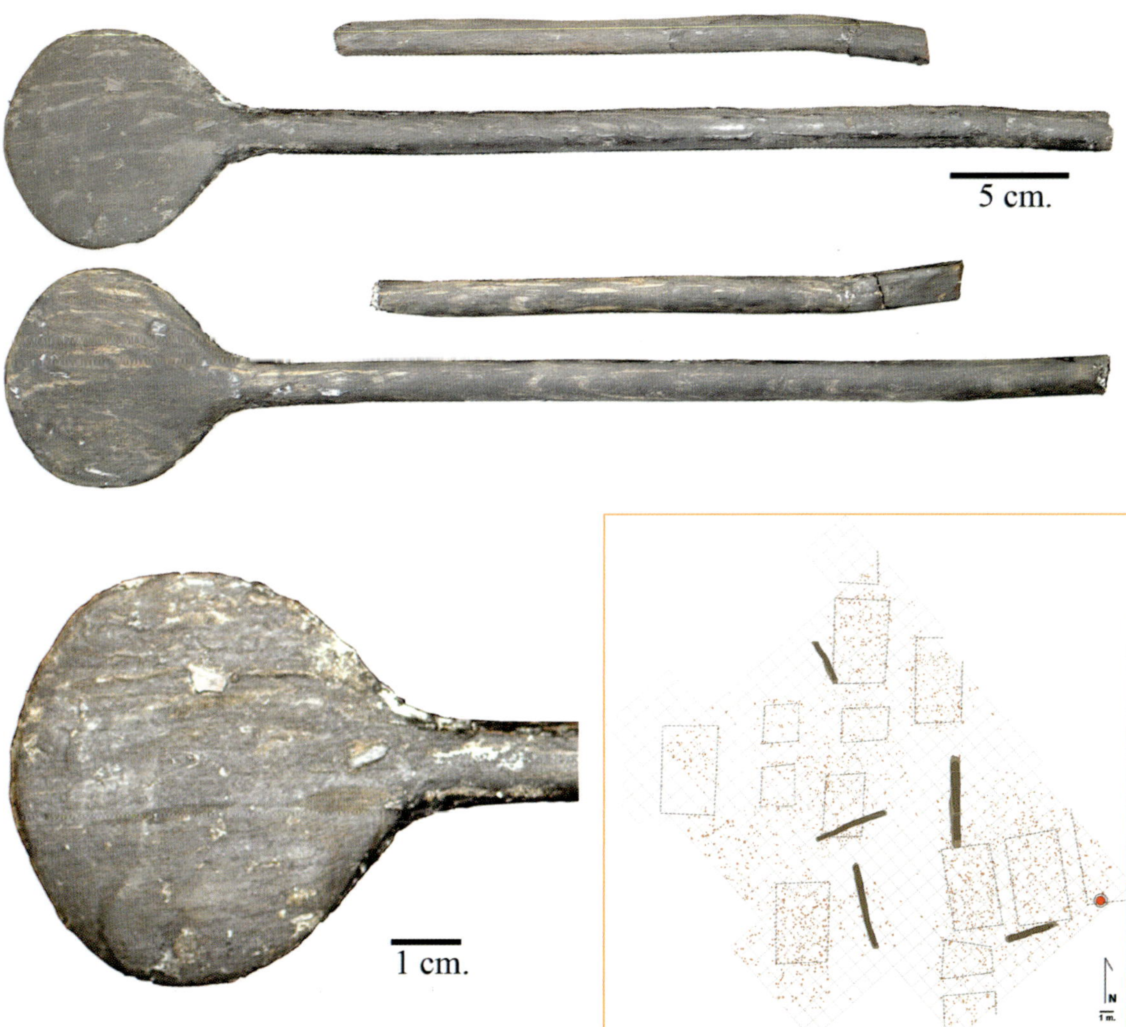

Figure 5.3.3. Circular spatula (Object No. 17903).

INFORMATION **11163**

OBJECT:	Semicircular spatula
YEAR:	1998
LEVEL:	I
SQUARE:	D288
NUMBER:	11163
SIZE:	218 x 60 x 9,2 mm

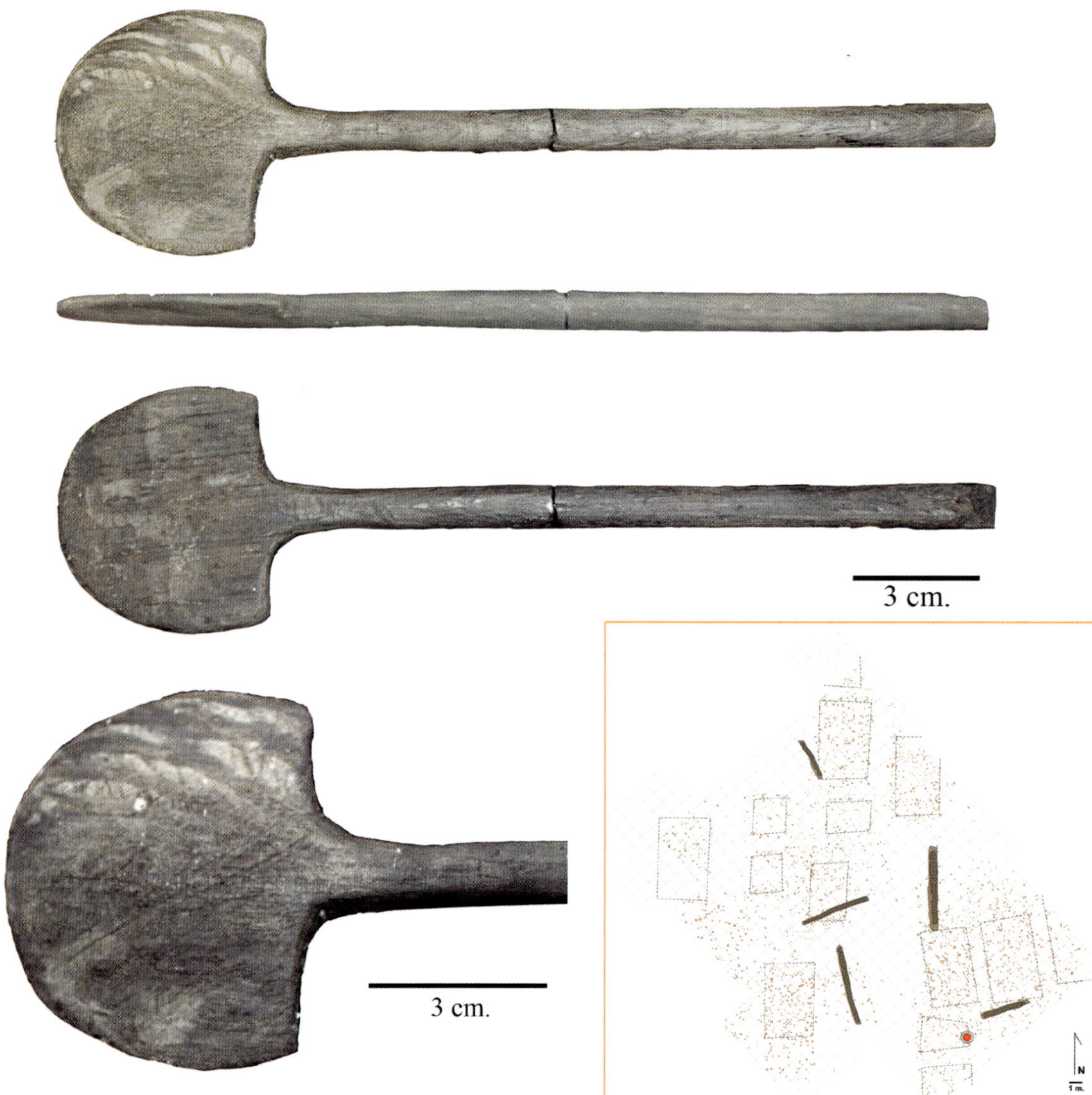

Figure 5.3.4. Semicircular spatula (Object No. 11163).

INFORMATION

17276

OBJECT:	Rhomboidal spatula
YEAR:	1999
LEVEL:	II
SQUARE:	D38
NUMBER:	17276
SIZE:	199 x 80 x 8,9 mm

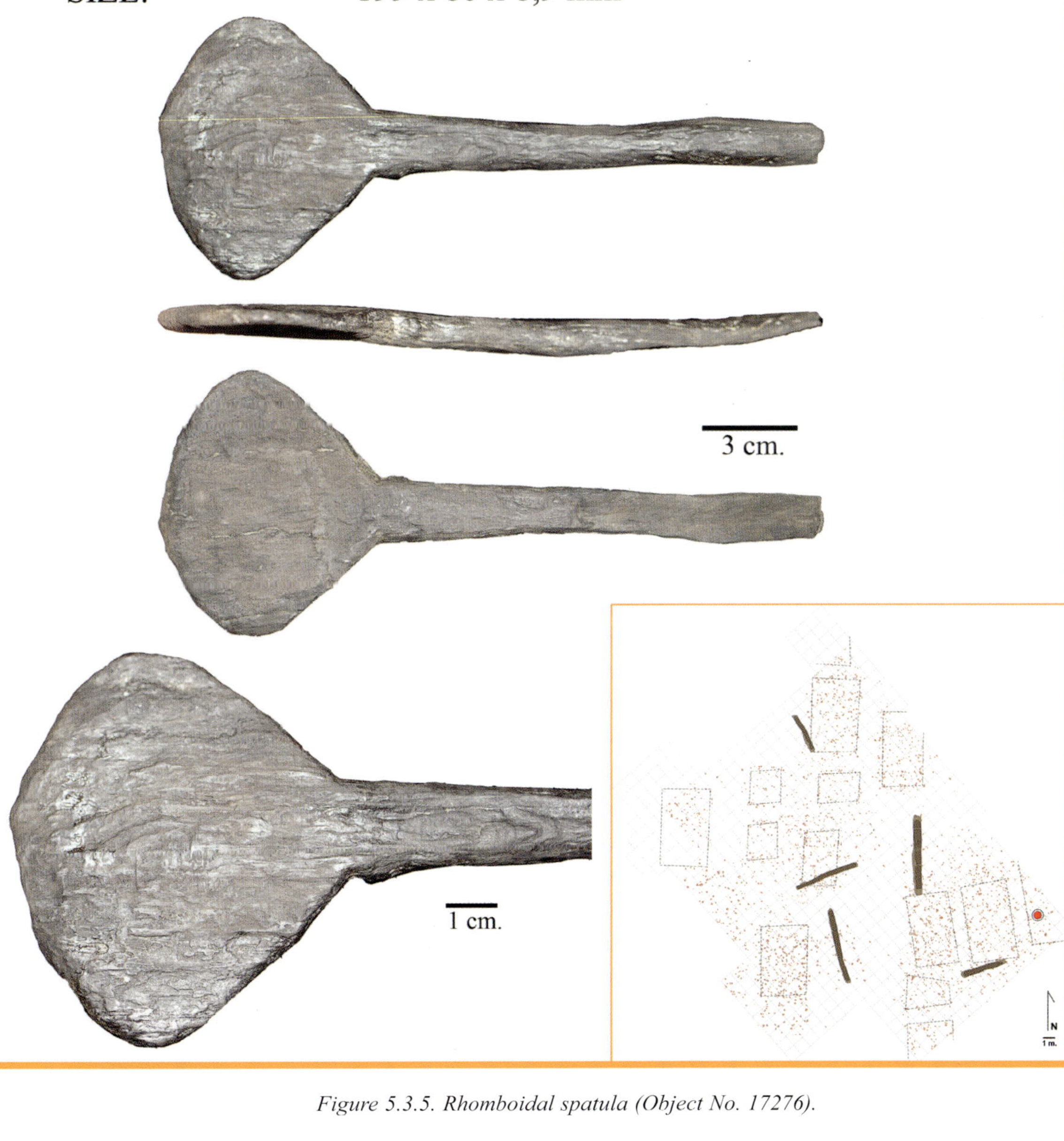

Figure 5.3.5. Rhomboidal spatula (Object No. 17276).

INFORMATION

6272

OBJECT:	Possible wooden mixer
YEAR:	1996
LEVEL:	I
SQUARE:	A55
NUMBER:	6272
SIZE:	230 x 50 x 11 mm

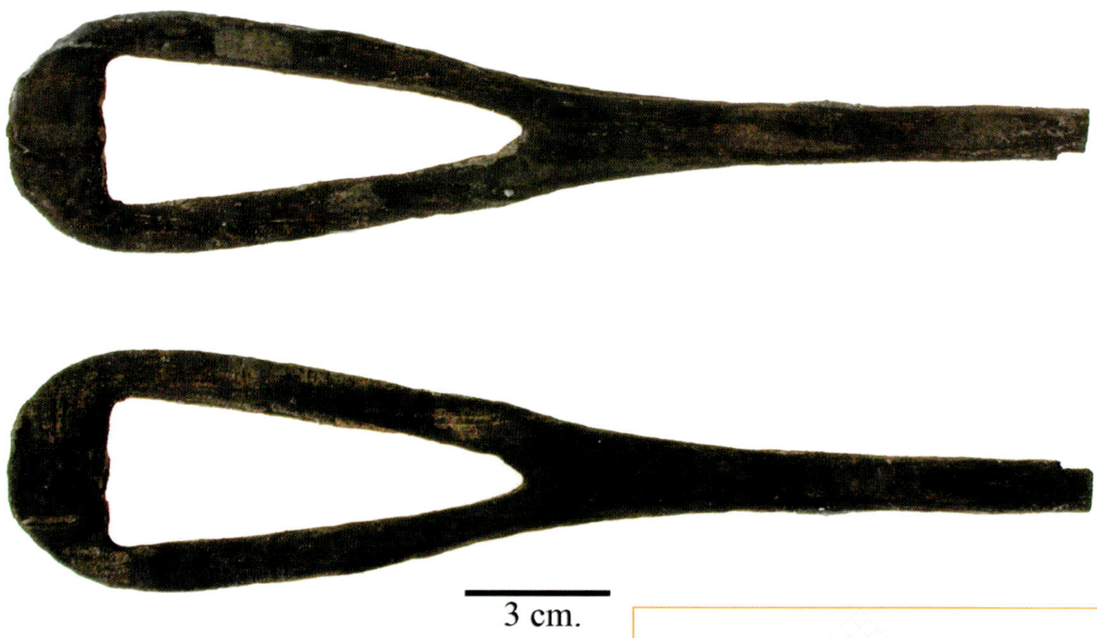

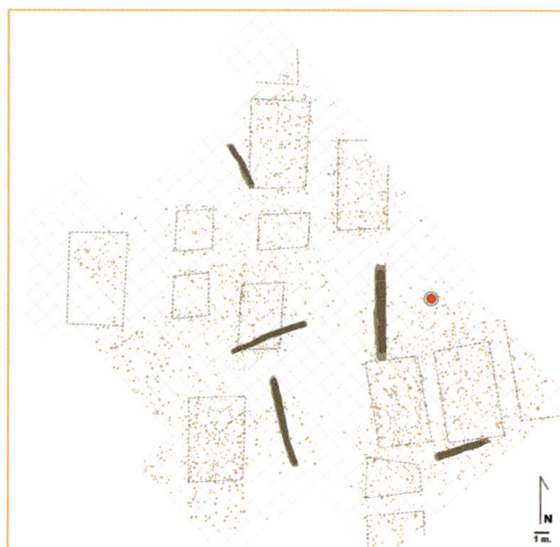

Figure 5.3.6. Possible wooden mixer (Object No. 6272).

INFORMATION

10136

OBJECT:	Wooden ladle
YEAR:	1997
LEVEL:	II
SQUARE:	D298
NUMBER:	10136
SIZE:	145 x 68 x 20 mm

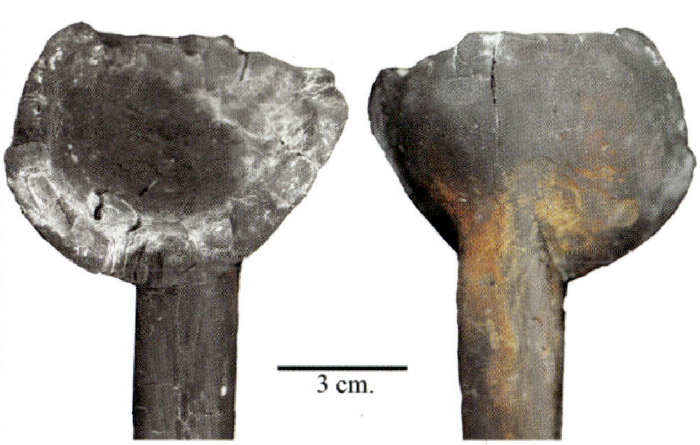

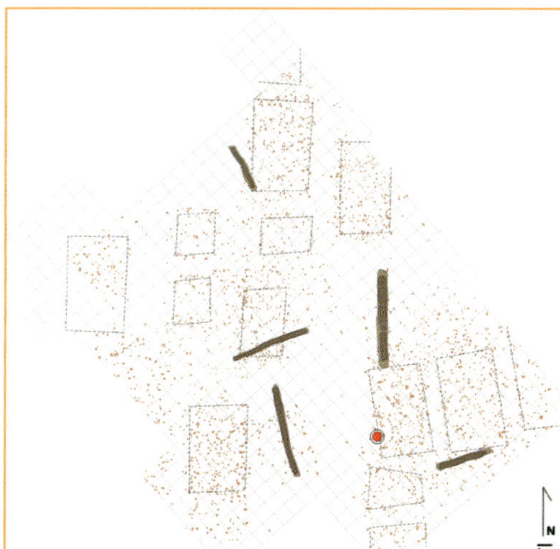

Figure 5.3.7. Wooden ladle. Much of the object is burnt, especially the bowl (Object No. 10136).

INFORMATION

45995

OBJECT:	Wooden ladle
YEAR:	2005
LEVEL:	II
SQUARE:	A510
NUMBER:	45995
SIZE:	365 x 70 x 11 mm

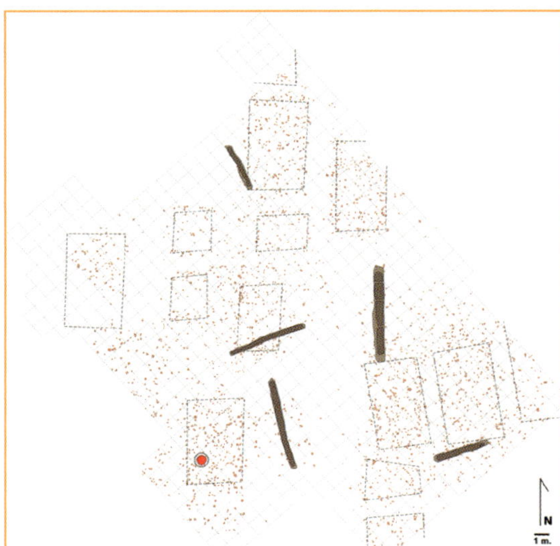

Figure 5.3.8. Complete wooden ladle (Object No. 45995).

blades and, less frequently, flakes were fixed diagonally to the sickle haft. These were all of a similar width to achieve a toothed edge.

Fortunately, the state of preservation of the sickles allows their sizes to be determined, as some of them are complete or practically whole. Thus, Type 1c for example, corresponding to Sickle 49965 (Level II, Square A611–A613), is 315 mm long, of which 146 mm correspond to the handle and 169 mm to the working edge where the flint pieces would be fitted. The handle is 62 mm wide and 12–25 mm thick. The upper part, where the flint pieces (which are not preserved) would have been, has a maximum width of 50 mm and thickness of 12 mm in the part where the teeth would be inserted and 3 mm on the opposite side. It therefore has a triangular cross-section.

Type 1d, represented by Sickle 7186 (Level I, Square D147) is 252 mm long: 115 mm correspond to the handle and 160 mm to the sickle blade. The handle is 80 mm wide and 22–24 mm thick. The sickle blade, in which three pieces of flint are still inserted, has a maximum width of 50 mm, excluding the flint blades, and is 15.3 mm thick on the side with the blades and 9.7 mm thick on the opposite side (Fig. 5.3.10).

The Type 2 sickles vary mainly in their different sizes and particularly in the lower appendix of the handle. Type 2a, represented by Sickle 23001 (Level II, Square A179) is 285 mm long, of which 104 mm correspond to the handle and 181 mm to the blade. It is 18–21 mm wide in the handle and 35–40 mm wide in the sickle blade. It is between 10 mm and 17 mm thick, depending on the part of the sickle. A series of small notches on the back edge of the sickle blade would have been decorative.

Type 2d, corresponding to Sickle 44297 (Level I, Square A507), is 365 mm long, 175 mm of which belong to the blade. While the handle is 20 mm wide and between 11 mm and 14 mm thick, the blade has a maximum width of 40 mm and thickness of 5–10 mm. The transversal appendix is 70 mm long and 8 mm thick. This sickle must have held eight blade fragments, although one of the pieces in the middle is missing. One matter that has not been resolved is the function of the pointed appendix. Was it used to separate the stems of the cereals? Was it connected with some activity involving the ground? If it was used to make holes in the soil, it would probably display numerous striations and small fractures, which are not seen. The questions remain unanswered because no similar archaeological, ethnographic or historical examples are known (Fig. 5.3.11).

The handles of these sickles all have a flat and smooth transversal appendix. An isolated fragment of this part of a sickle handle displays two holes (No. 20387, Level II, Square A114). This again suggests the use of a cord to grip the sickle more securely during harvesting and perhaps to hang it up.

These different types of sickles are indicative of a technical complexity not seen at contemporaneous or even more modern sites (Mazzucco *et al.* 2020; 2022a). Sickles were made with a huge degree of effectiveness in which the handles played several complementary functions, such as to protect the hand when reaping, secure the sickle with a cord so that it would not slip out of the harvester's hand, or with an appendix to separate the stems and ears when they were being cut.

These sickles represent a large investment of labour and were made to last. The flint blades, which would not have needed much work to make, could easily be replaced if

Table 5.3.1. Sickles. Size and state of preservation (all references with 'SR' are pieces without an archaeological number).

Object No.	*Layer*	*Square*	*Length (max. mm)*	*Width (max. mm)*	*Thickness (max mm)*	*With lithic tools?*	*Structural condition*
4279	I	A101	204	46	14	yes	almost complete
5151_1	Indet	Indet	101	39	12	yes	fragment
5151_2	Indet	Indet	95	17	3	not	fragment
6145	Indet	A105	89	15	14	not	fragment
6207	I	A105	245	34	11	not	almost complete
6507	I	D198	312	28	15	yes	complete
6693	I	D197	130	31	8	not	fragment handle
6899	I	D248	195	43	16	not	fragment
7110	I	D150	92	23	14	not	fragment
7186	I	D147	252	50	15.33	yes	complete
7290	Chiocc	D97	155	52	15	yes	fragment
7437	I	D48	200	28	10	not	almost complete
7560	I	D100	290	45	13.38	not	almost complete

(Continued)

Table 5.3.1. Sickles. Size and state of preservation. (Continued)

Object No.	*Layer*	*Square*	*Length (max. mm)*	*Width (max. mm)*	*Thickness (max mm)*	*With lithic tools?*	*Structural condition*
9042	I	D195	140	18	9	not	fragment handle
9649	I	D294	150	29	18	not	fragment
10853	Chiocc	D394	118	23	14	not	fragment handle
11354	I	D287	257	35	9	yes	almost complete
12020	I	D340	210	43	10	not	fragment handle
15046	I	D184	290	47	15	not	almost complete
15478	I	D184	313	38	13	yes	almost complete
15854	Ii	D184	175	23	17	not	fragment
17000	I	D42	152	44	16	not	fragment
17029	I	D45	111	30	14	not	fragment
19540	I	A126-A124	252	45	15.36	not	almost complete
19806	Ii	A114	111	38	14	not	fragment
20387	Ii	A114	115	22	11.48	not	fragment handle
20616	I	A164	247	32	15	not	fragment handle
22446	I	A129	248	29	6	not	almost complete
26684	I	A166	112	15	12	not	fragment handle
29190	I	A35	85	12	9	not	fragment
30041	I	A34	124	34	12	not	fragment
30156	Ii	A38	110	9	7.8	not	fragment handle
30394	I	A30	152	47	15	not	fragment
30413	I	A30	160	40	14	not	fragment
31188	I	A342	175	41	11	not	fragment
32756	I	A365	230	37	6	not	almost complete
37963	I	A488	290	35	14.8	not	almost complete
38051	I	A443	303	45	35	not	fragment
41748	I	A358	183	43	14	not	medial fragment
42921	I	A503	295	58	9	not	almost complete
44297_3	I	A507	365	40	10	yes	complete
44754	I	A515	246	50	5	not	almost complete
44766	I	A509	90	72	20	not	fragment handle
47443	I	A464	112	25	12	not	fragment
48526	I	A605	283	60	-	yes	almost complete
48721	I	A558	275	37	10	not	almost complete
49965	Ii	A611-A613	310	50	12	not	complete
30449A	I	A83	70	40	11	yes	fragment
SR003	I	A203	88	23	9	yes	fragment
SR017	Chiocc	Indet	130	11	9	not	fragment handle
SR018	I	A203	88	27	13	yes	fragment
23001	Ii	A179	285	40	15	yes	complete
182760	I	A65	260	20	26	yes	almost complete
1370	I	E19	225	27	15	yes	almost complete
SR008	Indet	Indet	42	24	8	yes	fragment (ceramic)

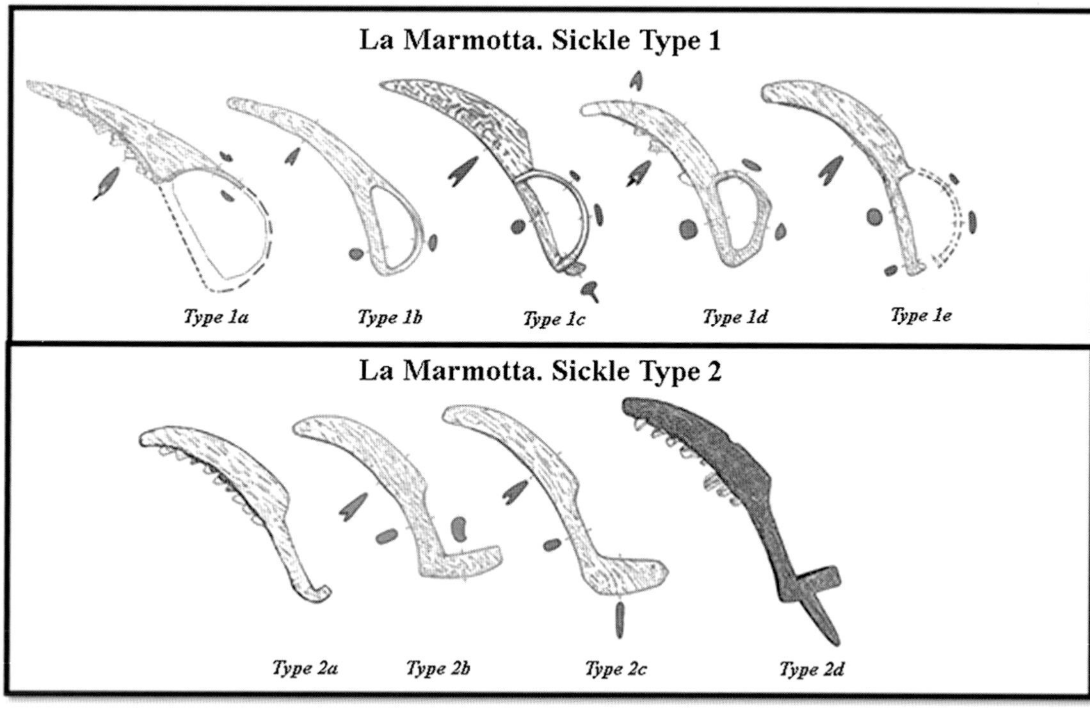

Figure 5.3.9. Typology of the sickles documented at La Marmotta.

they were lost, broken or worn out. It was only necessary to warm the part with the resin to remove the ones that were no longer effective and insert new blades or flakes.

One specimen stands out because it were made with clay. This is a small fragment (SR008) of a larger clay sickle. Although its full length cannot be determined, the fragment is 42 mm long, 25 mm wide (including the flint) and 10 mm thick. It only holds a small fragment of a blade inserted diagonally. The flint displays gloss showing that it was used to reap cereals. The intensity of the gloss can only have generated in the course of several hours of work, which means that the flint was used for a long time. The flint blade had been inserted in soft clay without any kind of resin.

The use of clay as a raw material to make tools in general, and sickles in particular, is absolutely unknown in Neolithic archaeology. We are not sure whether the clay was fired or only left to dry. The microscopic observation of the surface shows that the fabric contains few inclusions, apart from some small quartz grains that might even be naturally present in the clay.

This object is difficult to understand. Cereal harvesting is a task that exercises considerable force on the sickle and the hafted blades. This can be seen in the wear on wooden sickles, affecting both the blade and the handle. Wooden sickles require a great deal of adhesive to stop the flints moving and falling out of the haft. It is therefore difficult to imagine that this clay sickle, which would have been so fragile, could have been used to harvest cereals with the flint blades only fixed to the haft by the clay itself. During such hard work as harvesting, the flint elements would probably soon fall out.

It may therefore be wondered if its value and use was only symbolic. In the Neolithic, especially in the eastern Mediterranean, it is common to find clay models, normally miniatures of objects, animals, individuals, food, structures and architecture (Marangou 1996; Nanoglou 2009; Mazzucco *et al.* 2022b). These objects possessed no utilitarian function but were used to represent behaviour and practices that are largely unknown to us and which we usually regard as ritual. Clay miniatures of containers and canoes have been recovered at La Marmotta (Fugazzola 2004b).

It is true that ceramic sickles were used to harvest cereals in the Near East and they were even abundant in the El-Obeid and Uruk periods (Cauvin 1983; Benco 1992; Anderson and Formenti 1996). The blade of those sickles is a bevelled edge made by polishing the clay before it was fired (Benco 1992). No flint was hafted into them.

In conclusion, the sickle gloss on the flint in the clay sickle fragment at La Marmotta (SR008) can be explained in two ways: 1) the clay sickle really was used to harvest cereals until it broke; or 2) the flint blade was used for harvesting fitted in another tool, probably a wooden sickle. It was fixed in the clay sickle after being taken from its original haft. We now need to determine whether this clay object was fired or only left to dry. We also need to test its effectivity and resistance for cereal harvesting experimentally.

INFORMATION

7186

OBJECT: Sickle
YEAR: 1996
LEVEL: I
SQUARE: D147
NUMBER: 7186
SIZE: 115 x 44 x 15,3 mm

Figure 5.3.10. Almost complete sickle. It still conserves some of the flint teeth (Object No. 7186).

INFORMATION

44297

OBJECT:	Sickle
YEAR:	2005
LEVEL:	I
SQUARE:	A507
NUMBER:	44297
SIZE:	365 x 40 x 10 mm

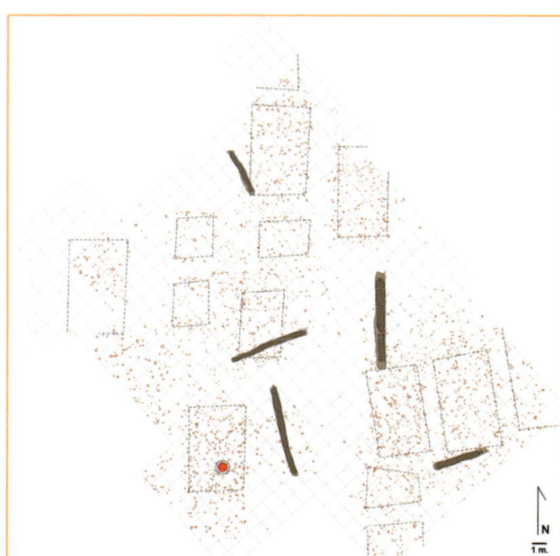

Figure 5.3.11. Complete sickle. It still preserves nearly all the flint teeth (Object No. 44297).

Pollen analysis of glue from sickles: first results

As mentioned previously, from the end of the eighth millennium cal BC agriculture began to spread from the eastern Mediterranean regions to the south of the Italian Peninsula, then expanded to central and northern Italy around 6000–5800 years cal BC and quickly reached also the westernmost maritime areas. Here, exploiting the newly acquired technological knowledge necessary for all farming practices, from soil preparation to sowing and harvesting, Neolithic groups began cultivation and cereal cropping (Rottoli and Pessina 2007; Buxó 2007; Zeder 2008; Bouby *et al.* 2020).

The main tools used for harvesting, a fundamental activity, mostly consisted of sickles which, being made from both perishable wooden elements and lithic components, in most archaeological contexts are not preserved entirely; the blades, often displaying gloss, are often the only preserved part but they are not sufficient to reconstruct the overall shape of the tool.

Only waterlogged and pile-dwelling sites have allowed finds of intact sickles which, in spite of some different features of the wooden support and, in particular, of the handle, consistently possess a groove to host the lithic blades, fixed with various types of adhesives (Piqué *et al.* 2015; Mazzucco *et al.* 2022a). Excavations at La Marmotta from 1989 to 2008 enabled the recovery of 52 wooden sickles, both fragmentary and intact, dated to the Early Neolithic (*c.* 5690–5260 years cal BC), forming the largest group of such Impresso-Cardial Culture artefacts within the whole Mediterranean basin.

The analysis of the glues which, due to their adhesive properties, trapped pollen grains, spores and other botanical micro-remains derived both from components of the glue itself (resins, waxes, charcoal powder) and from the harvested cultivated and weed species, has allowed specific data to be obtained about the activities of Neolithic farmers, which would not have been available studying only the plant macrofossil record and sediment samples from the area around the site. Out of the large number of sickles recovered, the adhesives from ten of the best-preserved artefacts are currently under investigation. This report presents the preliminary palynological results from three tools with different handle types which were found in two different stratigraphic units.

For pollen analyses we used a sickle (No. 23001) found in the oldest layer (II), and two sickles (Nos 44297 and 7186) from the grey unit of the overlying Layer I. Xylological analyses have identified deciduous *Quercus* sp. for the two more recent tools and Rosaceae Maloideae for the third one, characterised by a ring handle (Caruso Fermé *et al.* 2021). In order to reduce the damage as much as possible, the investigation was carried out on minimal amounts of glue (averaging 100 mg per sample). Both deep samples at the base of the lithic blades and superficial samples were taken from each sickle (Fig. 5.3.12).

The preparation procedure involved cold solubilisation in toluene for 24 hours, followed by washing through centrifugation in the decreasing toluene-ethanol series and then in the increasing ethanol-distilled water series, until complete hydration. The residue was subsequently treated by sieving through a 250 mm stainless steel mesh and standard acetolysis. To remove residual amounts of micro-charcoal and mineral particles, the 'swirling' method and dissolution with cold HF 40% for 24 hours and hot HCl 10% were used (Caramiello and Arobba 2003; Marshall 2005; Traverse 2007). The calculation of absolute pollen frequencies was

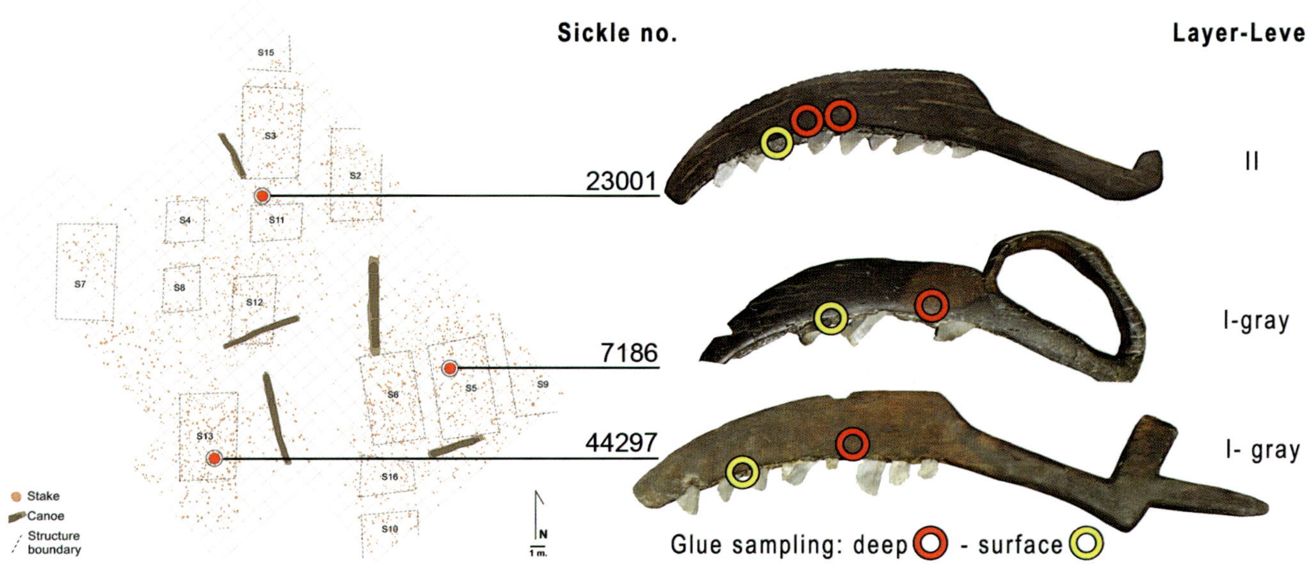

Figure 5.3.12. Position of the three sickles within the site of La Marmotta and sampling spots of the glue analysed.

obtained through calibrated sampling of 50–100 mL with a micropipette. The slides were observed in optical light microscopy at 400–630× magnifications.

The samples showed an optimal state of preservation of the pollen grains and good absolute frequencies, ranging between 6501 and 133,929 grains/g but usually higher in the inner glue samples than in the superficial samples. The diagrams in Figure 5.3.14: a and b (below) show the percentage values of individual tree-shrub taxa (AP), herbaceous taxa (NAP) and non-pollen palynomorphs (NPPs), while Figure 5.3.14: c shows the cumulative values of groups of taxa sharing particular ecological requirements and indicative of human impact.

Examples of pollen grains from the sickle glue samples are shown in Figure 5.3.13. Sickles No. 7186 and No. 44297 (Figs 5.3.10 and 5.3.11), both from the same grey unit of Layer I, are characterised by relatively similar pollen spectra. *Quercus* deciduous-type prevails among the arboreal taxa (AP=29.5–39.1%), paralleled by scant values of other components of the mesophilous oak wood, which include *Carpinus*, *Betulus*, *Ulmus*, *Ostrya/Carpinus orientalis*, *Corylus*, *Fraxinus ornus*-type and *Vitis*. There are only scarce traces of evergreen formations with *Quercus ilex*-type, *Olea*-type and *Pistacia*. The percentages of hygrophilous trees such as *Alnus glutinosa*-type, *Salix* and *Populus* are relatively high, as well as the percentages of plants typical of marshy environments, e.g., *Parnassia*, *Alisma plantago-aquatica*-type, *Typha*, *Callitriche*, *Potamogeton*, *Sparganium* and *Nymphaea alba*-type. Wild Poaceae display higher values in the superficial samples (22–23.1%) than in the deeper samples, as is the case of herbaceous ruderal taxa indicative of anthropogenic disturbance and cultivation.

Many pollen grains of cereals were grouped into different types according to their individual average diameter and size of the pore's annulus (Andersen 1979; Moore *et al.* 1991; Bottema 1992; Lagerås 1996; Beug 2004; Joly *et al.* 2007). Both *Hordeum*-type (d=40–50 mm and annulus=8–10 mm) and *Avena-Triticum*-type (d>50 mm and annulus>10 mm) were identified, reaching overall values of 4.4–8.6% and 5–10.6% respectively. In these two sickles the total cereal values are high in all samples, between 15.4% and 26%, along with frequent aggregates of cereal pollen.

From the third sickle, No. 23001, found in Layer II at the bottom of the archaeological sequence, three samples of glue were taken, one superficial and two from deeper within the mastic. They all show remarkable differences compared to the previous cases. The percentages of arboreal plants are very low (2.7–4.7%), with a prevalence of *Alnus glutinosa*-type, coupled with equally low levels of Cerealia (0.2–0.9%) and anthropogenic indicators (averaging 0.8%). However, the main characteristic of the pollen assemblages from the glue of this sickle consists of an unusually high amount of the herbaceous taxon *Oenanthe*-type (averaging 78.1%) paralleled by other species of humid habitats like *Alisma plantago-aquatica*-type (averaging 13.8%).

For the determination of *Oenanthe*-type, 50 grains were observed in glycerol 85%, obtaining the following measurements: P=33.4-(39.4)-48.4 mm; E=14.2-(19.4)-22.4 mm; *Apocolpium*=3.9-(5.5)-7.9 mm; P/E ratio=1.7-(2.0)-2.5; PAI ratio=0.22-(0.30)-0.39. Following Punt (1984), the main morpho-biometric features of the grains allowed them to be assigned to *Oenanthe aquatica* group and *Oenanthe peucedanifolia* group (Fig. 5.3.13: h).

In conclusion, the mastics from the sickles found at La Marmotta were found to act as good 'traps', able to incorporate and perfectly preserve a high quantity of pollen grains. This material enabled us to collect valuable information, especially as regards the type of cultivated plants of the earliest farming communities in central Italy and the local synanthropic flora.

For the first two sickles, in view of the abundance of both isolated pollen grains and pollen aggregates of Cerealia, it is possible to confirm their main function as harvesting tools for wheat and barley. It is well known how the pollen of such species can adhere to mature spikes, especially within the glumes of the caryopses of hulled cereals, even during harvesting. This pollen signature can therefore be still present significantly after flowering, and even in by-products of cereal grain grinding (Vuorela 1973; Robinson and Hubbard 1977; Hall 1988; Bottema 1992; Portillo *et al.* 2017).

The recording of both wheat and barley in the sickle glue, as well as some herbaceous taxa typical of autumn and winter weeds infesting cereal fields (wild Poaceae, *Papaver rhoeas* gr., *Galium* sp., *Polygonum aviculare*-type, *Rumex*-type, *Vicia*-type), is in accordance with the results from plant macrofossil data (Rottoli 1993; 2002; Rottoli and Pessina 2007). The low percentage of pollen from arboreal species testifies to the presence of clearings which might have been favoured or created by humans, who, after the collection of wood, used the resulting open areas for agricultural activities.

The exceptionally high pollen concentration of *Oenanthe*-type on sickle No. 23001 suggests that this tool was used also for harvesting this herbaceous species, rather than only for standard harvesting activities. The genus *Oenanthe* includes several species still present in marshes and wetlands of central Tyrrhenian Italy, such as *O. aquatica*, *O. fistulosa*, *O. globulosa*, *O. lachenalii*, *O. pimpinelloides* and *O. silaifolia*, although the most recent reclamation works have greatly reduced its distribution.

Oenanthotoxins, particularly abundant in fruits and roots of many *Oenanthe* species, are active substances similar to cicutoxins of *Cicuta virosa* (hemlock), which have pharmacological and neuro-enterotoxic properties. When consumed fresh, some of them can provoke alterations of

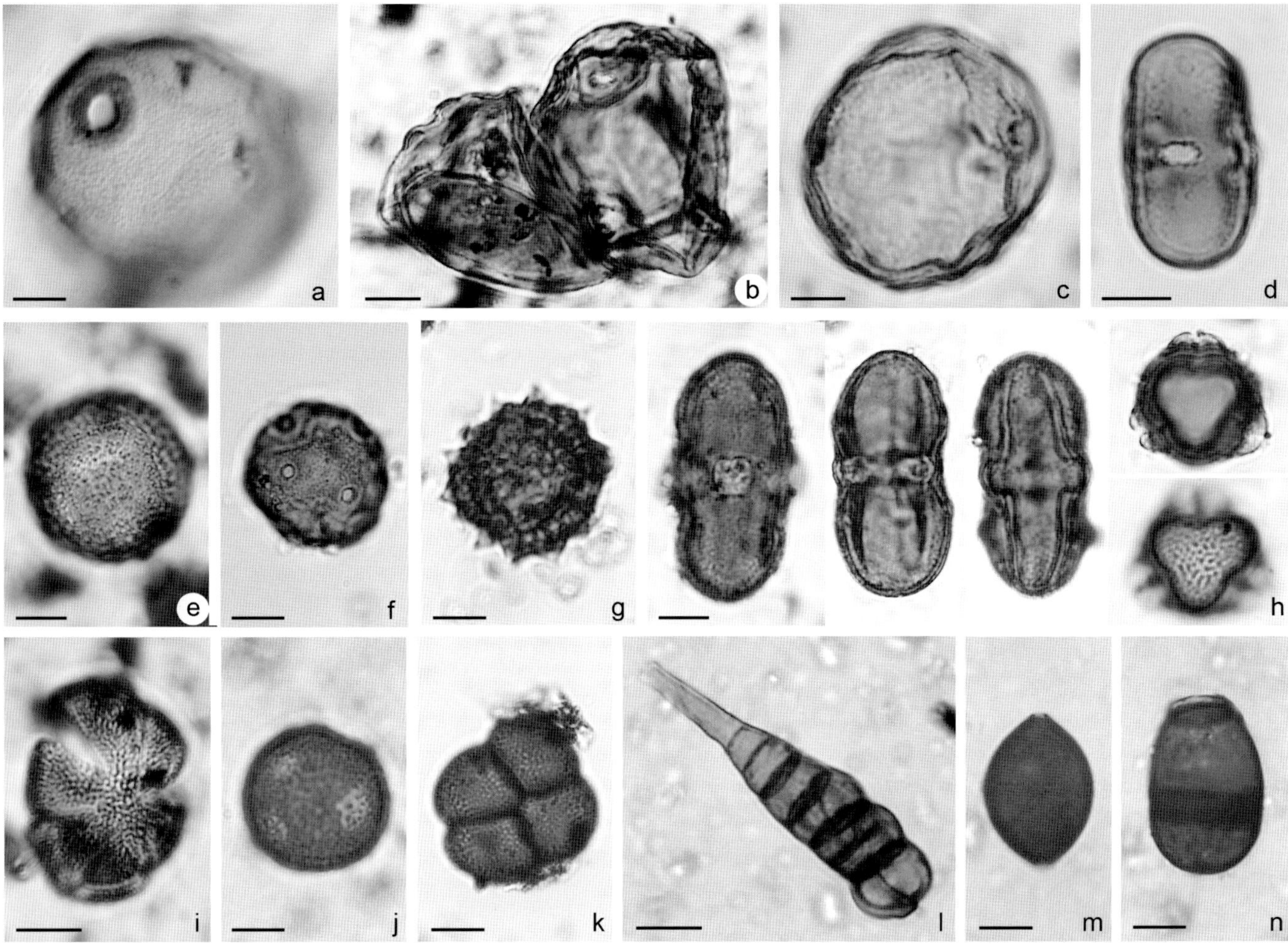

Figure 5.3.13. Selected palynomorphs from the sickle glue (scale bar = 10 micron). a. Avena-Triticum-*type; b.* Avena-Triticum-*type cluster; c.* Hordeum-*type; d.* Vicia-*type; e.* Papaver rhoeas-gr.*; f.* Plantago lanceolata-*type; g.* Cirsium-*type; h.* Oenanthe-*type; i.* Mentha-*type; j.* Alisma plantago-aquatica-*type; k.* Typha*; L.* Alternaria *sp.;* m. Sphaerodes-*type;* m. Bactrodesmium *sp.*

the mental state comparable to binge drinking, as well as nausea, vomiting and convulsions (Paris and Moyse 1981; Bulgarelli and Flamigni 2010). Not surprisingly, the term *oenánthe* derives from Greek *oínos-ánthos*, meaning 'wine-flower'. In more modern times, a citation of *Oenanthe* as a medical ingredient can be found in an eighteenth century herbarium, where it is referred to as *Cicuta palustre*, and in the text alongside it is indicated as '… *stirps ipsa venenata infamis*' (a species known for its poisonous properties) (Curti 1992).

If we take into account the state of drunkenness caused by the active substances of *Oenanthe*, we cannot rule out a ritual or shamanic use of these plants in the Neolithic community of La Marmotta. In this case, the pollen signal may have truly originated from intentional mowing of these plants, for purposes far removed from food production. This finding, which poses interpretative issues, increases the list of uncommon carpological finds from this site, such as *Papaver somniferum* (opium poppy), *Carthamus lanatus* (saffron thistle) and *Silybum marianum* (milk thistle), all species with officinal or medical relevance.

When interpreting pollen analyses of glues, one has to take into account also their origin from a mixture of various elements, such as pine resin, beeswax and charcoal powder. These substances possess, to a certain degree, natural adhesive properties which may have played a role in the incorporation of various components of the local aerial micro-particle assemblages, especially during harvesting in the hot season (Mazzucco *et al.* 2022a).

Moreover, prolonged and intense use of these tools may have required addition of new mastic and reworking of the old one to substitute worn-out lithic blades, a crucial practice for a successful use of the sickle, as demonstrated by our recent experimental work, soon to be published. These activities may have moved botanical micro-particles trapped on the surface towards inner parts of the glue, enriching the underlying layers, which, as often observed, would end up with higher absolute pollen frequencies (Fig. 5.3.14: c).

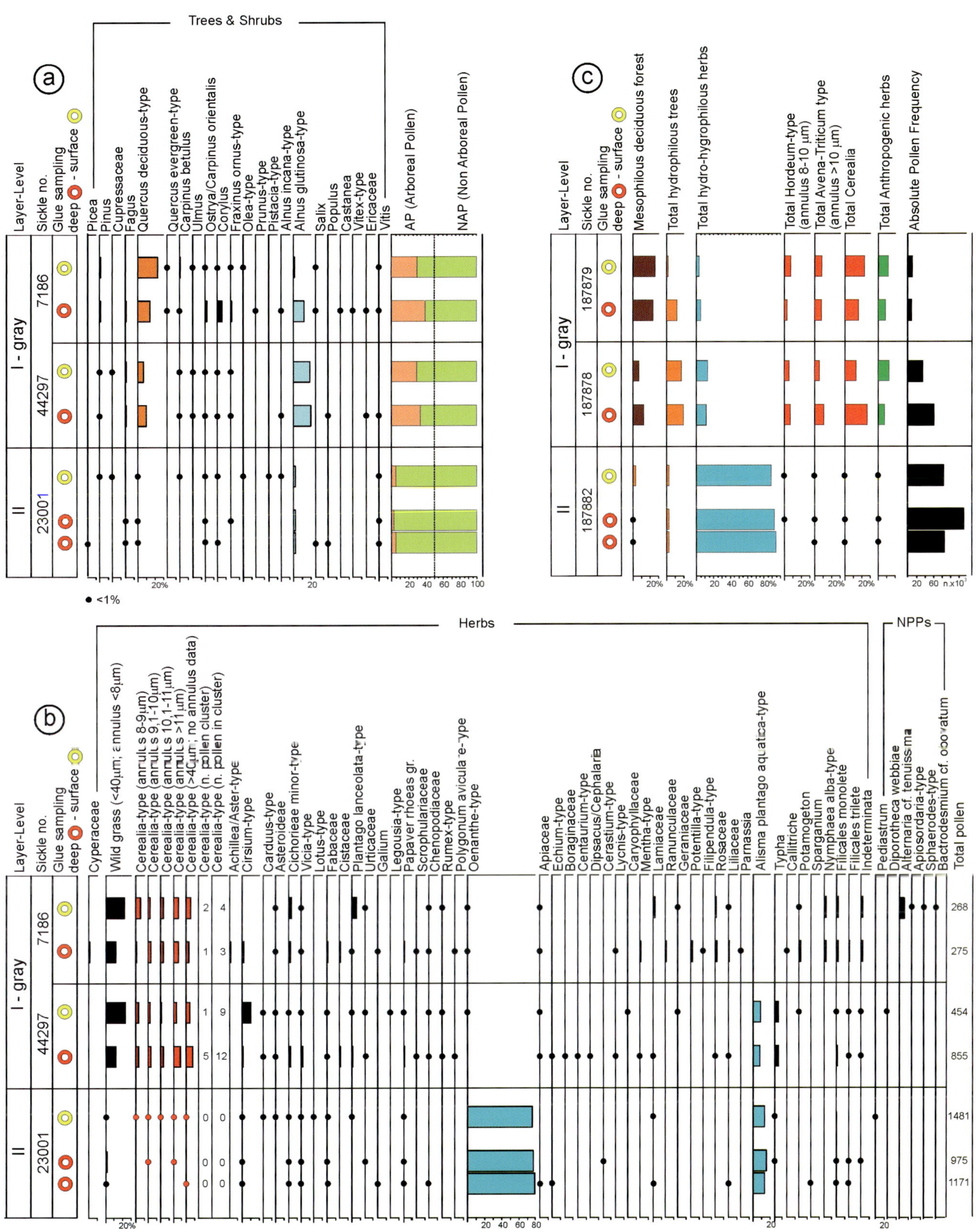

Figure 5.3.14. Pollen diagrams from the sickle glue samples: a. pollen percentage diagram of Arboreal Pollen (AP); b. pollen percentage diagram of Non-Arboreal Pollen (NAP) taxa; c. Cumulative pollen percentage diagram of selected categories of ecological and anthropogenic interest from the glues of three sickles.

Even when bearing in mind these considerations, the glues have proved to be efficient 'artificial traps' to capture and preserve several biological elements, and therefore this material seems suitable to integrate the floral scenario of cereal cultivation at the site and in the environments around the settlement, which so far had only been partially investigated through the macrofossil record from previous excavation campaigns.

Bows

The present study has been able to classify some semi-complete specimens, quite well-preserved, and about 43 fragments with a length from 300–700 mm (Table 5.3.2). Their morphology classifies them as components of small bows. These wooden bows are a singular discovery for their number, their antiquity and good conservation.

A total number of 18 bows has been calculated from the complete and broken specimens. In addition, another four possible bows are being assessed, as well as four intermediate fragments and nine pointed ends that might also be part of bows. While they are usually between 1.0 m and 1.2 m long, one exceptional specimen is as much as 2.2 m in length (No. 40609, Level I, Square A256-A305).

The analysed cross-sections are flat on one side and convex on the other. This suggests (as scientific literature referring to bows reports almost entirely indicates) that they belong to stickbows. A flat or flat-convex cross-section facilitates elastic flexion in one direction (the target) and, in the opposite direction, the accumulation/return of accumulated energy, which is needed to fire an arrow. Plane-convexity, consistent with the orientation of the growth rings, is a dominant feature of ancient bows in order to exploit the physical characteristics of the wood and the design geometry (Hickman 1947; Kooi and Bergman 1997; Brizzi 2002).

The measurements of the cross-sections allow the bows and their dynamic behaviour to be differentiated and classified, as well as enabling evaluation in predictive terms of the functionality or the risk of breakage in relation to the modulus of elasticity of the specific wood. Furthermore, analytical modelling is able to calculate the draw-force diagram of the object being examined. The classification criteria are based on measuring the widths and thicknesses every 50 mm along the bow and on the calculation of the width/thickness ratio. The higher its value, the flatter the section will be. Small errors in measuring these dimensions can have important consequences for our conclusions. For example, a 1 mm error in the thickness measurement would cause a 10% error in the draw-weight calculation and a 10% error in the thickness would cause a 30% error in the weight calculation of the draw-force diagram. From the dimensions, cross-sectional shape and assumed modulus of elasticity of the wood, we can compute the draw-weight and internal strain in the bow limbs versus draw-length of every single specimen. This is a fairly straightforward calculation that would be very familiar to a structural engineer.

Although the determination of the species used to make the bows is still provisional, some of them were shaped from *Carpinus* sp., *Viburnum lantana*, *Cornus* sp., *Fraxinus* sp., *Quercus* sp. and *Alnus* sp. Another interesting aspect concerns the six finds of *Viburnum lantana*. The presence of *Viburnum lantana* at archaeological sites is well known with regard to arrow shafts (Oeggl and Schoch 2000; Oeggl 2009). However, there is no evidence for its use as bows. *Viburnum lantana* L. is a shrub growing up to 4–6 m in height formed by adventitious shoots and rooting of branches in close contact to the ground. Despite the common name 'wayfaring tree', it seldom forms a single main trunk, but is usually much branched from near the base (Kollmann and Grubb 2002). Undoubtedly *Viburnum* has uncommon qualities of elasticity, resilience and lightness. The limit (and probably the reason) why it is not known as 'wood for bows' is due to the structure and physical dimensions of this shrub, which makes it difficult to identify trunks without knots and of such a size as to make a bow of any length. Other bow taxa (*Fraxinus* sp., *Cornus* sp., *Quercus* evergreen) are widespread in archaeological finds, while the discovery of a fragment of *Alnus* sp. remains doubtful, despite its geometric characteristics compatible with a terminal part of a bow. It would therefore seem that the choice of wood for the construction of these bows was linked to the ready availability of the raw material surrounding the settlement rather than a discriminating choice of the best possible wood. This would be consistent both with the large number of artefacts found and with their conditions (breakages, lack of accurate finishing). In an attempt to re-interpret some of these bows through physical approximations, we found that in 45 minutes' work with stone tools it is possible to obtain a perfectly functional product, efficient in hunting small and medium game.

Stickbows, both archaeological and ethnographic, vary in length quite dramatically. In the panorama of prehistoric bows found in Europe, Junkmanns (2013) enumerates 81 finds from the Upper Palaeolithic to the Neolithic and classifies a percentage of 29.6% as 'short', i.e. less than 1.30 m. On the other hand, depictions in prehistoric parietal art very often show hunting or fighting scenes in which archers are represented with short bows, depending on their height.

Three of the best preserved bows are:

- No. 9204 (Level I, Square D146). Fragment of a wooden bow made from *Viburnum lantana* with a flat-convex cross-section and a well-defined tip of a very particular type, curiously similar to the bow found in Nydam from

INFORMATION

14002

OBJECT:	Bow
YEAR:	1998
LEVEL:	I
SQUARE:	D190
NUMBER:	14002
SIZE:	1020 x 30 x 26 mm

Figure 5.3.15. Complete wooden bow (Object No. 14002).

INFORMATION

13794

OBJECT:	Wooden axe handle
YEAR:	1998
LEVEL:	I
SQUARE:	D141
NUMBER:	13794
SIZE:	275 x 56 x 70 mm

Figure 5.3.16. Wooden axe handle badly affected by fire (Object No. 13794).

INFORMATION

14177

OBJECT:	Adze handle
YEAR:	1998
LEVEL:	I
SQUARE:	D137
NUMBER:	14177
SIZE:	426 x 21 x 23 mm

Figure 5.3.17. Almost complete adze handle (Object No. 14177).

Table 5.3.2. Size and state of preservation of the bows.

Object No.	*Layer*	*Square*	*Width (30 mm from top)*	*Thickness (top, mm)*	*Width (max, mm)*	*Thickness (max, mm)*	*Length total (mm)*	*Structural condition*	*Estimated bow length ± 10% (mm)*
14002	I	D190	21	22	30	26	1020	complete	1020
40609	I	A256-A305	23.8	11.6	36.3	21.6	2200	complete	2200
9681	I	D195	18	21	23	26	373	intermediate	
7097	I	D147	23	21	24	26	223	intermediate	1200
7097	I	D147	22	17	20	22	340	intermediate	
7097	I	D147	23	20	16	18	184	intermediate	*
7372	I	D99	12	12	25	19	432	2 tips/extremities	1200
12729	I	D339	20	18	20	13	825	semi-complete	1000
4865	Indet	Indet	11	7	22	20	360	intermediate plus extremity	1080
30074	I	A31	20.1	11.8	22.9	16.5	510	intermediate + 2 Tips	1020
33004	II	A367	7.15	9.8	22.9	23.4	295	extremities	*
9204	I	D146	6	11	20	18	644	semi-complete	1200
9163	I	D143	6	13	11	15	930	semi-complete	1200
9236	I	D144	5	9	20	21	635	semi-complete	1200
9099	I	D195	14	19	20	24	241	intermediate	*
32992	I	A322	13.2	18.6	18.6	13.2	520	intermediate plus extremity	1100
32020	I	A183	10.8	9.1	24.8	18.8	320	intermediate + extremity	1100
9773	I	D144	10	11	28	25	681	intermediate + extremity	1200
30418	I	A30	25	17	31	26	820	intermediate + extremity	1300
18599	II	D285	17	13	30	23	681	intermediate + extremity	1200
32072	II	A185	19.6	9.7	19	22.6	534	intermediate + extremities	1200
35297	II	A327	10	10	30	26	445	intermediate + extremities	1200
9096	I	D195	25	21	11	10	445	intermediate + extremities	1000
9243	I	D146	11	13	18	26	535	intermediate + extremities	1200
12365	II	D240	15	16	20	22	520	intermediate	>1200
42164	I	A359	20	17	19	17	300	intermediate	> 1000
7157	Indet	D248	14	10	18	15	110	short intermediate	*
9196	I	D144	18	16	19	22	152	short intermediate	
9196	I	D144	19	22	19	22	123	short intermediate	>1000
9196	I	D144	18	21	19	21	118	short intermediate	
15417	I	D136	4	15	17	39	215	short tip	*
20534	II	A171	4	7	16	20	169	short tip	*
15415	I	D136	5	10	6	20	190	short tip	*
9671	I	D193	5	4	22	17	125	short tip	*
7400	I	D98	15	10	33	22	270	short tip	*
9680	I	D195	34	30	18	12	390	short tip	*
9242	I	D146	10	11	20	22	234	short tip	*
36581	I	A485	/	/	14	18	36	short tip	*
7121	I	D148	/	/	17	15	152	short tip	*

the third century AD. The upper part of the limb, 350 mm from the tip, has a plane-convexity index of 1.41 and this decreases to an average value of 1.10 towards the fracture. This suggests a presumed length of *c.* 1.20 m or 1.30 m in total, assuming a symmetrical distribution of stresses.

- No. 9236 (Level I, Square: D144). Fragment of a *Viburnum lantana* bow with a flat-convex cross-section without a well-defined tip. The upper part of the limb, 350 mm from the tip, has a plane-convexity index of 1.44, which decreases to an average value of 1.12 towards the fracture. This suggests an assumed length of *c.* 1.10 or 1.20 m in total, for a symmetrical distribution of stresses. Both surfaces, dorsal and ventral, are strongly degraded, presumably by contact with the organic sediment of the archaeological level.
- No. 14002 (Level I, Square D190). Fragment of a *Carpinus* sp. bow with a flat-convex cross-section. The upper limb part (in Figure 5.3.15) at 35 mm has a plane-convexity equal to 1.45, which decreases to an average value of 1.22 near the fracture. The lower part shows, 350 mm from the lower tip, a plane-convexity index of 1.18, which progressively decreases to 0.76. There are no shaped tips. The irregular surface comes from the desire to respect the natural structure of the wood, while a dimensional result and the sections are the result of a skilful design that aims to compensate for the asymmetries of the limbs. Evident traces of processing with a stone axe are visible on the whole surface of the bow.

Axe handles

Handle 13794 (Level I, Square D141) is the best preserved axe handle at La Marmotta. Although it is badly affected by fire, its shape is easily identifiable, with the central socket where the stone axe would have been fitted. Much of the handle is missing, and the object is now 275 mm long, 24 mm wide in the preserved part of the handle, and 56 mm wide in the area of the socket. Its thickness also varies considerably from 20 mm where it was gripped to 70 mm in the socket. This socket, which is 23 mm in diameter, does not conserve any remains of resin, probably because of the effect of the fire on the wood (Fig. 5.3.16).

Adze handles

Two adze handles have been documented; with very similar shapes, they differ greatly in their size. Their measurements are probably related to the size and weight of the stone adzes they were attached to, but unfortunately neither of them was found together with the tool.

The best preserved specimen is No. 14177 (Level I, Square D137), a practically whole adze handle. Elbow-shaped, it is 426 mm long, 20–21 mm wide and between 20 mm and 23 mm thick. It would have been larger because the proximal part of the handle is missing (Fig. 5.3.17). The part to which the adze was attached is 234 mm in length, of which 150 mm corresponds to the narrower area where the adze was hafted. This area is 18–19 mm wide and 24–27 mm thick. The widest and thickest part of the handle is the distal side of the elbow that joins the shaft to the area that held the adze. This would need to be thicker to withstand the force of the impacts when the tool was in use.

The second adze handle is less well preserved (No. 41771, Level I, Square A356). While it is also elbow-shaped, the proximal end and the area where the stone adze was attached are now missing. The handle is 210 mm long, the extension for the adze is 138 mm in length, and its width and thickness are between 14 mm and 20 mm. As before, the widest part is the elbow, which is 26 mm in width. Although the area that held the adze has not survived, the small diameter of the handle indicates that the implement would have been quite small. This is feasible because of the wide range of sizes, weights and raw materials of the stone axes and adzes found at the site (see Chapter 9.2)

Weaving swords and spadoni

Some of the most exceptional wooden implements found at La Marmotta are the *weaving swords* and *spadoni* (literal translation: 'large sword'). Those tools have been denominated as swords or *spadoni* by the excavators of the site because of their shape and size, like long wooden swords.

At La Marmotta, 38 whole or fragmented examples of weaving swords or *spadoni* have been documented (Table 5.3.3). They are all very similar from the morphological point of view: in the form of a long narrow spatula, with a sharp side and lenticular cross-section. One of the ends is always narrower so that it can be held, like a handle and, indeed, the surfaces are smoothed by contact with the hand. The handles sometimes end in an appendix so as to be held more easily. The whole weaving swords are no longer than 445 mm, 43 mm wide and 15 mm thick (Fig. 5.3.18). The *spadoni* are sometimes considerably larger, up to 1.34 m in length, 73 mm wide and 14 mm thick. Both ends of some of these *spadoni* were trimmed to create handles. Because of this and their large size, it is thought that they may have been used by two people (Fig. 5.3.19). All the *spadoni* were made in the same way from a wooden board cut out from a tree trunk.

Communities who used traditional looms employed long wooden tools to press down each row of the weft that was woven. In the twentieth century in northern Italy, an instrument like a wooden knife was used to work the textile (Scheuermeier 1980). However, this interpretation should be taken with precaution because those looms imply a much more complex and advanced technology. Even so, many other techniques detected at La Marmotta are not usually associated with the Neolithic and, so far, the site has revealed that Neolithic societies probably possessed more advanced technological knowledge than previously thought.

Table 5.3.3. The weaving swords and spadoni, size and state of preservation.

Tool	*Object No.*	*Layer*	*Square*	*Length (max. mm)*	*Width (max. mm)*	*Thickness (max. mm.)*	*Structural condition*
weaving swords	10581	I	D238	551	32	16	complete
weaving swords	14446	II	D142	490	51	15	complete
weaving swords	19260	I	A125	460	43	15	complete
weaving swords	8884	I	D246	682	37	25	complete
spadoni	10749	Chiocc	D291	730	36	15	complete
spadoni	11364	I	D242	705	25	11	complete
spadoni	13853	I	D88	272	61	15	fragment
spadoni	15545	I	A233-A184	905	78	15	complete
spadoni	16941	I	D93	499	61	15	fragment
spadoni	17384	I	D33	860	51	13	fragment
spadoni	19042	I	A119	465	52	16	fragment
spadoni	19355	I	A76	820	37	16	complete
spadoni	20418	I-II	A70	439	58	20	fragment
spadoni	26976	I	A271	457	33	7	fragment
spadoni	29903	I	A40	757	71	13	fragment
spadoni	36902	I	A487	1110	70	15	fragment
spadoni	37231	I	A471	1065	79	8	fragment
spadoni	37357	I	A422	1130	57	12	complete
spadoni	38404	I	A492	1173	82	14	complete
spadoni	41632	I	A361-A363-A314	434	32	5	fragment
spadoni	41637	I	A312	570	32	7	fragment
spadoni	12128	II	D289-D290	1232	57	15	complete
spadoni	14076	I	D190-D191-D192	1340	73	14	complete
spadoni	19103	Chiocc	A74	482	60	15	fragment
spadoni	22649	I	A172	1245	38	10	fragment
spadoni	29124	I	A31-A33	936	55	9	complete
spadoni	31791	II	A183	474	53	30	fragment
spadoni	37679	I	A469	857	33	10	fragment
spadoni	38161	I	A447	1112	51	18	fragment
spadoni	38365	I	A541-A543	1327	62	14	complete
spadoni	41265	I	A357	1012	47	13	fragment
spadoni	42615	Chiocc	D450	918	54	15	fragment
spadoni	44670	I	A518	1212	65	16	fragment
spadoni	45850	I	A461-A462	943	60	15	complete
spadoni	8994	I	D243	1140	63	14	complete
spadoni	28992	I	A29-A31	785	45	10	complete
spadoni	41770	I	A261	821	69	15	fragment
spadoni	11351	I	D288	367	51	16	fragment

Similar objects have been discovered at other lacustrine sites, albeit of later date. For example, weaving swords have been cited at locations in Switzerland (Greifensee, Niederwil-Egelsee and Robenhausen-Wetzikon), Italy (Fiave) and China (Tianluoshan) (Bazzanella *et al.* 2003; Cameron and Guoping 2022).

Draghetti

Other, rather enigmatic, wooden tools are the so-called *Draghetti* (so-called because of their toothed shape like a dragon's back). This is a very particular kind of tool and relatively similar objects have only been found at the lacustrine site of La Draga in Spain. One the possible hypotheses that have been proposed to explain the function of those tools is a use for the processing of plant fibres.

In total, seven complete or fragmented *draghetti* have been documented at La Marmotta. They all display the same morphological characteristics (Table 5.3.4). They consist of two parts, one straight and the other curved. The former is a straight, wide handle with a hole. The latter is formed by a concave inner surface and a convex outer face with a line of triangular teeth. The hole in the handle suggests two possible interpretations. First it may have been used to hang up the tool with a string through the hole. Alternatively, a string through the hole may have helped the user to hold on to the tool. The curved active part of the *draghetti* displays two very different surfaces: the internal concave surface is smooth and worn by use, while the external convex face displays a series of aligned triangular teeth, some with longitudinal striations and distinct rounding, also probably caused by use.

Although the whole specimens are between 230 mm and 255 mm long, one of the broken examples (No. 12240, Level I, Square D241) must have been much larger because it is 245 mm long despite missing much of the distal end. The proximal areas are between 48 mm and 65 mm wide while the convex distal part varies from 55 mm or 65 mm in its widest section to 20 mm or 30 mm in the pointed end. The proximal part is 11–16 mm thick and the distal part 22–28 mm thick.

To give some examples, of the two objects with a complete line of teeth, one has ten teeth (No. 7559, Level I, Square D98; Fig. 5.3.20) and the other seven (No. 7558, Level I, Square D100). The teeth had been used to very different degrees. Some are badly worn and have almost been removed, while others are much more complete. This row of teeth may have been continually sharpened with not all of them needing to be repaired at the same time, only the most worn ones. Thus, the less rounded teeth were the last ones to be resharpened. It is thought that the teeth were used to open the fibres of some plants, such as flax. Historical and ethnographic research has shown that a metal plate with spikes was traditionally used to work with flax (Loi 2012). Although it is difficult to make comparisons, the teeth of these *draghetti* may have been utilised for a similar function.

In turn, the internal concave face is extremely smooth, as can be with by the naked eye. Because of its shape, it is proposed that this face rested on the worker's thigh while the plant fibres were being pulled over the toothed surface.

Relatively similar objects have been found at the Neolithic lacustrine site of La Draga (Spain). The difference is that while some of them at La Draga do not possess the toothed convex part (in the case of objects Nos 35 and 85), others seem to conserve some teeth (Nos 37 and 86) (Bosch *et al.* 2006).

Indeterminate objects

Axe handles in the process of being shaped?

Object No. 31545 (Level I, Square A238) is broken in its active zone and therefore its function cannot be determined. This area might have been used to hold an adze but its shape and state of preservation do not allow a definite identification. The opposite side displays the impact marks and removals made by axes or adzes when it was being shaped. The active part is 163 mm long, 65 mm wide and 59 mm thick. The handle, of which only a small part has been preserved, is 60 mm long, 25 mm wide and 18 mm thick.

Table 5.3.4. Draghetti, Size and state of preservation.

Object No.	*Layer*	*Square*	*Length (max. mm)*	*Width (max. mm)*	*Thickness (max. mm)*	*Structural condition*
7558	I	D100	230	87	23	complete
7559	I	D98	240	65	16.5	complete
9262	I	D144	255	60	26	complete
9400	Indet	D243-D245	140	54	17	fragment
12240	I	D241	245	75	19	fragment
17902	I	D38	177	75	27	fragment
30415	II	A30	35	39	23	fragment

INFORMATION

19260

OBJECT:	Weaving swords
YEAR:	2000
LEVEL:	I
SQUARE:	A125
NUMBER:	19260
SIZE:	445 x 43 x 15 mm

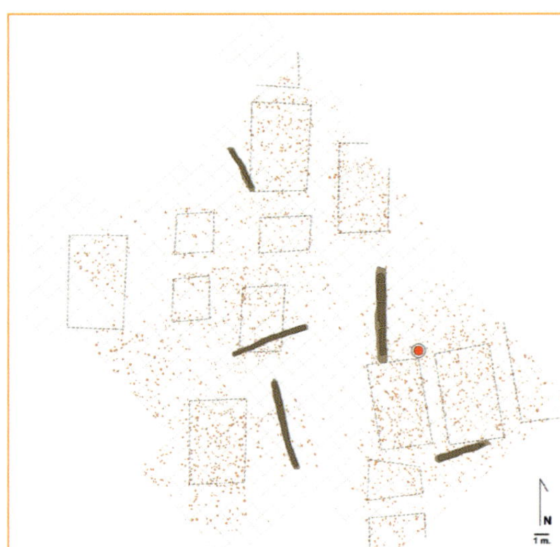

Figure 5.3.18. Complete weaving swords with decoration in their active zone (Object No. 19260).

INFORMATION

14076

OBJECT:	*Spadoni*
YEAR:	1998
LEVEL:	I
SQUARE:	D190-D191-D192
NUMBER:	14076
SIZE:	1340 x 73 x 14 mm

Figure 5.3.19. One of the largest and best conserved spadoni *from La Marmotta (Object No. 14076).*

INFORMATION

7559

OBJECT:	*Draghetto*
YEAR:	1996
LEVEL:	I
SQUARE:	D98
NUMBER:	7559
SIZE:	240 x 65 x 16,5 mm

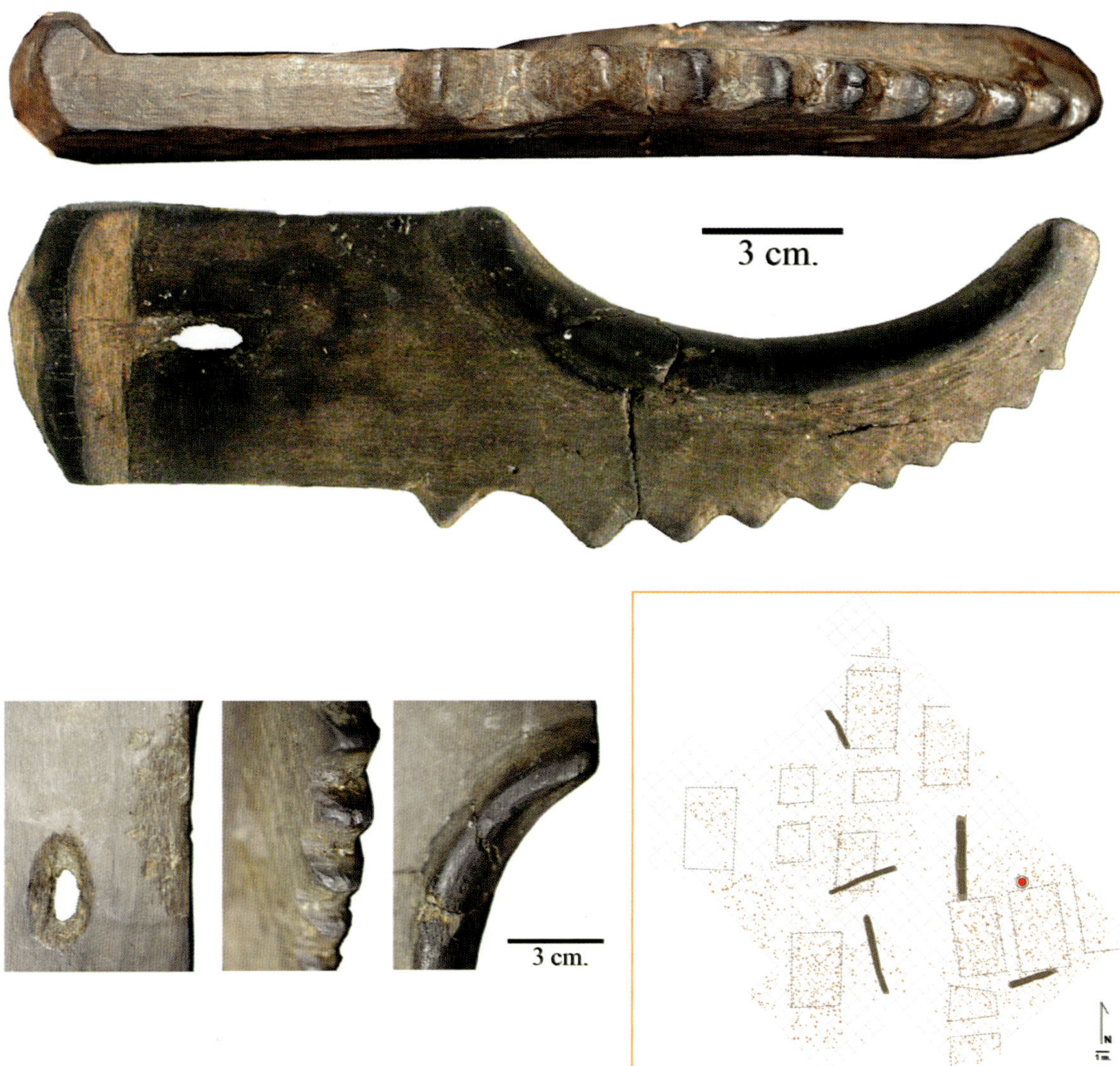

Figure 5.3.20. Draghetto *made of wood (Object No. 7559).*

INFORMATION

12370

OBJECT:	Possible distal part of a wooden adze handle
YEAR:	1998
LEVEL:	I
SQUARE:	D239
NUMBER:	12370
SIZE:	149 x 102 x 56 mm

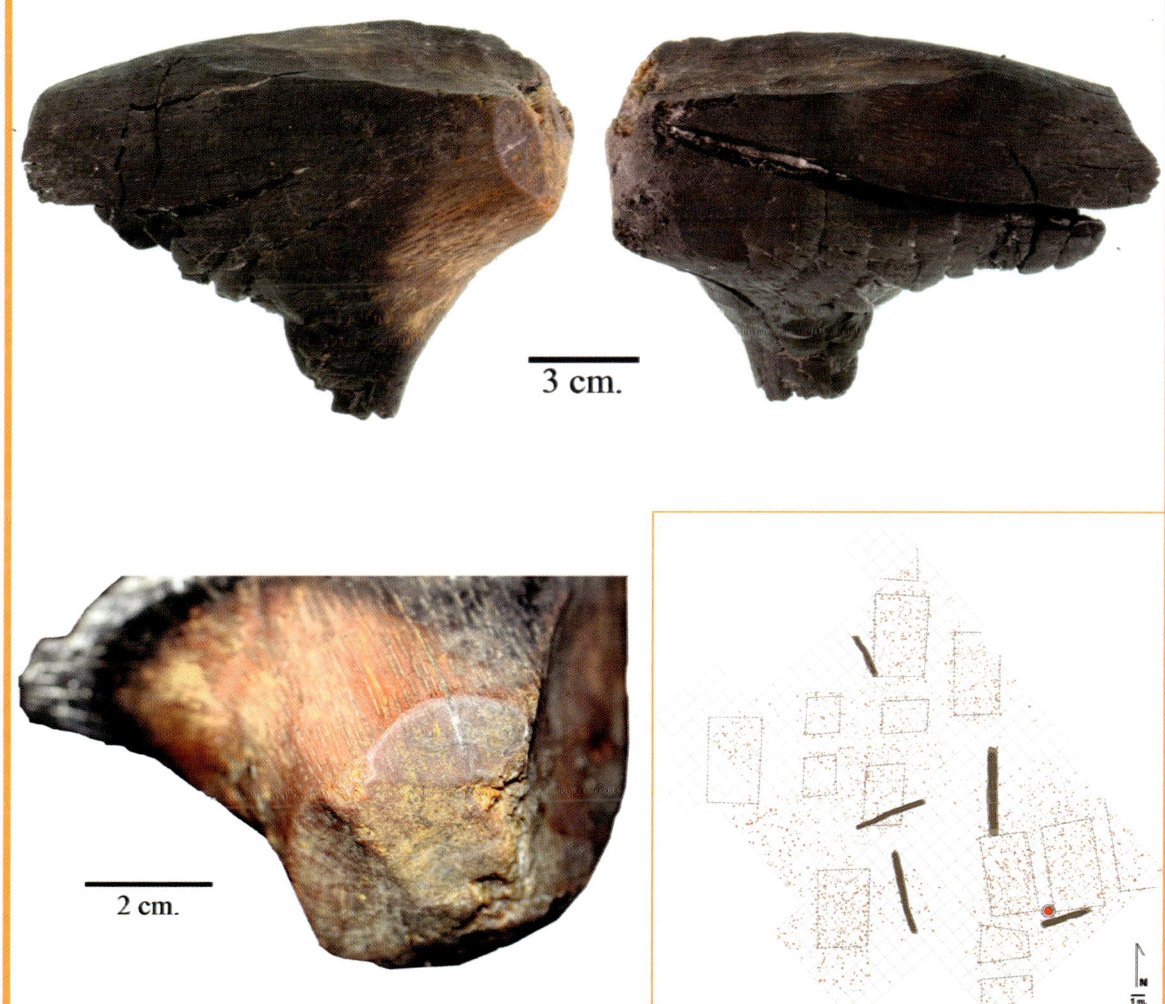

Figure 5.3.21. Possible distal part of a wooden adze handle. It is affected by fire (Object No. 12370).

A similar tool, No. 12370 (Level I, Square D239), is even less well preserved and more affected by fire than the previous object (Fig. 5.3.21). However, the preserved part of handle is 149 mm long, 102 mm wide and between 45 mm and 56 mm thick. A small fragment of the haft 25 × 35 × 31 mm in size has been preserved. What would have been the working area is completely missing so it is impossible to imagine its appearance and whether it was prepared for holding a ground stone tool such as an adze. The marks left by an axe or adze, forming a small cone, can clearly be seen on the anterior part of the object.

Lastly, No. 6299 (*Chiocciolaio* Level, Square D248) was abandoned as it was being prepared, as it is not fully shaped. It is 225 mm long, between 110 mm and 120 mm wide and 30–45 mm thick. A small fragment of what would have been the handle has been preserved; its small width (21 mm) and thickness (16 mm) must have caused it to break.

Mallets?

Four tools seem to have been mallets or a resistant implement used for striking or stirring something. They are formed by a quite long handle ending in a round, rectangular or slightly trapezoidal head. Their general characteristics are:

- Object No. 7311 (*Chiocciolaio* Level, Square D97) has a slightly trapezoidal head (Fig. 5.3.22). It is 335 mm long and the head is 53 mm wide and 28 mm thick. The handle is 20 mm wide and 23 mm thick. It is broken in the handle.
- The head of Object No. 8291 (Level I, Square D194–243) is also trapezoidal. The slightly curved handle has a triangular cross-section with an upper part that tends to be rectangular. It is 410 mm long, with a width and thickness of 20 × 18 mm in the handle and 80 × 13 mm in the head.
- Object No. 19042 (Level I, Square A119) has a rectangular upper part and is quite flat. Although it is 465 mm long, 55 mm wide in the head and 20 mm in the handle, and 9–10 mm thick, it must have been longer because it is broken at both ends.
- Implement No. 26867 (Level I, Square A216) is the largest of these tools. It has a very long handle which ends in a round head. With a length of 785 mm, the head is 50 mm wide and 12 mm thick, and the handle is 35 mm wide and 23 mm thick.

Ard?

One of the most interesting objects found at La Marmotta because of its possible historical repercussions if its purpose is finally confirmed, is an ard share. No. 24088 (Level I, Square A273) is 540 mm long, with a width of 141 mm at its base and 36 mm at its tip, and a maximum thickness in its middle of 38–40 mm (Fig. 5.3.23).

The object is triangular in shape with a concave base that was deliberately hollowed out. This work at the base has two appendices of very different widths (40 mm and 13 mm), which means that the cavity is not located on the axis of the object but towards one of its sides. Its cross-section is slightly triangular as the middle part is thicker. Microscopic observation has identified removals and striations made to cut back the sides and obtain this particular shape.

A large curved branch pointed at one of its ends was found next to this object. This might have been the beam of the ard. With No. 23373 (Level I, Square A226), it is 1.15 m long, with a maximum width of 59 mm and maximum thickness of 61 mm. This oval cross-section shows that the branch was trimmed considerably to obtain two quite flat faces.

Conclusions

This chapter, and those devoted to the canoes, dwellings and implements used to work with textiles and cordage (see Chapter 6), have made known the quantity and diversity of wooden artefacts at the site. However, they must be only a tiny portion of the implements that the Neolithic communities at La Marmotta used every day. Despite the outstanding preservation conditions, many wooden objects must have been lost.

This has raised a doubt about the name that has always been used to define the first agropastoral communities: the Neolithic. Ground and polished stone axes and adzes, the elements that support the name of Neolithic, are not only quite scarce at most sites belonging to this period but they are also largely linked to working with wood. This is a raw material that is easy to obtain and work with, predictable, renewable, recyclable, with different hardness and properties, and simple to conserve if treated correctly. Bearing in mind La Marmotta and other Neolithic sites in Europe, perhaps we should wonder if it would be more correct to speak of a 'Wood Age' (Bocquet and Noël 1985).

In any case, this array of objects and the technology involved in their manufacture is changing our view of those Neolithic societies. We are accustomed to studying their pottery, lithic tools and osseous remains of the animals they consumed. La Marmotta, however, brings to mind a much more complex picture of the Neolithic. They were communities that were much closer to contemporary rural societies or those that our grandparents knew. In this way, La Marmotta takes us back in time to discover a very different reality from the one we had envisaged in our minds from the archaeological remains usually found at most dry sites.

INFORMATION

7311

OBJECT:	Probable wooden mallet
YEAR:	1996
LEVEL:	Chiocciolaio
SQUARE:	D97
NUMBER:	7311
SIZE:	335 x 53 x 28 mm

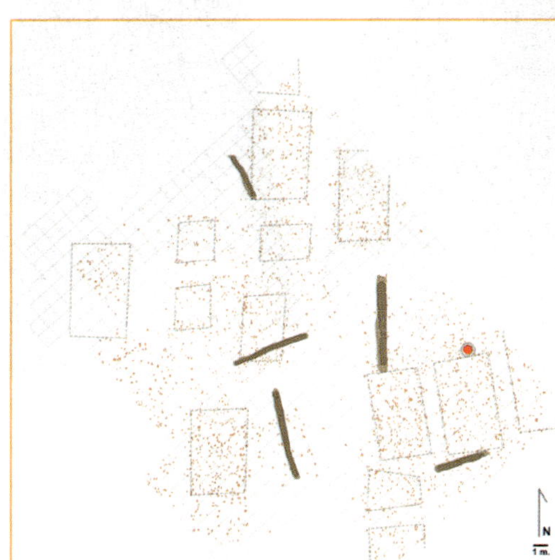

Figure 5.3.22. Probable wooden mallet (Object No. 7311).

INFORMATION

24088

OBJECT:	Wooden ard share?
YEAR:	2001
LEVEL:	I
SQUARE:	A273
NUMBER:	24088
SIZE:	54 x 14,1 x 4 cm

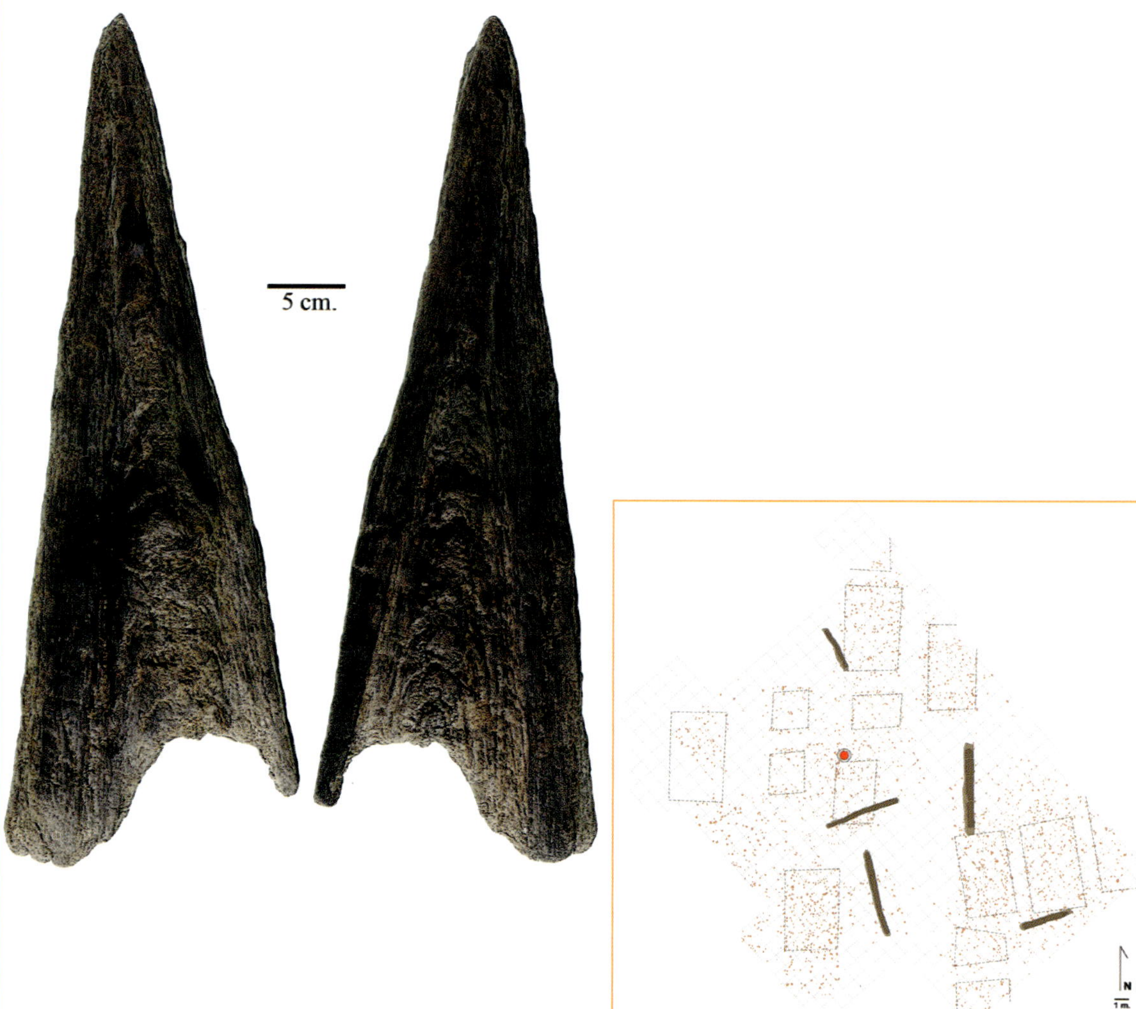

Figure 5.3.23. Possible wooden ard share (Object No. 24088).

6

Working with plant fibres: textiles, basketry and cordage

Juan F. Gibaja, Mario Mineo, Niccolò Mazzucco, Laura Caruso-Fermé, Vanessa Forte, Millán Mozota, Christina Margariti and Eva Andersson

Plant and animal materials used to make textiles, cordage and basketry are preserved at few prehistoric sites in the world. Bacterial decay means that at most archaeological sites these types of objects disappear in a few years. The result is that we do not obtain a clear picture of their importance, their diversity and of the different materials and techniques employed to make them.

Therefore, when they are found, such materials are able to revolutionise archaeological understanding. They open a window to the past and help us to understand the major role they must have played and the wide-ranging knowledge that was handed down from generation to generation. The first part of this chapter will review some of the examples of these materials that have been found at archaeological sites. Despite their scarcity, they are suggestive of their importance even for very old, hunter-gatherer societies in the Palaeolithic. Thus, in Dzudzuana Cave (Georgia) several fragments of flax fibres were found in levels dated between 30,000 and 11,000 BC (Kvavadze *et al.* 2009). In 1953, Abbot André Glory discovered a 30 cm long rope with an approximate age of 20,000 years in Lascaux Cave (Breuil 1955). In Ohalo II (Israel), three fragments of 2–3 mm fibres were interpreted as part of a rope made from a monocotyledon plant. This site is about 19,000 years old (Nadel *et al.* 1994).

During the Mesolithic, most of the evidence of these kinds of objects has been found in northern Europe, preserved in wet conditions, in lakes or peat bogs. This is the case of sites like Tybrind Vig (Denmark), dated to 5400–4000 BC, Friesack (Germany), with an approximate chronology of 7700 BC, and Dabki 9 (Poland) dated to 5000 BC. Cords used to make fishing nets, bows, arrows and ornaments have been documented in these and similar sites (eg, Fischer 1985; Gramsch 1992; Myking *et al.* 2005; Kabaciński and Terberger 2015). In the western Mediterranean, preservation is achieved by opposite conditions: aridity. In this way, the fragments of cords found in Cuevas de Santa Maira (Spain), dated between 11,200 and 8200 BC, are an outstanding discovery (Aura *et al.* 2019).

Aridity and particular combustion processes explain the preservation of remains of cords and baskets at sites belonging to the first Neolithic occupations in the Near East. Some of the best known examples are:

- The funerary context in Nahal Hemar Cave (Israel), where several fragments of cords and baskets made of *Phragmites australis*, *Juncus* and *Linum usitatissimum* are attributed chronologically to *c.* 7900 BC (Schick 1986).
- In Çatalhöyük (Turkey) direct and indirect evidence of textiles and basketry is dated in 5500–5000 BC (Marciniak *et al.* 2015; Rast-Eicher *et al.* 2021).
- In Tomb 98 at Tell Halula (Syria), in a chronology of 7600–7300 BC, fragments of textiles were made of flax and hemp (*Linum usitatissimum*, *Cannabis sativa*) (Alfaro 2012).

The expansion of the Neolithic towards Europe from the 9th millennium BP is often associated with communities that frequently settled next to lakes and other waterbodies. Those societies sought locations next to water for their farming activity and other forms of subsistence. Thanks to that circumstance, some of the best preserved sites have been documented near or in lakes. Some of the most important are:

- Charavines, on Lake Paladru (France), with a Neolithic occupation that began in 4000 BC. Numerous remains of cordage, textiles and basketry made from flax, rushes and nettles have been found (Bocquet and Berretrot 1988).

- Arbon-Bleiche 3, next to Lake Constance (Switzerland), dated in about 3400–3300 BC, has yielded cordage and basketry made with fibres made from the bast of lime trees (*Tilia* sp.) and from flax (*Linum usitatissimum*) (Médard 2003).
- Egolzwil, on the former lake of Wauwilermoos (drained in 1856), was occupied in about 5200 BC. It is one of the sites where most plant remains have been preserved. Numerous remains of textiles, cords and baskets made from flax and the bast of oak (*Quercus* sp.) and lime trees have been documented (Vogt 1951).
- La Draga (5300–5000 BC) next to Lake Banyoles, Spain, is another of the best preserved sites in Europe. Several cords and baskets also made from the bast of lime and from *Clematis* sp. have been recorded (Piqué *et al.* 2018; Romero *et al.* 2021a; 2021b).

Aridity and particular taphonomic conditions also facilitated the preservation of similar objects in Cueva de los Murciélagos in Albuñol, Spain. Attributed chronologically to about 4000 BC, the assemblage of remains found in the 19th century included sandals and baskets, some of them painted, made from esparto grass (*Stipa tenacissima*) (Cacho *et al.* 1996). We must also cite the case of 'Ötzi the Iceman' (3300 BC). Found in the icy summits of the Alps, many items in his equipment were made of lime bast: the dagger sheath, cords and a knotted net of twined strings, as well as the inner nets of his three-part shoes (Spindler 1995).

Plant fibres were used for many purposes, from the most resistant, which were employed as building materials and for transport, to finer and more flexible fibres, used to make bows, baskets, nets, clothes, sandals, handles and in utensils and ornaments. They all reflect their importance in the activities carried out by past societies and the knowledge they acquired over time to work with them. This knowledge is still put to use by artisans in many villages in Europe today (as seen, for example, in the containers on display at Castelsardo Museum in Sardinia: http://www.mimcastelsardo.it). These materials are so common in our daily life, just as in the past, yet are extremely ephemeral in archaeology because of their rapid decay.

Textiles

Some of the most important finds from La Marmotta are four fragments of textile (Fig. 6.1), discovered in 1995 when Canoe Marmotta 1 was recovered (Fugazzola and Mineo 1995). Their dimensions are rather small: No. 1 (SR011), 11.01 mm; No. 2 (SR012), 27.09 mm (there is a probable hole in it); No. 3, 11.50 mm; and No. 4, 12.92 mm. Although they are small, the excellent technique with which they were made can clearly be seen. These remains, incredibly well preserved, show the wide knowledge acquired by the inhabitants of La Marmotta for the manufacture of textiles and basketry. Scanning electron microscope (SEM) analysis indicated the textile fragments are made of cellulosic bast fibres (see *infra*).

Cordage

As many as 29 fragments of cordage of different thicknesses and lengths were found in the course of the excavations at La Marmotta. Their different sizes would be related to their uses: strings for bows and nets to obtain food, twine to fasten some implements and containers, and ropes for

Table 6.1. Examples of cordage.

Object	*Object No.*	*Level*	*Square*	*Length (mm)*	*Weight (g)*
Cord	7186	I	D147	66.3	6
Cord	7027_1	I	D197	57.1	2.1
Cord	7027_2	I	D197	54.7	2.1
Cord	7320	Chiocc	D99	31.4	2.8
Cord	9517	I	D247	27.5	3.3
Cord	9637	I	D245	big roll cord	8
Thread	9993	I	D93	–	–
Cord	10153	I	D298	small roll cord	6
Cord	12090	I	D292	199.6	4
Cord	13803_1	I	D94	81.3	6.7
Cord	13803_2	I	D94	62.1	8.6
Cord	14045	I	D139	106.6	5
Cord	14046	I	D139	170.4	18.3
Cord	14181	I	D141	22.9	5
Cord	15688B	I	D183	96.2	8.1
Cord	16373	II	D240	440	7.4
Cord	16480	I	D85	small roll cord	1.7
Cord	16998	I	D89	48.7	4.9
Cord	17573	I	D85	76.7	6.5
Cord	22928	I	A132	174.3	1.8
Cord	26112	II	A286	small roll cord	0.4
Cord	26314	II	A273	small roll cord	6.5
Cord	26333	II	A276	123.2	9.5
Cord	31225	I	A288	25.8	4.6
Cord	32162	II	A187	29.2	11.6
Cord	36217	I	A41	–	–
Cord	41614	I	A356	24	2.8
Cord	42607	Chiocc.	A401	21.6	6
Cord	Indet	Indet	Indet	22.9	2.4

hanging objects or used in the construction of houses, among others (Fig. 6.2). These materials were used by joining short discontinuous fibres to create long threads which were made into cords by three methods: twisting, braiding or knotting.

The length of the cords varies considerably, depending on their original size and the degree of preservation. Thus, both small fragments a few centimetres long and a bundle, whose length cannot be calculated because it is coiled up, have been documented (Table 6.1). Their thickness is equally diverse, because they include very fine threads and thick strong ropes capable of supporting heavy weights and tensions (Figs 6.3–6.5).

Although information about the types of plants used to make these objects is still quite limited, analyses have identified plants from the Poaceae (or Gramineae) family of monocotyledonous flowering plants (grasses) (see *infra*). An initial study of a 6 mm fragment of string (No 36217), found in Level I, Square A41, was performed some years ago. The microscopic observations by Dr Maria Rita Giuliani and Giulia Gaietta (ISCR Biological Research Laboratory) determined that this string with its two ends twisted towards the left was made from flax fibres (*Linum* sp.).

Basketry

We only need to think of the houses of modern farmers in some parts of the Mediterranean or remember our grandparents' country homes to appreciate the importance that basketry has enjoyed until very recently. It must have been equally or more important in the first Neolithic societies. The know-how achieved over the years about the properties of different crops and the wild plants in their surroundings was crucial to make the various types of baskets documented at La Marmotta. Thus, among the 49 basketry remains discovered, several techniques have been identified, from weaving and pseudo-weaving to sewn spirals and binding (Mineo 2019) (Table 6.2). The most common technique was weaving concentric spirals with the 'continuous growth' method. The spiral starts in the middle of the base of basket, and then continues to be woven to build up the recipient (Figs 6.6, and 6.7). In some cases, as seen in Figure 6.8, remains of food are still preserved on the bottom of the basket.

In addition, several possible pieces of bread have been found at La Marmotta with the imprint of basketry on one of their sides. This is undoubtedly indirect evidence of the importance of baskets in the processing and storage of such a basic foodstuff as bread (Fig. 6.9). Indeed, just ad today, baskets must have been used for numerous purposes: gathering and processing food, storing products, transportation, etc

Brushes

This short section describes some unique utensils that are only known because of the outstanding state of preservation of the remains at La Marmotta. These are two small brushes. Observing their appearance, which resembles modern brushes so closely, we realise how much these utensils have persisted over time. They are so simple and so effective that technological developments in the history of humankind have hardly affected them.

The first brush is No. 14398 (Level II, Square D142). It comprises a group of plant stems (the species has not yet been determined) tied by string in their proximal and medial parts (Fig. 6.10). While the cord in the proximal part creates a rounded shape that would be held in the hand, that in the middle holds together the active part of the brush. It is 141 mm long and 39.5 mm wide. The two strings have a similar width: between 4 and 4.9 mm.

The second brush, No 22232 (Level I, Square A132), is quite similar. Also consisting of a bundle of plants (the species has not yet been determined), they are only tied in the middle by a string that wraps around three times (Fig. 6.11). It was made in a very simple way. The stems were bent over in the middle and tied together with the cord. This formed a brush with a rounded proximal part and the loose ends of the stems in the active part. It is 124 mm long and 54 mm wide. In its widest part, the string is about 5 mm wide.

Tools used to make cordage, basketry and textiles

At archaeological sites with excellent conditions for the preservation of remains, like La Marmotta, we can find wooden implements that can be associated with the processing of materials and the manufacture of baskets, cords and textiles. Hypotheses about their use can be proposed but, owing to the lack of similar archaeological or ethnological artefacts, the interpretation of their purpose cannot be regarded as definitive.

Spindles

The spindles found at La Marmotta must have been used to make threads. The central part is a small piece of wood, slightly conical in shape and pointed at the ends (Table 6.3). Nine examples have been documented, of which one is complete and the other eight are fragments with or without remains of threads.

These are exceptional objects because hardly any other similar objects have been found in European prehistory. In other exceptional sites such as Fiavé (Italy –Bronze age) spindles with different morphology have also been found (Perini 1987, Bazzanella *et al.* 2003).

Three of the best preserved spindles will be here described:

- Complete spindle (Fig. 6.12 No. 6762, Level I, Square D299–D250, length 256 mm and width 35 mm) consisting of a cylindrical piece of wood with thread wound around it. This creates a final biconical shape. As the most perfectly conserved spindle at La Marmotta it is an example of how well these artefacts have survived.

INFORMATION **SR011-SR012**

OBJECT:	Textile fragments
YEAR:	1995
LEVEL:	SR011: ?; SR012: I
SQUARE:	SR011: A204-A206; SR012: A202
NUMBER:	SR011 and SR012
SIZE:	SR011: 11,01 mm; SR012: 27,09 mm

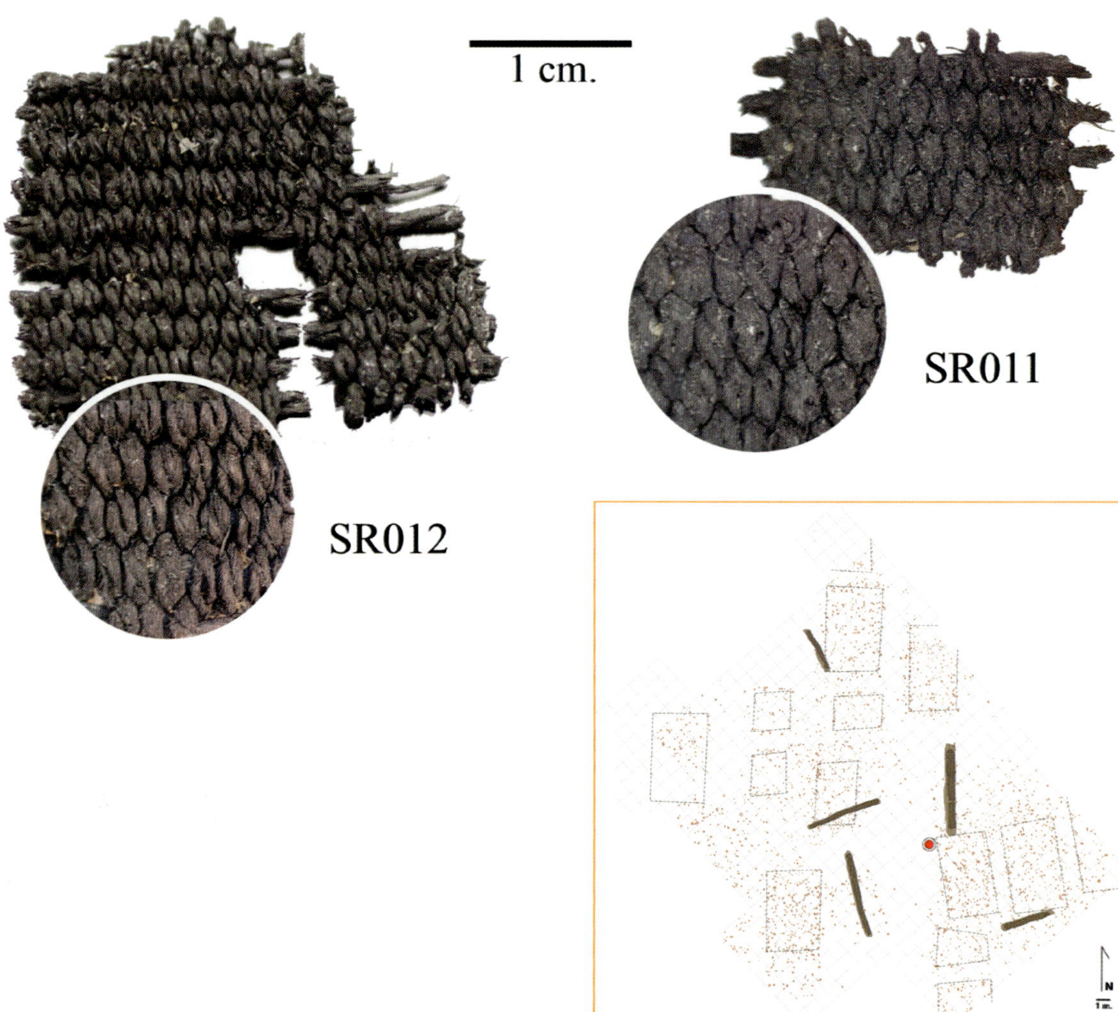

Figure 6.1. Textile fragments 1 and 2. Although they are small, the technique with which they were made can clearly be seen (Object Nos SR011, SR012).

INFORMATION

40214

OBJECT: Use of rope to join various wooden elements
YEAR: 2004
LEVEL: I
SQUARE: A445
NUMBER: 40214
SIZE: 330 x 60 x 40 mm

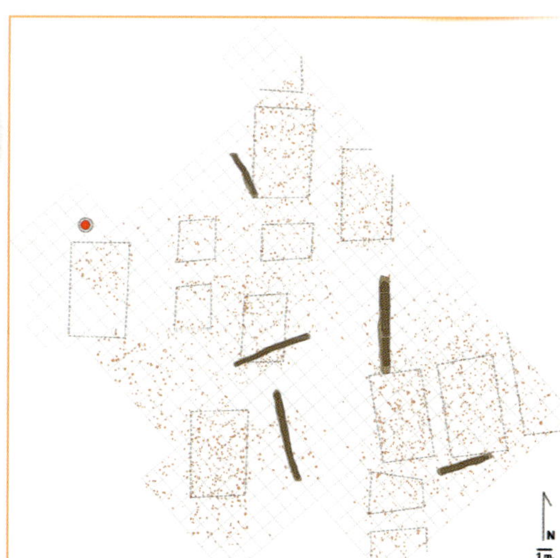

Figure 6.2. Use of rope to join various wooden elements (probably vine stems, Object No. 40214).

INFORMATION

9637

OBJECT:	Bundle of cord
YEAR:	1997
LEVEL:	I
SQUARE:	D245
NUMBER:	9637
SIZE:	Big Roll Cord

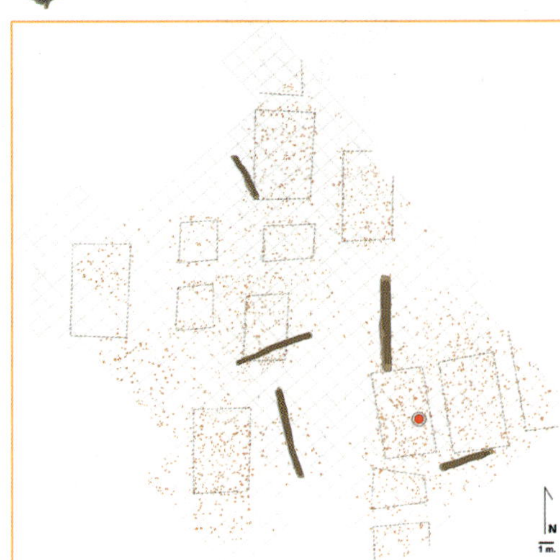

Figure 6.3. Bundle of cord. It was probably a ball of string (Object No. 9637).

INFORMATION

14046

OBJECT:	String
YEAR:	1998
LEVEL:	I
SQUARE:	D139
NUMBER:	14046
SIZE:	170,4 x 18,37 mm

Figure 6.4. Very thick string that would be ideal for supporting weights or tension (Object No. 14046).

INFORMATION

14181

OBJECT:	Thin string
YEAR:	1998
LEVEL:	I
SQUARE:	D141
NUMBER:	14181
SIZE:	22,9 x 5 mm

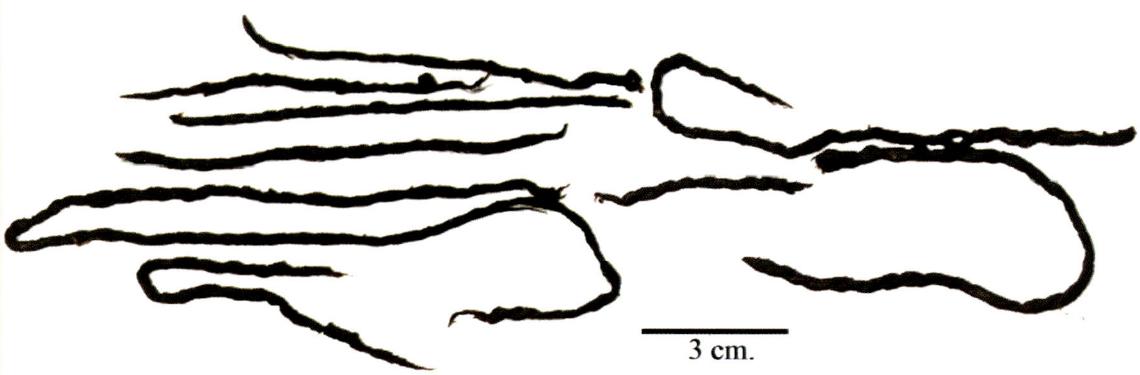

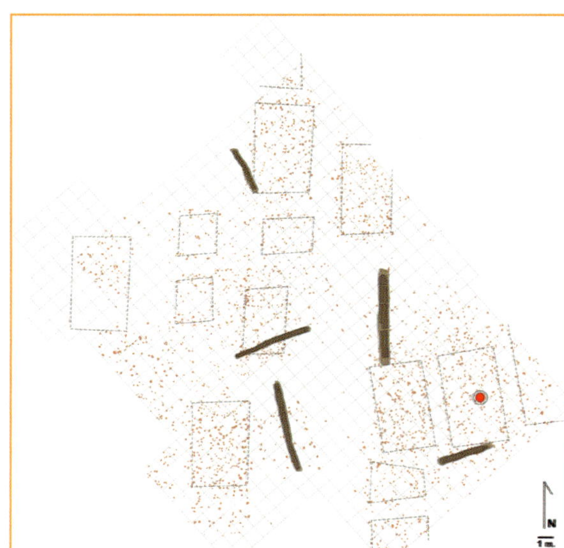

Figure 6.5. Thin string made by twisting (Object No. 14181).

INFORMATION

11355

OBJECT:	Base of a basket
YEAR:	1998
LEVEL:	I
SQUARE:	D287
NUMBER:	11355
SIZE:	126,7 x 103,7 mm

Figure 6.6. Base of a basket. The weaving method can be clearly observed (Object No. 11355).

INFORMATION

46471

OBJECT:	Fragment of the side of a basket
YEAR:	2005
LEVEL:	I
SQUARE:	A531
NUMBER:	46471
SIZE:	189,8 x 118,5 mm

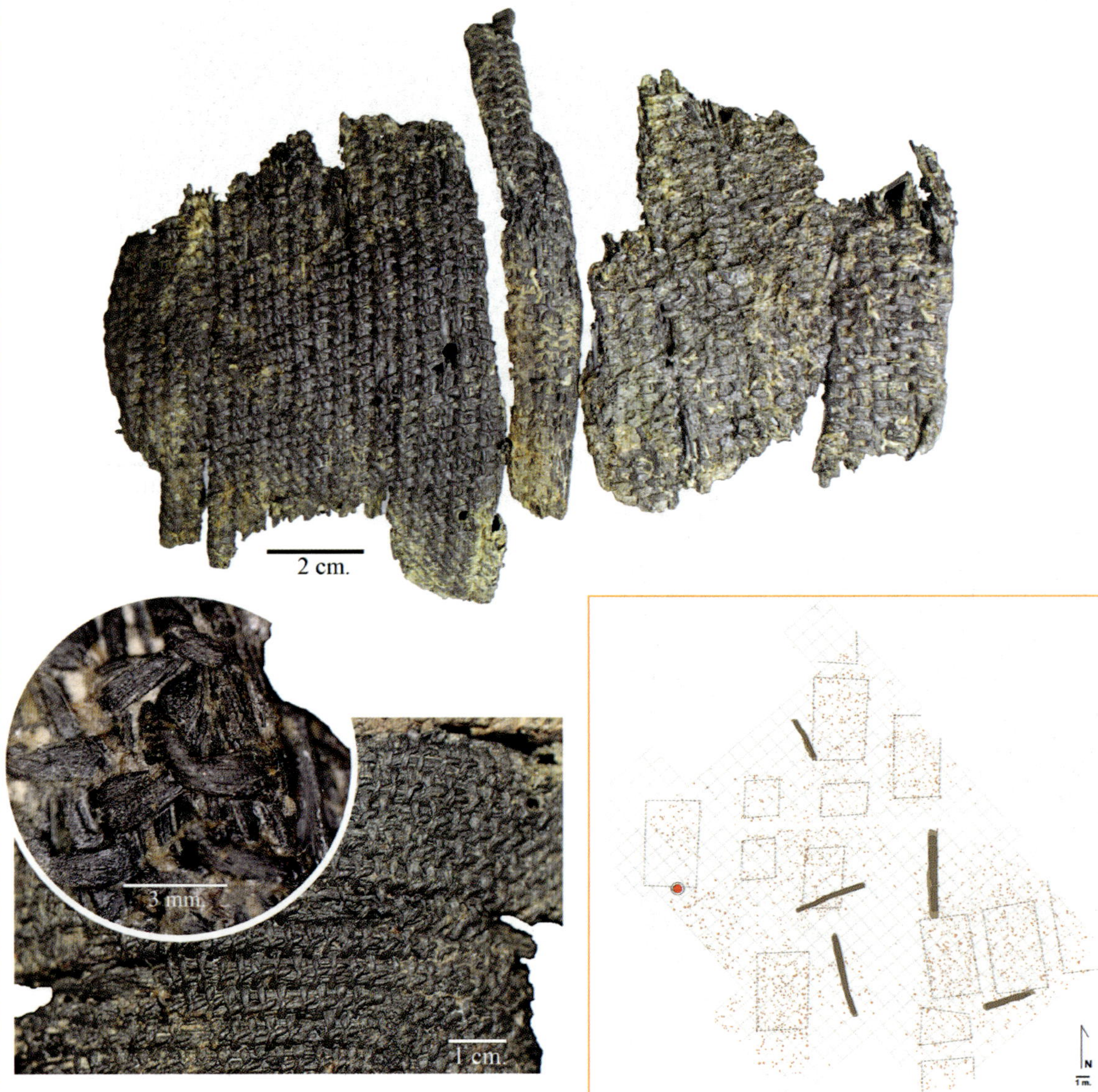

Figure 6.7. Fragment of the side of a basket (Object No. 46471).

INFORMATION

17572

OBJECT:	Bottom of a basket to which remains of food
YEAR:	1999
LEVEL:	I
SQUARE:	D38
NUMBER:	17572
SIZE:	171 x 169 mm

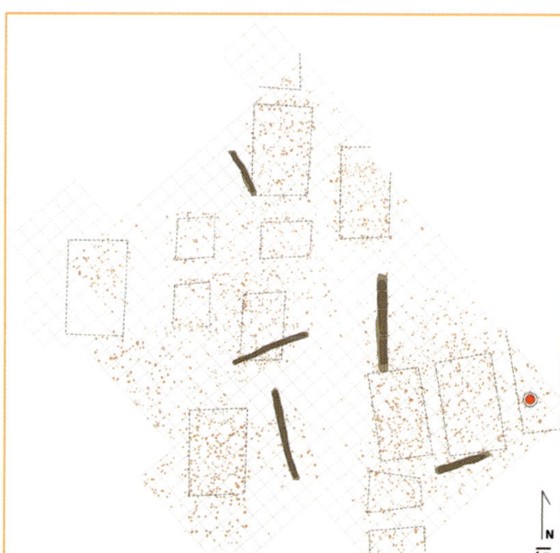

Figure 6.8. Bottom of a basket to which remains of food still adher (Object No. 17572).

Table 6.2. Basketry specimens.

Object	*Object No.*	*Level*	*Square*	*Length (mm)*	*Weight (g)*
Small basket fragment	3418_A	I	A158	41.6	6.4
Small basket fragment	3418_B	I	A158	36.4	10.6
Small basket fragment	3418_C	I	A158	32.5	9.2
Small basket fragment	3418_D	I	A158	28.2	12.8
Small basket fragment	3418_E	I	A158	35.4	21.5
Small basket fragment	3418_F	I	A158	40.3	9.5
Small basket fragment	6603	I	D199	42.7	51.9
Basket fragment	7139	I	D148	275	262
Small basket fragment	7139 (*bis*)	Indet	D148	18.4	11.2
Small basket fragment	8816	I	D343	73.9	55.6
Basket fragment	8862	I	D296	93.9	53
Basket fragment	11355	I	D287	126.7	103.7
Basket fragment	12008	I	D346	334.3	307
Small basket fragment	13330	I	D142	23	20.8
Basket fragment	13750	I	D140	351.7	56.8
Small basket fragment	13859	I	D90	25	6
Small basket fragment	14041	I	D90	97.7	21
Basket fragment	15512	I	D233	318.2	264.7
Basket fragment	16814	I	D91	91.1	80
Small basket fragment	16982	I	D44	70	8.5
Small basket fragment	17210	II	D42-D44	44.5	42.5
Basket fragment	17572	I	D38	171	169
Small basket fragment	17590	I	D37	79.5	67.2
Basket fragment	17594	I	D36	151.7	64.2
Small basket fragment	17595	I	D36	55.4	40.3
Small basket fragment	17809	I	D36	45.7	54
Basket fragment	17883	I	D34	90.3	88.2
Small basket fragment	17876	I	D85	61.4	9.2
2 small basket fragment	17912	I	D37	59.3	68
Small basket fragment	17920	II	D38	77.8	24.2
Small basket fragment	30581	II	A89	29.8	28.2
Small basket fragment	19240	I	A163	49.6	40.2
Small basket fragment	20772	II	A164	58.2	26.1
Basket fragment	20777	II	A214	63.4	42
Basket fragment	26682	I	A166	127.7	61.3
Small basket fragment	29825	I	A88	38.5	21.3
Small basket fragment	34501	I	A335	34.6	32.8
Small basket fragment	36954	I	A483	73.4	19.8
Small basket fragment	45155	I	A530	52.9	46.2
Basket fragment	45823	I	A529	196	110.2
Basket fragment	46471	I	A531	189.8	118.5
Small basket fragment	47642	I	D349	87.1	19.4
Small basket fragment	47810	I	D350	43.4	8.8

(Continued)

Table 6.2. (Continued)

Object	*Object No.*	*Level*	*Square*	*Length (mm)*	*Weight (g)*
Small basket fragment	47903	I	A254	42	43.8
Small basket fragment	50145	II	A560	30.7	20.3
Small basket fragment	50399	I	D300 Bis	46.9	20.7
Small basket fragment	SR001	I	Indet	29.6	14.8
Small basket fragment	SR020	I	Indet	29.3	10.6
Small basket fragment	Indet	I	D197-D199	23	8.8

Table 6.3. Spindles.

Object No.	*Layer*	*Square*	*Length (mm)*	*Width (max. mm)*	*Thickness (max. mm)*	*Structural condition and material*
6846	I	D297	55	14.5	14.5	fragment: wood and cord
17573	I	D85	82	11	11	fragment: wood and cord
17912	I	D37	73	6.4	6.4	fragment: wood and cord
35547	II	A327	110	6	6	fragment or complete? wood
SR013-1	Indet	Rimosso	80	15	15	fragment: wood and cord
SR013-2	Indet	Rimosso	123	10	10	fragment: wood and cord
6762	I	D299-D250	256	35	35	complete: wood and cord
16864	I	D44	176	7.8	7.8	fragment or complete? wood
46316	I	A482	163	8	8	fragment or complete? wood

Figure 6.9. Fragments of food remains, possibly bread. The imprint of the basket in which they were kept is still preserved on one of their surfaces.

- Fragmented spindle (No. SR013-2, Indeterminate Level, length 123 mm and width 10 mm) of which the central wooden part is slightly bent as a consequence of a post-depositional alteration. The thread wound in a conical shape is still seen around the wooden axis.
- A spindle of which part of each end is missing. It preserves part of the thread in the middle (No. 17573, Level I, Square D85, length 82 mm and width 11 mm). This was one of the first objects for which it was attempted to determine the plant species used to make the thread (see *infra*). However, the consolidant used did not allow a precise identification.

Loom or net weights

Spindle whorls and loomweights are objects commonly associated with textile activity (eg, Rast-Eicher 2005; Mazare 2012; Forte and Lemorini 2017; Grömer 2018; Grabundžija *et al.* 2021). During the study of the archaeological material unearthed from the site of La Marmotta, 81 weights and 3 spindle whorls were identified (Fig. 6.13). Nevertheless, this is a provisory number since the documentation of the ceramic materials is ongoing and other tools could be identified. The corpus documented so far is formed by objects that vary in their shape and measurements (Table 6.4).

Spindle whorls are biconical in shape with a length range of 28–31 mm and a weight range of 3.6–3.8 g, while the central vertical hole measures 5 mm in each (Fig. 6.14). The surfaces are damaged by post-depositional conditions and use-wear has only been identified around the central hole in one case (1911; Fig. 6.13). A horizontal polished area, located above the hole edge, suggests a prolonged use of the tool caused by a repeated interaction of the whorl surface with the spindle (Forte and Lemorini 2017). The weights are more variable in their size and shape (Fig 6.13).

INFORMATION

14398

OBJECT:	Brush fragment
YEAR:	1998
LEVEL:	II
SQUARE:	D142
NUMBER:	14398
SIZE:	141 x 39,5 x 35 mm

Figure 6.10. Brush fragment (Object No. 14398)

INFORMATION

22232

OBJECT:	Brush fragment
YEAR:	2000
LEVEL:	I
SQUARE:	A132
NUMBER:	22232
SIZE:	124 x 54 x 50 mm

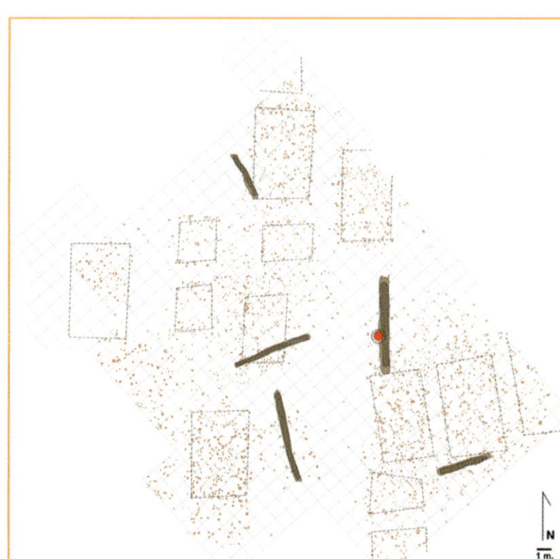

Figure 6.11. Brush fragment (Object No. 22232).

INFORMATION

6762

OBJECT:	Spindle
YEAR:	1996
LEVEL:	I
SQUARE:	D299-D250
NUMBER:	6762
SIZE:	256 x 35 x 35 mm

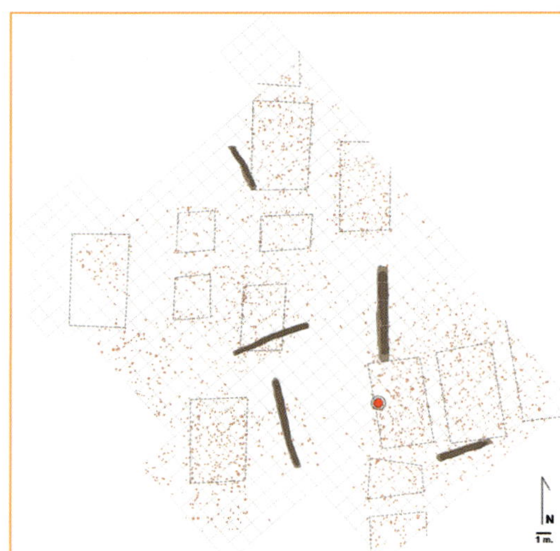

Figure 6.12 Whole spindle. Photographs taken during the excavation and after its restoration (Object No. 6762).

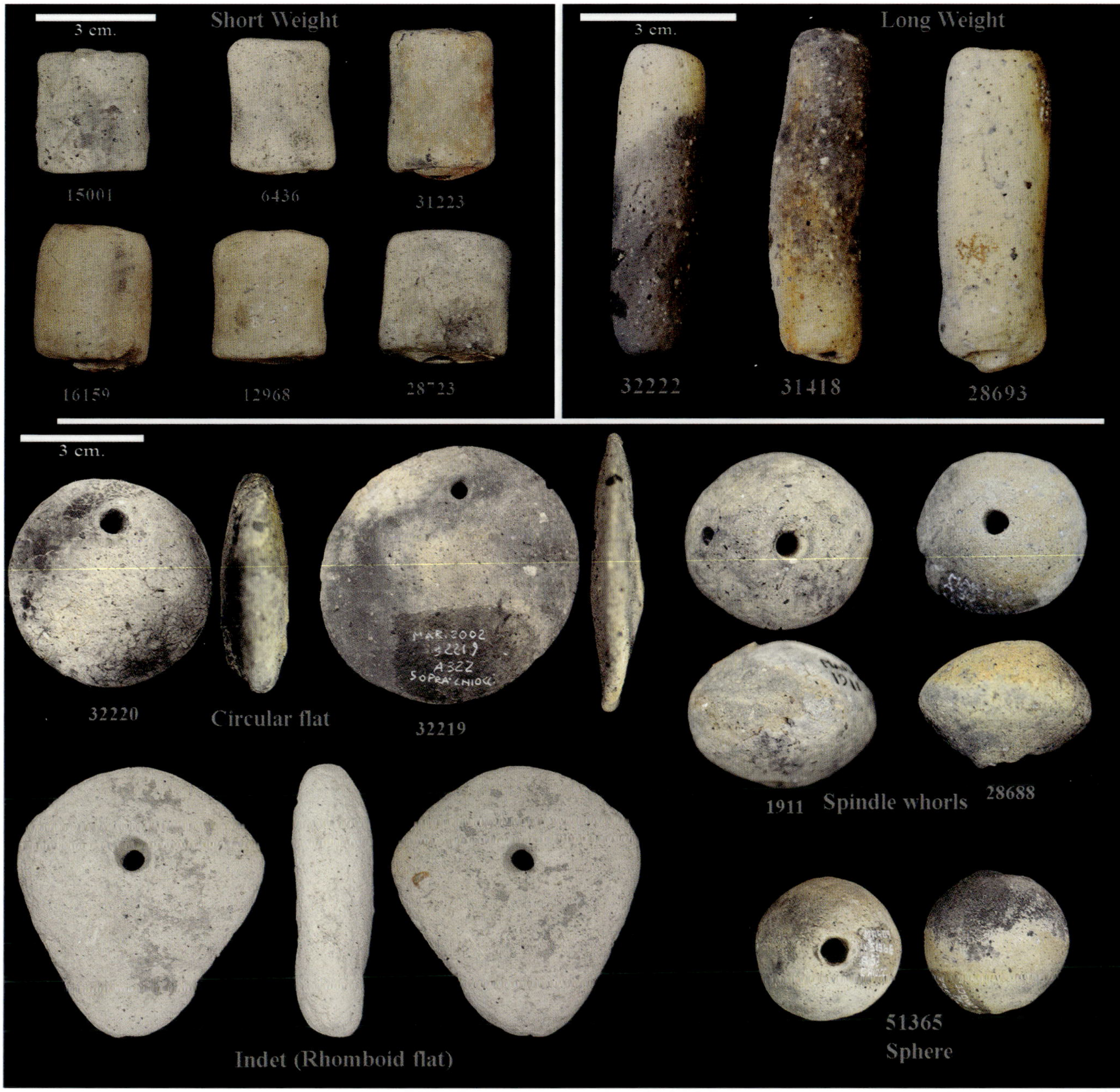

Figure 6.13. Spindle whorls and weights.

They include tubular and cylindrical weights (respectively long and short) with a round longitudinal hole, circular flat weights with a transversal hole, and a group of variable shapes (triangular, trapezoidal, rhomboid morphologies) with a transversal hole. The range of weight is between a minimum of 0.9 g and a maximum of 29 g. Observing the three main types of ceramic weights, the most homogeneous is the group of cylindrical (short) weights with a mean of 7.17 g, followed by the circular weights, with a mean of 8.53 g, and finally the most numerous group, the tubular (long weights), with a mean of 6.39 g. Overall, however, the circular weights are lighter than the tubular and cylindrical ones (Fig. 6.14).

The weights and spindle whorls were shaped by hand using a fine or semi-fine clay paste with volcanic inclusions. Both spindle whorls and weights were pierced with a stick or shaped around a stick while wet. Preserved surfaces show traces of smoothing as the finishing treatment, applied at a leather-dry state of the clay. The triangular, trapezoidal and rhomboid-shaped weights differ from the largest groups not only because of their peculiar and variable shapes but also for the raw material, probably stone,

Table 6.4. Spindle whorls and loom-weights. Three (*) could not be weighed.

Object	*Object No.*	*Level*	*Square*	*Lenght (mm)*	*Width (mm)*	*Thickness (mm)*	*Diameter hole (mm)*	*Weight (g)*
Short weight	46	Indet	A II-III	47	29	29	7	55.23
Short weight	133	Indet	A III	44	22	22	5	26.57
Short weight	134	Indet	A III	43	27	26	6	38.98
Long weight	135	Indet	A III	61	18	18	4	23.78
Short weight	185	Indet	A IV	42	22	25	6	33.70
Long weight	368	Indet	C II	55	21	20	6	29.16
Circular flat	452	Indet	CIV	53	53	12	5	33.61
Long weight	508	Indet	C V	63	21	19	6	30.00
Short weight	509	Indet	C V	33	25	25	4	23.70
Spindle whorls	1911	Indet	A24	31	38	38	5	48.05
Circular flat	1915	Indet	Indet	55	50	10	4	26.69
Circular flat	2093	Indet	Indet	51	55	7	4	19.24
Spindle whorls	2197	Chiocc.	A24	40	35	30	5	39.00
Long weight	4131?	Indet	Indet	52	18	16	4	21.32
Trapezoidal flat	4202	Chiocc	A53	63	53	12	5	37.54
Triangle flat	4203	Chiocc	A51	62	49	14	5	34.17
Short weight	6003	Indet	D97-D98	38	24	25	4	31.60
Short weight	6436	Chiocc	D147	34	27	25	4	32.02
Circular flat	8202	Chiocc	D143	57	54	12	4	35.40
Short weight	8375	Chiocc.	D296	41	22	20	5	26.29
Short weight	10330	Chiocc.	D240	29	33	33	5	44.84
Long weight	10331	Chiocc	D289	66	20	18	8	28.77
Short weight	10332	Chiocc	D289	48	29	28	7	46.09
Long weight	10333	Chiocc	D289	63	21	20	7	28.23
Short weight	10334	Chiocc.	D339	46	26	26	6	47.00
Long weight	10362	Chiocc	D340	63	20	20	6	30.23
Short weight	10656	Chiocc	D292	48	23	23	7	37.21
Long weight	12847	Chiocc.	D142	73	18	18	6	29.79
Short weight	12968	Chiocc.	D139	34	29	29	8	40.45
Short weight	12969	Chiocc.	D139	37	27	26	4	36.47
Short weight	15001	Indet	D35	33	28	28	5	38.22
Long weight	15002	Indet	D35-D37	75	31	30	6	84.57
Long weight	15087	Chiocc.	D134	47	18	18	6	18.90
Long weight	16012	Chiocc.	D235-D238	38	20	20	7	17.90
Short weight	16159	Chiocc.	D37	37	29	29	7	35.92
Short weight	16610	Chiocc.	D40	38	32	32	7	42.22
Short weight	18291	Chiocc	D336	30	27	26	6	30.61
Short weight	18479*	I	D384	41	19	20	7	Indet
Long weight	18913	Chiocc.	D437	64	18	18	6	27.23
Short weight	18971	Chiocc	A125	38	27	27	9	35.42
Long weight	19231	Chiocc.	A127	61	25	25	5	61.55
Long weight	20850	Chiocc.	A129-A131	50	17	17	6	15.90

(Continued)

Table 6.4. (Continued)

Object	*Object No.*	*Level*	*Square*	*Lenght (mm)*	*Width (mm)*	*Thickness (mm)*	*Diameter hole (mm)*	*Weight (g)*
Circular flat	20959	I	A73-A74	47	47	8	4	22.86
Short weight	23204	Chiocc.	A86	36	30	30	4	46.12
Long weight	23205	Chiocc.	A282	64	27	27	6	53.00
Long weight	23206	Chiocc.	A224	67	27	27	7	57.76
Short weight	23410	I	A86	41	23	22	10	21.50
Long weight	24073*	I	A133	33	13	11	7	Indet
Long weight	24207*	I	A133	31	13	13	10	Indet
Long weight	26364	Chiocc.	A270	52	16	16	5	16.70
Long weight	26366	Chiocc.	A268	48	27	27	5	53.72
Short weight	26440	Indet	Indet	33	32	32	10	44.00
Long weight	28639	Chiocc.	A85	79	29	29	06	79.07
Spindle whorls	28688	Chiocc.	A30	31	38	38	5	29.59
Long weight	28693	Chiocc.	A239	63	21	21	6	35.48
Long weight	28694	Chiocc.	A257	58	18	17	5	25.12
Short weight	28723	Chiocc.	A191	33	34	34	7	49.77
Long weight	28725	Indet	A237-A239	46	14	14	4	12.45
Short weight	30248	Chiocc.	A237	52	30	30	5	65.19
Short weight	31223	I	A288	51	18	18	7	17.27
Short weight	31223 bis	I	A288	39	26	26	6	38.09
Long weight	31418	I	A338-A340	67	19	19	6	27.87
Long weight	31418 bis	I	A338-A340	55	20	20	7	27.50
Circular weight	32219	Chiocc.	A322	58	56	9	6	30.00
Circular weight	32220	Chiocc.	A318	47	44	14	5	Indet
Long weight	32221	Chiocc.	A318	57	20	20	6	25.22
Long weight	32222	Chiocc.	A373	62	18	18	4	23.92
Long weight	32223	Chiocc.	A324	39	18	18	4	16.00
Long weight	32224	Chiocc.	A316	65	21	20	8	28.47
Long weight	33330	Chiocc	A336	71	18	19	5	30.08
Long weight	39990	Chiocc	A412	35	26	26	7	33.20
Circular flat	42612	Chiocc	D450	45	33	10	4	20.91
Long weight	42923	Chiocc	A453	55	15	14	6	15.83
Long weight	42969	Chiocc	A506	64	19	18	6	23.89
Long weight	45566	Chiocc	A476	60	20	18	7	30.78
Circular flat	47641	Chiocc	D350	61	56	11	0,4	36.21
Circular flat	50397	Chiocc	D349 (*bis*)	54	50	13	0,4	33.04
Sphere	51365	Chiocc	A52	35	34	33	0,6	39.91
Long weight	SN1	Chiocc	A52-A54	57	19	19	0,7	24.82
Short weight	SR009	Indet	Indet	44	27	27	0,7	47.25
Short weight	SR010	Indet	Indet	37	27	27	0,4	41.80
Rhomboid flat	SN3	Indet	Indet	62	57	18	0,7	39.14
Triangle flat	SN4	Chiocc	A52	82	52	20	0,7	59.47
Trapezoidal flat	SN5	Chiocc	A54	63	60	12	0,6	37.32

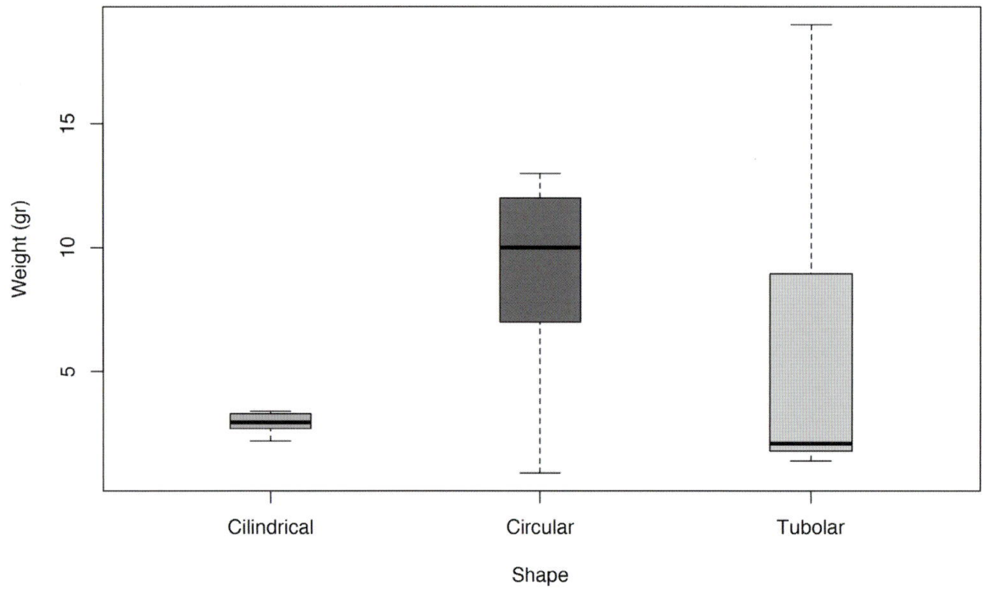

Summary statistics of weights (gr)

Shape	Min	Mean	Max	Std
Cilindrical	2.2	7.17	29	9.38
Circular	0.9	8.53	13	4.30
Tubolar	1.4	6.39	21	7.62

Figure 6.14. Boxplot of weights (g).

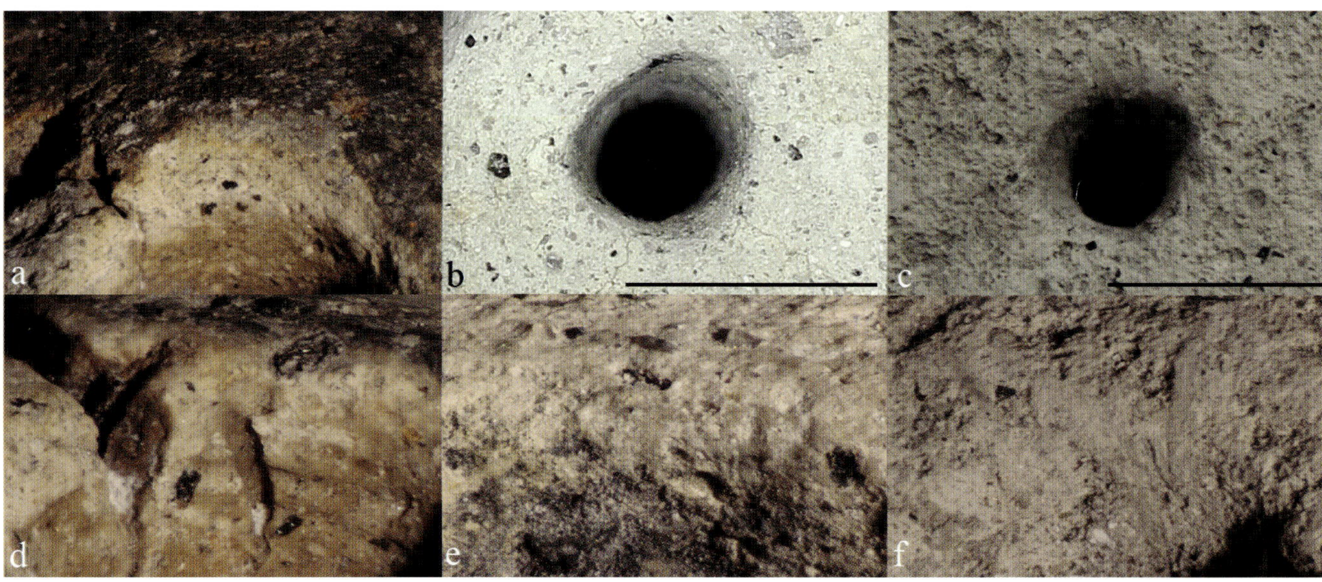

Figure 6.15. a, d: Extended abrasive wear along the spindle-whorl hole's edge (inventory number 1911), a: 8×, d: 15×; b,e: Extended abrasive wear along the weight hole's edge, deformation of the original hole (inventory number 39990), b: black bar is 1 cm, e: 15×; c-f: Vertical striations along the weight hole's edge (inventory number 4203), c: black bar is 1 cm, f: 6.7×.

which still has to be characterised in detail. Like the spindle whorls, the weights' surfaces are also altered: 17 show use-wear along the hole edges associable with suspension traces such as vertical striations, or deep abrasions changing the morphology of the edges (Fig. 6.15). The small number of items with preserved use-wear limited the interpretation of the actual use of these objects. Nevertheless, on one hand the position of use-wear in specific places of the holes could suggest the use of suspended weights, as in case of looms, while, on the other hand, the peculiar shape of the tubular weights, along with the lack of localised use-wear around the hole, could suggest a use of these weights even as net sinkers. Similar clay weights were used by the Arabs in the 8th century AD in the Iberian Peninsula (Merino 1986).

Lithic and bone instruments

Lithic and bone tools also participated in the processing of vegetal fibres. This can be assessed from the study of the use-wear traces preserved on their surfaces. Functional analyses have been performed on an assemblage of 233 lithic artefacts, of which 133 had been used (see Chapter 9.1). Of these, as many as 87 were employed with plant matter: 34 (with 41 used surfaces) to harvest cereals, 24 (with 33 used zones) to cut or scrape non-woody plants, and 29 (with 46 used zones) to scrape wood. Most of these lithic tools are blades whose edges were retouched for greater efficacy. Although sharp edges are very useful at first, after a period of work, numerous scars appear and make the tool less effective. In the case of blades forming part of a sickle, they are not retouched or only slightly so at their two ends. Many of these objects with cereal use-wear display retouched active edges because they were frequently resharpened to prolong the life of the sickle. When an edge became too blunt, the other edge of the blade was used, or the blade was replaced with another.

The use-wear study of the lithic tools is ongoing. The lithic assemblage at La Marmotta consists of 12,139 chipped pieces of flint and obsidian. This large number of objects to be studied is a guarantee of magnificent results, even though their study involves a large investment in labour. The importance and characteristics of the tools used in different activities will be understood better and it may be possible to distinguish activity areas linked with the various houses (see Chapter 9).

The bone tools have been studied with standard methodology, combining the use of stereo- and metallographic microscopes (Mozota and Gibaja 2015). An initial study has detected a group of 39 artefacts:

- Twenty small awls made from longitudinal sections of metapodials from medium-sized animals (probably ovicaprids in most cases).
- Six robust awls made from bone shafts of medium-sized animals, conserving the whole circumference of the shaft except at the pointed end.
- Six gracile needle-like awls, highly eroded and fragmented.
- Two robust smoothers made from fragments of bone shafts from medium-sized animals.
- Two awls that had not been fabricated or were improvised from bone shaft fragments.
- A flat awl made from a rib of a medium-sized animal.
- Two indeterminate utensils.

Evidence of use-wear is very difficult to identify in the bone assemblage because of the poor preservation of cortical surfaces. Of the typical metapodial awls, seven were possibly used, four display modifications caused by their use, and for the others there are no criteria to determine whether or not they were used. Among those that had been utilised, the modifications observed do not allow a determination of the substance they were worked with. In turn, five of the six robust awls exhibited clear evidence of their use. However, it was only possible in one case to determine that it had been employed in working with plant matter, probably fibres, with a predominantly transverse movement. The other tools had probably been used, but their state of preservation does not allow this to be affirmed definitively (Fig. 6.16).

Approach to the plant species that were utilised: an initial study

Carpological information

To date, only five flax seeds (out of more than 20,000 determinations) have been found at La Marmotta. Underestimation of flax can be due to several causes. Many of the samples analysed derive from the *vaglio* (sieve); samples were treated as soon as the sediment was brought to the surface of the lake by sieving, probably with a mesh size of a few millimetres, which allowed the recovery of cereals and fruits but not of smaller seeds. Poor preservation of flax seeds is a known problem in literature: the high oil content often causes the fragmentation of waterlogged seeds; there is a high likelihood of seeds being carbonised under reducing conditions, while under oxidising conditions the probability is very low (Märkle and Rosch 2008).

The plant material kept at the Museo delle Civiltà suggests that linen (fibres and plants with capsules) was, instead, particularly abundant. Many seeds from La Marmotta still remain to be studied in the Como laboratory. Their analysis will help to assess the representativeness of the flax remains.

Among the species documented at La Marmotta, several may have been used for dyeing (*Hypericum perforatum*, *Phragmites australis*, *Persicaria maculosa*, *Prunus spinosa*, *Sambucus* spp., etc.) but until now no accumulations of seeds or other parts of these plants have been found that can support this use. *Carthamus lanatus* seeds are frequent at the site (Rottoli 1993; 2002). It is a species similar to *C. tinctorius* (safflower), which may have been used for dyeing and/or for the extraction of an edible oil; but safflower spread in Europe only from the Bronze Age onwards (Marinova and Riehl 2009). *Carthamus lanatus* seeds (charred and waterlogged) are widely distributed throughout the excavated area, but they are larger than those of flax and may therefore have been favoured in sampling. *Carthamus lanatus* has not been documented in other Italian Neolithic sites.

Textile and cordage analysis

Over two decades after the discovery of La Marmotta, the raw material used to make the textiles and cordage found there is now being analysed. Thus, the following information represents the first stage in the series of analyses that will be performed. The finds were studied by the naked eye and with a Breukhoven BMS 74958 stereo-microscope, an Hirox stereo-microscope, and a Tescan Vega 3 Oxford Inca x-act (at UniVac 15Pa with no coating) scanning electron microscope (SEM) (operator Dr Daniela Ferro).

Figure 6.16. Robust awl that had hardly been shaped, slightly eroded by taphonomic processes. It was made from a long bone that preserved its whole circumference. The working area was prepared by abrasion from a deliberate oblique fracture near one of the epiphyses. The microscopic use-wear traces (100×) suggest it was used to work with plant fibres.

Textiles

Small textile fragments (*c.* 15 × 30 mm) have been preserved (eg, Nuo SR011, Level Indet, Square A204–A206; Fig. 6.1). They all display similar technological characteristics: they are intertwined, with 60 × 80/mm^2 weave count, with 2ply S2z threads of 500±80 µm diameter, and 350±80 µm diameter of each ply (Fig. 6.17: 1). Scanning electron microscope (SEM) analysis indicated the textile fragments are made of cellulosic bast fibres, as they are polygonal with nodes (Rast-Eicher 2016) although the condition and consolidation of the fibres did not allow a more precise identification. They are generally separated but some fibres still occur in bundles (Fig. 6.17: 2).

Threads on spindles

A large volume of threads has been preserved still coiled around the spindles. The threads on the spindles can be divided into two categories based on their diameters. One is finer: 2ply S2z of 350±50 µm diameter, with a 240±30 µm diameter of each ply (Fig. 6.18: 1), made of separated cellulosic bast fibres. Some of the fibres seem to occur in bundles but the heavy impregnation by the consolidant does not allow a clearer image of the sample (Fig. 6.18: 2). The other category is coarser: 2ply S2z of 830±160 µm diameter, and 560±80 µm diameter of each ply, that seem to be spliced (Gleba and Harris 2018) (Fig. 6.19: 1), made of most probably bast fibres still in bundles, where the epidermis seems to have been retained although this observation could be a mis-interpretation of the consolidation of the find (Fig. 6.19: 2).

Cordage

A very large amount of cordage has been preserved, both plied and braided examples. The plied cordage is generally 2ply S2z and Z2s with different diameters of each ply recorded at 1 mm, 2.5±0.5 mm and 5 mm (eg, Fig. 6.20: 1); while there is one 3ply z3S example with 4.5±0.5 mm diameter of each ply, and a much coarser (rope?) example of 3ply Z3s with 8±1 mm diameter of each ply (Fig. 6.20: 2). For the braided cordage, the widths of the plaited strands are generally 3.5±0.5 mm (Fig. 6.20: 3). All cordage seems to have been made of plants from the Poaceae (or Gramineae) family of monocotyledonous flowering plants (grasses), as indicated by the outer structure and the papilla-like formation observed (Khan *et al.* 2017) (Fig. 6.21: 1–3).

Figure 6.17. 1. Detail of one of the textile fragments (Object No. SR011); 2. SEM micrograph of a textile thread sample.

Figure 6.18. 1. Detail of one of the spindles with the finer coiled thread (Object No. 17573); 2. SEM micrograph of finer coiled fibres, where the fibres seem to be separated.

Figure 6.19: 1. Detail of the coarser thread from spindles (Object No. SR013-2); 2. SEM micrograph of a thread sample from coarser spindle thread, where the fibres seem to be preserved in bundles.

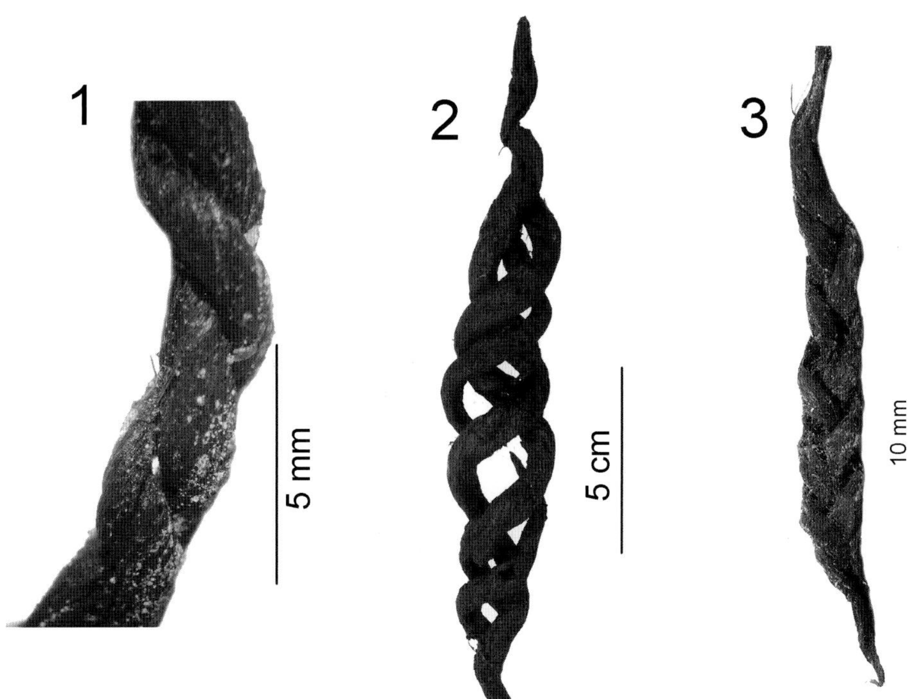

Figure 6.20: Cordage: 1. Object No. 7027_1 (Level I, D197); 2. Object No. 14046 (Level I, D139); 3. Object No. 15688B (Level I, D183).

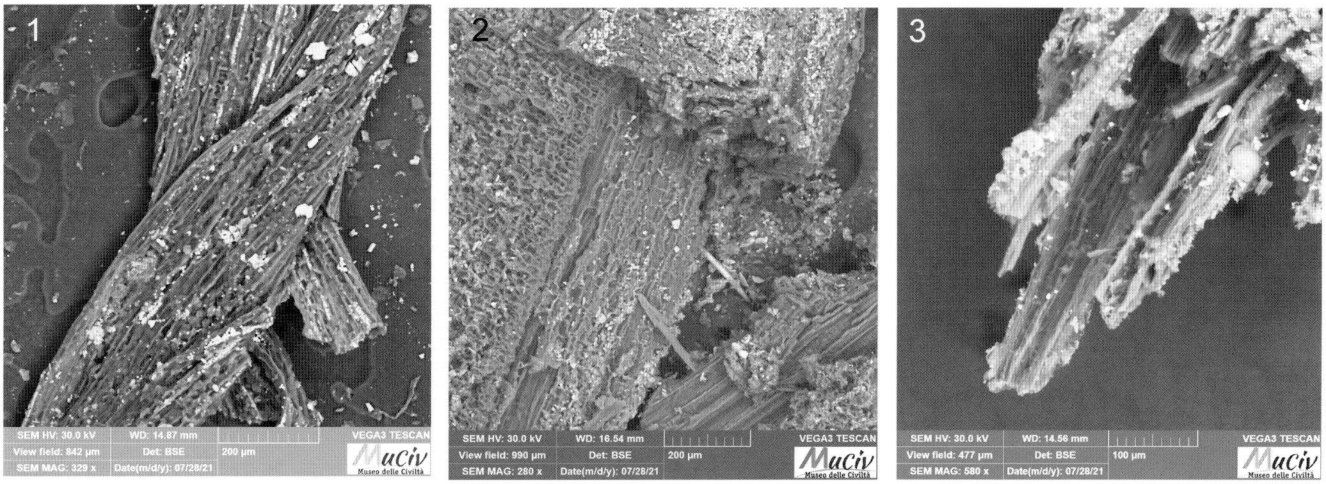

Figure 6.21. SEM micrographs: 1. sample finer 2ply cordage (Object No. 16373, Level II, D240); 2. Sample of 3ply cordage, where alternating layers are observed (Object No. 26333, Level II, A276); 3. Sample of braided cordage, where a formation corresponding to papilla was detected (Object No. 16998, Level I, D89).

7

Food remains, phytotherapics and psychotropics remains

Mauro Rottoli and Amaia Arranz

Neolithic vegetation around La Marmotta

Neolithic pile dwelling sites are renowned for the excellent preservation conditions of organic material: wooden tools, textiles, fruit remains and foodstuffs have been preserved in many of them. In Italy only three reliably-dated settlements of this type have been documented: Isolino Virginia (Lake Varese, Lombardy, Antolín *et al.* 2022), Palù di Livenza (Friuli, Micheli *et al.* 2018) and La Marmotta, the oldest and the only one in central Italy (Fugazzola and Tinazzi 2010; Salavert *et al.* 2020), where the presence of water allowed exceptional preservation of the botanical macro-remains.

Up to now, more than 35,000 seeds and fruits found in La Marmotta have been analysed, allowing an accurate reconstruction of the environment around the site and of the plants used for food or other purposes. The dataset from La Marmotta has also allowed us to determine the first farming in the area of central Italy near the Tyrrhenian coasts, helping to clarify a still little-understood issue.

At the end of the last glaciation, the area of volcanic lakes north of Rome (Sabatini volcanic district) was covered by dense forest vegetation. Pollen analyses (Ciuffarella 1996; Kelly and Huntley 1991; Giardini 2007) have partially reconstructed the composition of those forests which, in addition to deciduous and evergreen oaks, hazel (*Corylus*) and hornbeam (*Ostrya/Carpinus orientalis*), were characterised by the presence of laurel (*Laurus nobilis*) and other species, scarce producers of pollen, which represent a legacy of the tertiary flora now almost completely disappeared from Italy (Pignatti *et al.* 2015).

The start of Neolithic colonisation was not discouraged either by the dense forest cover or by the hilly landscape and absence of real flat land: the advantages were too substantial. Particularly fertile soils were formed thanks to volcanic activity, which had ceased some tens of thousands of years before (80–40 ka BP; Bertagnini *et al.* 1993; De Rita *et al.* 1993). The volcanic lakes had clear water full of fish and the presence of marshy areas, which were formed in the oldest calderas, allowed the development of highly varied vegetation, which in turn favoured the frequentation of a wide range of wild animal species and the possibility of obtaining pastures for livestock.

Along the shores of the lake there was a dense reed bed consisting mainly of *Phragmites australis* with different species of sedges (*Carex pseudocyperus*, *C. elata* type). Common reed appears to have been widely employed in the construction of the village huts. Various plants thrived in the often-submerged areas (*Ceratophylllum demersum*, *Cladium mariscus*, *Cyperus longus*). In the lake, aquatic plants included *Potamogeton* spp., *Nuphar lutea*, various Najadaceae (*Najas marina*, *N. minor*, *N.* cf. *flexilis*) and Characeae. At the edge of the lake, alternating with alder groves, were wet meadows (with *Cyperus fuscus/flavescens*, *Cerastium fontanum* and so on).

The village stood on the shore of the lake, the best area from an 'ecological' point of view, although the lack of an outlet led to certain variability in the lake level. For the construction of the houses, poles obtained from deciduous oaks (*Quercus sz. Robur, i.e. Q. robur, Q. pubescens* or *Q. petraea*), laurels (*Laurus nobilis*) and ash trees (*Fraxinus* spp.) were mainly used. The assemblage of species in the forest included other plants that denote the presence of a mosaic landscape where wetter areas alternated with better drained ones and where the slopes might benefit from better or less favourable exposure. Wood, charcoal and macro-remains document the use of alder (*Alnus glutinosa*), hornbeam (*Carpinus betulus/orientalis*), beech (*Fagus sylvatica*) and forest species with edible fruits. Thus, the different plant and animal resources growing in the area and available to the inhabitants of La Marmotta were used as plant foods, psychotropic plants and ornaments.

Plant-foods: edible seeds, fruits and nuts

The array of fruits and nuts represented at La Marmotta suggests that wild plant resources were important components of the diet during the Early Neolithic. Wild fruits, which could be eaten raw, dried, cooked or in processed form to remove toxins, were identified in the assemblages, including: hazelnuts (*Corylus avellana*), acorns (*Quercus* spp.), apples (*Malus sylvestris*), sloes and plums (*Prunus spinosa, P. domestica insititia*), pears (*Pyrus* sp.), cornelian cherries (*Cornus mas*), common dogwood berries (*Cornus sanguinea*) and strawberries (*Fragaria vesca* agg.).

However, it is the remarkable abundance and the exceptional preservation of cereals that represent the most interesting data from the site. Huge quantities of intact whole ears together with already cleaned grains ready for use were found in the burned layers. It is difficult to establish which cereal was most abundantly cultivated at the site: two-row barley (*Hordeum distichon*), emmer (*Triticum dicoccum*), naked wheat (*T. durum/turgidum*) and einkorn (*T. monococcum*) are present in almost pure and mixed accumulations. Naked wheat has a very ancestral morphology that is little differentiated from emmer: the spikelets are two-grained and the glumes still tightly wrap the grains. These are only a little more rounded than those of emmer but the distinction is often problematic.

The harvesting of cereals took place with wooden sickles. The pollen of arable weeds (*Avena* sp., *Bromus cf. secalinus, Capsella bursa-pastoris, Galium cf. aparine*) was discovered inside the glue used to fix the flints on the wooden handle of the sickles (Mazzucco *et al.* 2022a). However, weeds rarely appear in the carpological assemblages, suggesting that cleaning operation were made before that the harvested yield was stored at the village.

The seeds of cultivated pulses, namely lentils (*Lens culinaris*), peas (*Pisum sativum*), grass peas/chickling vetches (*Lathyrus sativus/cicera*) and vetches (*Vicia sativa* agg.), are much rarer than cereal grains. Lentils and peas are the most abundant. The cultivation of broad bean (*Vicia faba minor*) is documented with uncertainty. as discussed above, up to now, only a few flax seeds (*Linum usitatissimum*) have been found.

Grape macro-remains (seeds, wood and charcoal) are very common on the site. The grapevine was naturally very widespread: palynological data show that wild grapevine (*Vitis vinifera sylvestris*) was common and sometimes very abundant in the natural Mediterranean riparian vegetation in the form of a climber (Magri *et al.* 2019). We do not know if the La Marmotta inhabitants were able to produce wine but the grape harvest was certainly a well-organised activity. Indeed, to determine the types of meals and foodstuffs that the inhabitants of La Marmotta produced, other data proxies have to be examined.

Food remains

Whilst the analyses of plant macro-remains have traditionally centred on the study of wood charcoal and non-woody plant remains, in the last decades a ground-breaking discovery has been made: not only seeds, fruits, nuts and pieces of wood charcoal can be found in archaeological sites but also accidentally charred food remains. The implication of this is nothing short of revolutionary. The study of 'amorphous' carbonised food remains has allowed archaeobotanists to provide, for the first time, direct evidence of plant-food ingredients (*e.g.*, cereals, wild plants, legumes), cooking techniques and final food products like bread, beer, bulgur and porridges, as well to gain crucial new insights into the socio-cultural significance of food, including the identification of daily food, ritual meals and offerings (Valamoti *et al.* 2008; 2011; 2021; Heiss *et al.* 2015; 2017; 2020; Kubiak Martens *et al.* 2015; Gonzalez-Carretero *et al.* 2017; Arranz-Otaegui *et al.* 2018).

In Europe, the analysis of carbonised food remains has started to develop through the effort of several archaeobotanists and research projects (see summaries in Popova 2016; Gonzalez-Carretero *et al.* 2017). Methodological advances include in-depth tissue-based analyses of the remains using SEM and X- ray Computed Microtomography to identify the plant ingredients and cooking methods (Valamoti *et al.* 2008; Heiss *et al.* 2015; 2017; 2019; 2020; Gonzalez Carretero *et al.* 2017); as well as the first residue analyses of charred food lumps, using Gas Chromatography-Mass spectrometry (GC/MS) to characterise their chemical composition and detect the presence of food components invisible to the naked eye, such as dairy products, vegetal oils, honey or animal fats (Kubiak Martens *et al.* 2015; Heron *et al.* 2016).

The tissue-based analysis of archaeological food remains follows specific procedures. Under the SEM, different plant parts are observable, such as the testa (seed coat), aleurone layers (cells located between the starchy endosperm and the seed coat), as well as energy storage starch granules. These are genera/family-specific and inform on the plant ingredients used as food in the past. The anatomy of the archaeological plant tissues is compared with modern reference materials to achieve highest level taxonomic identifications. In addition, some of the taphonomic features present in the microscopic plant tissues are recorded. For example, the cell wall breakdown in the grain's aleurone layer can be used as a general marker for malting processes (Heiss *et al.* 2020), whilst the characterisation of the state of starch granules (*e.g.*, intact, gelatinised, pitted) informs on cooking processes such as baking, soaking and fermenting (Henry *et al.* 2009). Apart from studying plant tissues, the SEM analyses allow the characterisation of the micro-structure or 'matrix' of the food remains under study. This involves the measurement of the size and density of plant inclusions (*e.g.*, cereal tissue) and other features like air or gas bubbles, micropores and channels through image analyses. The proportions with which these elements appear in the matrix are later used to identify specific food products like dough, flat and leavened breads and porridges (Heiss *et al.* 2015; 2017; Gonzalez Carretero *et al.* 2017; Arranz-Otaegui *et al.* 2018).

Despite their potential to provide first-hand empirical data on the types of food products consumed by prehistoric societies, the visibility of archaeological food remains is still limited. These remains have been (and continue to be) confused with parenchymatous tissue, dung, or simply referred to as 'indeterminate remains' or 'amorphous charred objects' in archaeobotanical studies. As a result, the analysis of food remains is not yet systematic. With few exceptions, most of the case studies so far derive from regions such as central Europe and Greece and chronologies starting from the Neolithic onwards (Valamoti *et al.* 2008; 2019; 2021; Heiss *et al.* 2015; 2017; 2020; Kubiak-Martens *et al.* 2015; Gonzalez-Carretero *et al.* 2018). As a result, very little is known about regional differences in terms of plant-food consumption practices and their evolution though time. Besides, most of the archaeological food remains analysed so far are usually small in size (*e.g.*, 4 × 4 mm) and found mixed with other plant macro-remains in flotation samples. Except for the complete bread loaves preserved in Egypt (Samuel 1996) and the cereal-based foods discovered in a select number of Neolithic, Late Bronze Age and Roman sites in Europe (Heiss *et al.* 2015; 2017; 2019), the presence of large pieces of food remains is commonly an exception rather than the rule.

In this sense, the finds from La Marmotta are exceptional. During field excavations, at least 90 large fragments of carbonised food remains were recovered. These vary from 20 mm to 180 mm in length and 10–80 mm in width, and have a thickness of 7–80 mm. Besides, many of these food fragments still preserve their original shape including rectangular remains, dough-type flat pieces, often with rounded edges, as well as circular remains (Fig. 7.1).

The evidence indicates that the inhabitants of the site produced and consumed a range of different plant-based foodstuffs. Variations in terms of micro-texture and plant inclusions allow us to establish at least four main categories:

1. Remains that represent the contents of pots, which commonly show rounded shapes with smooth edges and clearly differentiable bottom parts and upper surfaces. Here plant remains are present, but they are overall rare and the matrix is dense and compact.
2. Cereal-based foods, which comprise at least baked bread and dough-like remains. These remains include a large proportion of cereal impressions, as well as embedded grains and chaff remains. So far, the use of both einkorn and barley has been identified in these food preparations. Cereal-based foods like bread represent the most common type of food category at broadly contemporary Neolithic sites (Heiss *et al.* 2017; 2020; Valamoti *et al.* 2019; 2021).
3. In addition, there are remains that show oily or greasy micro-structures, with a large number of small pores and very vitrified surfaces.

Figure 7.1. Food fragment (Object No. 9047; Level II, Square D194) showing square impressions in the lateral section.

4. Fragments that have layered or laminated and crackly matrixes with large numbers of fragmented seeds embedded. Preliminary analyses indicate that the latter may represent the remains of oil extraction activities.

A key feature to be highlighted from the La Marmotta food assemblage is that, unlike the discoveries made so far, many of the food remains from the site still preserve fibre remains and/or plant impressions, suggesting that food was regularly stored in baskets and other plant-made containers. Whilst the detailed and interdisciplinary analysis of these food remains is currently ongoing, it is clear that the evidence recovered in La Marmotta will not only provide key new insights into the selection, processing and consumption of plant food resources during the Early Neolithic, but also into how food was stored and served, activities that are not commonly identified in the archaeological record.

Phytotherapics, psychotropics

The use of drugs is an extended activity in the animal kingdom. Cats, reindeer, foxes and dolphins among many other species have been observed exploiting plants, mushrooms, and even manipulating other animals like blowfish to obtain psychotropic substances. Humans are not an exception in this sense. The archaeological evidence shows that even in the Upper Palaeolithic, the species *Homo sapiens* was using poisons like ricinoleic acid from mature castor beans (*Ricinus communis* L., Euphorbiaceae) in incised sticks for hunting purposes, in a similar way to the modern Kalahari San (D'Errico *et al.* 2012). However, clear-cut evidence for the use of plant-derived drugs in Europe is only attested from the Neolithic onwards.

There are a number of plant species and fungi that could have been used as medicines and in ritual activities during the Neolithic:

- The presence of seeds of *Hyoscyamus niger* (henbane), a species that produces a strong psychotropic effect and causes hallucinations, has been attested at several sites dated from the Neolithic onwards in Bulgaria (Marinova 2009; Marinova *et al.* 2013), Scotland (Long *et al.* 1999; 2000) and Switzerland (Martin 2015). However, clear evidence for its use is attested during the 3rd millennium BC in a burial cave in Calvari d'Amposta, Tarragona, Spain. Here alkaloid hyoscyamine and traces suggestive of barley beer were documented in a Bell Beaker and interpreted as a hallucinogenic beer that could have been consumed during mortuary ceremonies (Fábregas 2001).
- Seeds of *Atropa belladona* (deadly nightshade) have been documented at Early Neolithic sites at La Planta in Switzerland (Martin 2015) and, later, at Măgura Gorgana in Rumania (Toderas *et al.* 2009). At this latter site, thousands of seeds were found in several rooms probably linked to religious activities.
- It is also known that, since the Neolithic period, people in northern Europe were familiar with *Claviceps purpurea* (ergot). This is a parasitic fungus that grows in cereals and wild herbs and produces hallucinogenic alkaloids (LSD-25 is a semi-synthetic derivate of this fungus). Ergot remains have been found in Neolithic sites in Germany and the Netherlands, although its presence increased considerably from the Iron Age onwards (Guerra Doce 2006; Guerra Doce and López-Sáez 2006; Hellmund 2008).

Nevertheless, the first clear evidence for the use of psychoactive plants in Europe belongs to a key species: poppy (*Papaver somniferum*). This genus comprises more than 80 species of poppy that currently grow in central and south-western Asia, central and southern Europe and northern Africa (Kadereit 1988). The opium poppy is an annual species, 30–150 cm high, and the evidence indicates its wild relative is *Papaver somniferum* subsp. *setigerum*, an annual plant, 60 cm high which is native to the Western Mediterranean and commonly inhabits cultivated fields and disturbed ground.

In Europe, *Papaver somniferum/setigerum* seeds are reported in the archaeological record starting from the 6th millennium cal BC, that is, during the Early Neolithic (see Guerra Doce and López-Sáez 2006; Zohary *et al.* 2012; Salavert *et al.* 2020). Poppy remains were first recorded in excavations conducted in 1852–1854 at the Neolithic village beside Lake Pfäffikersee near Robenhausen in northern Switzerland (Heer 1865; Keller 1866), and shortly after, at the cave site of Cueva de los Murciélagos in Albuñol, Spain (Góngora 1868; Neuweiler 1935). In the first case study, the presence of poppy-seed cakes suggested that Neolithic communities used opium poppy as a source of food (Keller 1866). In contrast, in Cueva de los Murciélagos, several poppy capsules were found in a funerary context, stored in woven bags made of esparto grass and associated with human skeletons. This evidence shows a clear link between the effects that the opium poppy produces in the human mind and body (*e.g.*, relaxation, somnolence, stillness) and the 'state' of the dead. Apart from its use as food or as a medicinal or symbolic plant, the seeds of opium poppy have also been found embedded as temper in the fabric of clay pots at the Neolithic site of Vaux-et-Borset in Belgium (Bakels *et al.* 1992). Taken together, this evidence indicates that, even if the opium poppy is nowadays known and exploited primarily as a source of opium, its use in the past seemed to have been more diverse than at present.

Although this species has been documented in a number of Neolithic and later sites in Western Europe, the origins of opium poppy domestication are still unclear (Salavert *et al.* 2020). As highlighted recently (Jesus *et al.* 2021), most of the archaeological finds reported so far make reference to *P. somniferum,* but do not always provide clear evidence of domestication (*e.g.*, an increase in the size of the capsule and seeds, and capsule indehiscence). Whilst it was traditionally thought that this species was domesticated in south-west Asia, along with the other key 'Founder Crops' of Neolithic agriculture, researchers now consider that opium poppy could actually represent one of several species domesticated outside the Fertile Crescent (Salavert 2010; Salavert *et al.* 2020). In this sense the remains found at La Marmotta are helping to elucidate the origins and diffusion of this key species.

At La Marmotta large quantities of well-preserved charred and waterlogged opium poppy seeds, capsules and stigmatic discs were recovered from different archaeological contexts (Rottoli 1993; Rottoli and Pessina 2007). It is possible that wild opium poppies (*Papaver setigerum*) grew naturally along the central and western Mediterranean coasts and were taken into cultivation by the first Neolithic farmers that settled in the area (Fig. 7.2). The number of finds and their overall ubiquity, the presence of stigmatic discs with a number of rays greater than those typical of the wild form and some indehiscent capsules (*i.e.* closed at the time of ripening), are all arguments for the cultivation of poppy at La Marmotta. The domestication process was still ongoing when, after hundreds of years of exploitation, this species could have been relocated to other regions. In fact, a recent study suggests that the poppy from a pile-dwelling site in Switzerland had not yet been fully domesticated at the end of the 4th millennium BC (Jesus *et al.* 2021).

Whether wild or in the process of domestication, the poppy remains from La Marmotta represent the oldest evidence for the cultivation and exploitation of this species in Europe. This has recently been confirmed by a research project directed by the archaeobotanist Aurelié Salavert. A total of 20 radiocarbon samples were taken from 12 different Neolithic sites located in Western Europe (Salavert *et al.* 2020), including one sample consisting of opium poppy capsule fragments from La Marmotta. The radiocarbon analyses confirmed the antiquity of the capsules from La Marmotta with dates around 5690–5260 cal BC, linking them to the early stage of the site's occupation (Fugazzola and Tinazzi 2010). Opium poppy is later attested *c.* 5620–5480 cal BC in other Mediterranean Neolithic sites, such as Le Täis (southern France) and La Draga (north-eastern Spain), as well as in central Europe, at sites such as Momalle (central Belgium), Vaihingen an der Enz and Nieder-Mörlen (Germany) and the Geleen-Janskamperveld (Netherlands; Salavert *et al.* 2020). Whilst the origins and dispersal of this species are currently being disentangled, the reasons that led Neolithic populations to cultivate this particular plant, as well as the uses it was given by the different communities (*e.g.*, as a drug, food, oil etc.) remain to be investigated.

Apart from poppy, the evidence recovered at La Marmotta also attests the exploitation of other plant resources and fungi that could have been used as phytotherapics and psychotropics. In terms of plant species, the archaeobotanical assemblage from the site includes two species of thistle: milk thistle (*Silybum marianum* and downy safflower (*Carthamus lanatus*) (Rottoli 1993; 2002). The quantity and frequency of burnt and waterlogged seeds indicate that these species, which grow spontaneously in the area around the site, were in great demand and probably cultivated (Rottoli 2002). Many parts of the *Silybum* plant are edible and medicinal substances can be obtained from the seeds. Downy safflower is closely related to the true safflower (*C. tinctorius*) so it is possible that this spontaneous species was used for dyeing too.

In addition to these plants, potential medicinal fungi remains have also been recovered at La Marmotta. During the excavations in the 1990s, ten cut pieces of bracket fungus were identified (Bernicchia *et al.* 2006). Five were located inside the domestic structures and the rest were found outside the habitation areas but in close vicinity to the wooden structures. The shape and size of the remains varied but they were on average 30–90 mm long, and 30 mm in thickness. The remains had a broad chronological assignation, meaning that they could have been used in different occupation phases at the site. The macro- and microscopic examination of the remains and DNA analyses indicated

Figure 7.2. Two opium poppy capsules and seeds.

that the fungi remains belong to the species *Daedaleopsis tricolor* (blushing bracket). They were interpreted as being gathered for their pharmacological properties and use as a symbolic offering (Bernicchia *et al.* 2006; Fugazzola 2004a).

The presence of fungi has been attested at several Mesolithic, Neolithic and Bronze Age sites in northern Europe (Kreisel and Ansorge 2009; Robson 2018) and the circum-Alpine region (Roussel 2005; Kreisel and Ansorge 2009). However, most of the finds belong to polypores that grow on fallen trunks or trees and their intentional use has been demonstrated at few sites, often linked to firemaking. The most emblematic case study refers to Ötzi, a man who died around 3350–3100 cal BC in Hauslabjoch, on the Austrian–Italian border. Among his belongings a bag was found that contained the fungi *Fomes fomentarius* with clear evidence of preparation to be used as tinder (Peinter *et al.* 1998), a practice that is well documented in historical records (Piqué *et al.* 2020). Clear evidence for the use of fungi, including the presence of charring and cut marks, has been attested at other Neolithic sites such as Star Carr, England (Robson 2018) and La Draga, Spain (Berihuete *et al.* 2018; Piqué *et al.* 2020). At the latter, 86 fruiting bodies were studied that belonged to six different taxa including: *Ganoderma adspersum*, *Daldinia concetrica*, *Daedalea quercina*, *Lenzites warniere*, *Copriolopsis gallica* and *Skeletocuti nivea*. The remains were interpreted as gathered and dried materials to be used as tinder by the inhabitants of the site, a practice that seems to have been very common according to modern ethnobotanic and ethnomycological studies (Berihuete *et al.* 2018; Piqué *et al.* 2020).

Overall, the richness and variety of plant and fungal remains at La Marmotta provide new insights into the use of plants in the ancient Neolithic. Whilst in other Neolithic sites only charred plant remains are preserved (commonly comprising cereals, legumes, weeds and particularly fruits with resistant shells and stones), the data from La Marmotta attest a much more varied and complex use of plant resources during this crucial time period.

8

The botanical ornaments of La Marmotta

Cristiana Petrinelli Pannocchia and Alice Vassanelli[1]

La Marmotta yielded over 300 personal ornaments, differing in shape and raw material. The abundance and the high quality of these artefacts have no comparison within the Neolithic landscape of the central Mediterranean area.

Adorning oneself with objects, pigments, and manipulation of the body is a widespread practice in all current and ancient populations, reflecting choices related to personal tastes and cultural traditions. Over time, personal adornments have varied in forms and materials. During prehistoric periods, beads, pendants and bracelets were made from stones, clay and hard animal matter (Baysal 2019). However, the possible use of botanical materials in ornament production can be assumed through ethnographic comparisons. The observation of the decorative objects worn in a settlement context helps us to understand the complexities of ornament biographies, from manufacturing techniques and formation of wear traces (Falci *et al.* 2019) to their intrinsic value. Beyond the aesthetic role of this practice, the ornamental elements can in fact reflect different meanings related to the wearer and the society to which he or she belongs (Vanhaeren 2005; Van Gijn 2017).

The morphology and the choice of the raw material used for their realisation can hide multiple meanings related to age, social role, power, and gender of the wearer (Kuhn and Stiner 2007; Hodder 2011; Bar-Yosef Mayer 2015; Mueller Epstein 2017). At the same time, they may also have had a magical or apotropaic connotation.

In addition, ornamental objects can inform us about several aspects of ancient communities. As products of human behaviour, these items are an expression of craft knowledge and skills, and of technological and economic choices. They can reveal important information about raw materials, exchange networks, finished products, and at the same time can testify to the existence of identity traditions, changes, persistence, and possible transcultural ties.

Due to the paucity of archaeological evidence, information about Early Neolithic ornamental habits in Italy is still fragmentary. This scarcity is related in part to the fragility of these elements. Although durable materials have often been used to make them, the small size of many objects has often favoured their fragmentation. In addition, excavation methods play a primary role in the recovery of these items. The tiny size of many beads means that they may not be recovered if sieving and flotation are not performed, which was largely the case in old excavations.

There is also a lack of data on a large part of products made from botanical materials because of their perishability. For this reason, the extraordinary preservation of organic remains at the site of La Marmotta has provided a unique witness to Early Neolithic ornamentation practices that are still quite unknown.

Personal ornaments in prehistory: a brief overview

As many authors point out, personal ornaments can be considered 'tangible signs of the existence of symbolic material cultures' (Bouzouggar *et al.* 2007), and for this reason, establishing their beginning and evolution is important to understand the origins of culturally modern behaviour. Recent discoveries testify to the earliest proof of ornamental practices in North Africa and Asia around 100,000 BC. The evidence from these areas (Grotte des Pigeons, Morocco; Bouzouggar *et al.* 2007; Blombos, South Africa; Henshilwood *et al.* 2002; Oued Djebbana, Algeria, Es Skūhl, Israel; Henshilwood *et al.* 2004, Vanhaeren *et al.* 2006) attest the use of beads made from perforated shells all of the same genus (Taforalt, Djebbana, and Skūhl) or similar ones (Blombos), often covered with red ochre.

In Italy, as in Europe, in recent years increasing evidence may indicate practices with ornamental purposes before the arrival of anatomically modern humans (Zilhão 2007; Peresani *et al.* 2011; 2013; Romandini *et al.* 2014). However, the systematic use of specific objects as ornaments started with the earliest phases of the Upper Palaeolithic. The assemblages consist mainly of perforated shells, almost exclusively of marine gastropods and bivalves. A preference for red or yellow shells has been observed, probably because of their correlation to particular meanings (Álvarez-Fernández 2002). The use as pendants of perforated bones or teeth, mostly red deer canines or their lithic imitations, is also attested.

Changes occurred in ornamental traditions from the last phase of the Upper Palaeolithic to the Mesolithic. *Columbella rustica* shells gradually increased in importance (Cristiani *et al.* 2014; Perlès 2018) and became almost the exclusive ornament of Mesolithic groups. At the end of the 7th millennium cal BC, with the spread of Neolithic groups in Western Mediterranean regions, the first farmers who landed on the eastern coasts of the Italian Peninsula brought with them an innovative variety of personal ornaments in the so-called 'Neolithic Package'.

The ornamental custom of these newcomers shows continuity in the use of *Columbella rustica*, perforated animal teeth, including red deer canines or, in general, the use of hard animal matter, recalling previous traditions. However, a significant increment in the use of stone materials, connected to an increase in manufacturing complexity, is clearly observable (Petrinelli Pannocchia and Vassanelli 2021). The morphology of the ornaments became ever more defined and new models, the discoidal bead and the ring bracelet, were introduced (Micheli 2021).

Attributable to the Neolithic is the first archaeological attestation of botanical ornaments in the Mediterranean area. We cannot rule out their presence in previous periods but, probably due to their perishability, no traces have been found so far. The earliest wooden beads attested came from Nahal Hemar (Werker 1988). The production of beads from various botanical materials is attested also at the site of Çatalhöyük (Turkey, Vasic *et al.* 2021).

In the Italian Peninsula, the discovery of botanical ornaments in prehistoric contexts is rare. Before the discovery of La Marmotta, the only known evidence had been found in the Early Bronze Age level at the pile-dwelling settlement of Lucone (Lake Garda). The investigated layer preserved a necklace, formed by at least 25 beads, 12 made with bladdernut seeds (*Staphylea pinnata)* and 13 from marble.

The impressive number of ornamental items collected at La Marmotta allows us to observe the relevance of shaped ornaments and the use of organic matter in their production in the first Neolithic phase in the central Mediterranean area, as well as the development of types that will become increasingly standardised in successive phases.

The ornamental assemblage at La Marmotta

A rich ornament collection of beads and pendants (over 300 items), characterised by a relatively restricted typology, reflects a standardised and serial production of many of these items. All ornaments have been measured with callipers to record the length, width, thickness and diameter of perforation. The weight was also recorded. The beads have been photographed in several projections with a Nikon EOS 550D camera equipped with a macro lens. The specimen surfaces have been observed by the naked eye and with an optical binocular microscope (BMS 7458), to which the Nikon camera was connected, to detect the manufacturing traces and use-wear. Multifocal reconstructions of the images have been realised with the Helicon Focus program. A selection of beads has been analysed with a Bruker Tracer III–SD handheld XRF to determine the raw materials used for their production and the nature of the residues found on some surfaces.

According to the nature of the raw materials, the ornamental assemblages can be divided into three main groups: minerals, hard animal matter, and plant materials. A general preference for soft materials, easier to shape, has been observed.

To the first group belong stone and clay beads. Black and dark green steatite, probably obtained from the south of Tuscany, was selected to produce disc and short cylindrical beads. Brown clay was used to make regular cylindrical pottery beads, while a grey paste, rich in calcareous and volcanic tempers, was employed to model irregular ovoid beads.

Shell was the principal hard animal matter used. Long ovoid specimens were produced from *Spondylus*, while discoidal items were produced from other genera of shells. Some animal teeth have a perforation through the root, probably used for suspension. A number of these items show lateral breakage. No bone beads have been collected.

Botanical personal ornaments

At La Marmotta, three different types of plant matter, wood, seeds and nuts, were chosen to produce 56 beads (Table 8.1). The plant taxa determination of the single objects is still ongoing. The first results point to the use of *Vitis vinifera* and *Fraxinus*. All these items were found charred. It is unclear if this happened accidentally or whether they were deliberately heated to achieve a black colour, as supposed for the wooden beads found in a burial at Çatalhöyük (Asouti and Kabukcu 2012; Vasic *et al.* 2021). Moreover, the transformation of the vegetal tissues into carbon would have ensured their preservation against the aggression of biological or chemical agents (Märkle and Rösch 2008). The seeds chosen to make beads seem to belong to the same botanical species, not yet identified. However, similarities with both Pinaceae and Rosaceae seeds have been noted. The only nut bead was made from a hazelnut (*Corylus avellana*).

Wooden beads

The wide typological differentiation of the few wooden beads recovered reflects the entire ornament production at the site (Fig. 8.1): short (1) and long (1) cylindrical shapes, ovoid (1) and discoidal (2).

Cylindrical beads (Fig. 8.1: b) show straight sides, convex faces, and round to oval cross-sections. They display tubular perforations with a diameter that differs significantly between the two specimens: 2 mm in the long bead and just under 4 mm in the short item. The ovoid bead has convex sides and faces, with a thin tubular piercing 1 mm in width (Fig. 8.1: a).

Two of the beads have an irregular disc shape. Among the wooden artefacts, these two have the largest diameter which, however, does not exceed 14 mm. One of these beads has an ovoid piercing, regular in width, while the second has a conical-shaped perforation, with the starting side displaying deep concentric grooves. The rim of the perforation is irregularly denticulated, suggesting that this bead was not finished and probably never used.

The preservational status of the wooden beads has seriously compromised the possibility of obtaining information on their use or the manufacturing process

Table 8.1. Summary of the botanical bead types.

Material	*Typology*					
	Disc	*Short cylinder*	*Long cylinder*	*Ovoid*	*Automorphic*	*Total*
Wood	2	1	1	1	–	5
Hazelnut	–	–	–	–	1	1
Seeds	–	–	–	–	50	50
Total	2	1	1	1	51	56

Figure 8.1. Wooden beads: a. the ovoid bead and detail of the perforation where deep concentric striations made by the drilling tool are visible; b. the long cylindrical bead.

through microscope observation. The surfaces appear vastly degraded. In a few cases, it is possible to observe the presence of sporadic smooth spots revealing their original aspect. The dimension and shape of these wooden beads allow some consideration about the operational chain followed to produce them.

The manufacturing process started with the selection of thin branches from hardwood species (*Vitis vinifera* and *Fraxinus*). Their bark was removed and they were abraded to obtain sticks with regular thickness. They were later cut into segments of the desired size and perforated. The irregular circumference of some beads suggests that not all the items underwent a finishing process, probably because it was not always deemed essential.

Seed and nut beads

The seeds and nuts have undergone minimal processing to preserve their automorphic shape. Small, shiny and perforated seeds (50) represent the majority of the botanical beads (Fig. 8.2). Fourteen of the 50 collected seeds were found tied together by an organic string (Fig. 8.2: a). During the recovery operations, it was not possible to preserve this string entirely; nevertheless, residues have been left inside the perforation of some seeds (Fig. 8.2: b).

The collected items are brown with an irregular ovoid shape. Their lengths are between 4 mm and 7 mm, with widths of 4–6 mm, and their weight does not exceed 0.03 g. The perforations are on the wide part of the seeds, not always perfectly centred. This area exhibits an abraded surface that accentuates the drop shape of the items and suggests the perforation technique utilised, performed in two steps. First, by abrasion, a flat and thin area was obtained with a tool moved circularly. The pecking technique was then employed to obtain the hole, a choice probably linked to the fragile nature of the material. The holes are large and often have irregular and notched rims, resulting from the force used to hit the seed surface. In some specimens, the holes were enlarged, and their rims appear regularised. A few seed beads show the presence of smoothed and glossy areas on the rim of the holes, probably due to their use (Fig. 8.2: c).

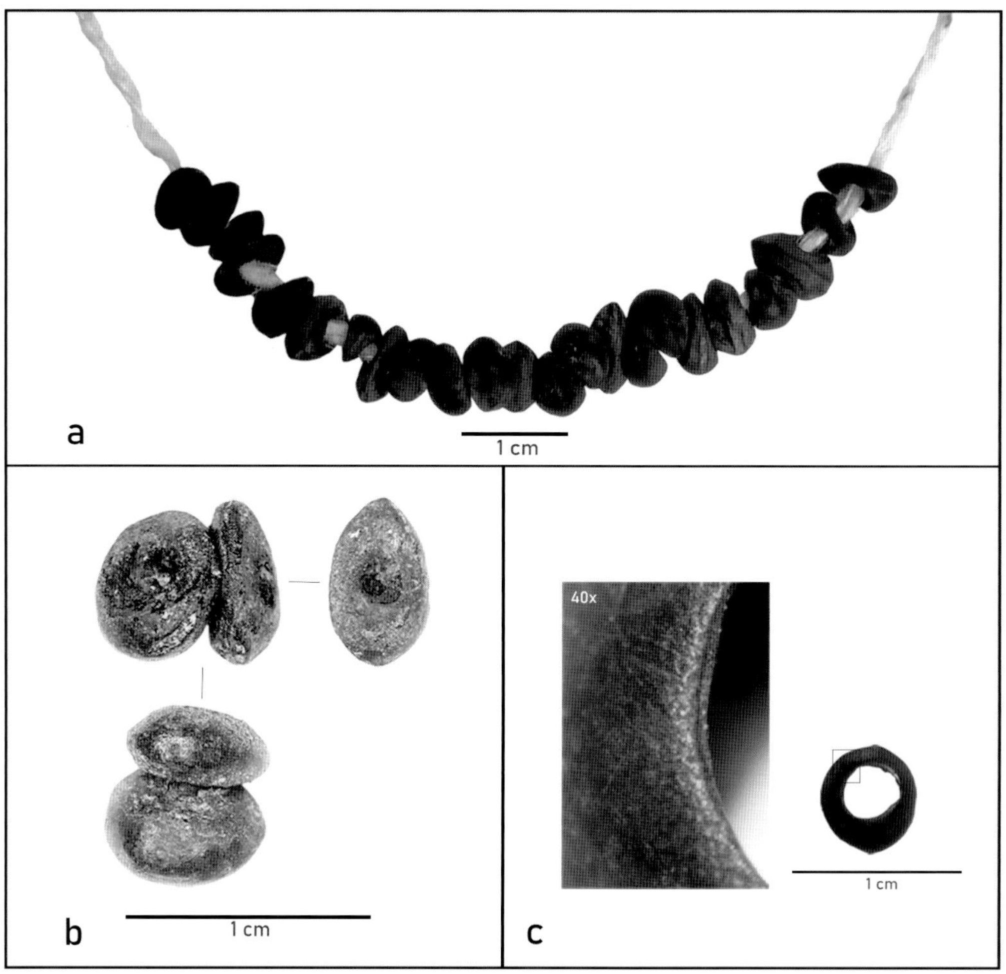

Figure 8.2. Seed beads: a. reconstruction of seed bead necklace; b. different views of two seed beads belonging to the necklace recovered; c. seed bead and detail of the smoothed perforation rim resulting from prolonged use.

A unique example is a perforated hazelnut, presumably used as an ornamental element. It is a perfectly preserved ripe hazelnut shell about 16 mm high, 13 mm in width, and 12 mm thick. The item has two holes: one on the top and the other centred on one of the wide sides. The regular shape of both holes suggests intentional drilling, performed by a lithic drilling tool with alternated rotational movements.

Final considerations and conclusions

Only sporadic evidence of ornaments produced from organic matter has been recovered in the Mediterranean region. As mentioned above, the earliest Neolithic evidence of wooden beads in the Near East comes from Nahal Hemar Cave (Bar-Yosef and Alon 1988), a Pre-Pottery Neolithic site dated in the mid-second half of the 8th millennium cal BC. The beads, at least 11 of them, usually have an ovoid shape, with a length between 20 mm and 50 mm and a width of 10–25 mm. Their surfaces were coloured with one or two pigments: red and green. The difference in type and dimension of these items compared with the La Marmotta ones can be explained by their geographical and chronological distance.

Wooden and nut beads have also been discovered in Africa. A rich assemblage of beads was found in Njoro River Cave in Kenya. Nuts (*c.* 300) were employed to produce principally disc beads and two barrel-shaped beads. In the same cave numerous beads (*c.* 4000) were made from sedge seeds (*Scleria racemosa*). As at La Marmotta, the seeds maintain their automorphic shape although their preparation was different and consisted of merely removing the coat at each end (Wandibba 1988), followed by the perforation. Njoro River Cave is related to the Neolithic-Elmenteitan culture; its chronological attribution, nevertheless, is still under debate (Cole 1954; Ambrose 1984).

At La Marmotta it is possible to observe the same choice of only one species, selected probably on physical criteria such as colour, hardness, and size. However, it is not possible to know if these seeds came from plants that grew in the surrounding area or were collected far from the site, as supposed for the Njoro River Cave.

A wooden bead was also found at the site of GaJj I, located in the east of Lake Turkana. This irregular disc bead has a large triangular-shaped perforation (Wandibba 1988).

The botanical bead production at La Marmotta represents, as highlighted above, the earliest and largest Early Neolithic dataset in the central Mediterranean area. The analysis of this assemblage has offered essential information about the typology and raw materials used for body ornamentation in this period. Data reveal a standardised production consisting of small and regular elements. Although only five wooden beads were found, they show strict affinities in shape and size with steatite and clay products.

Information about how these items were worn, tied, and combined is scarce. At La Marmotta, necklace making with a single type of bead is certainly attested by the discovery of 14 attached seeds. However, the alternate use of different kinds of beads to produce complex creations cannot be excluded. Outside the Mediterranean area, at the site of Harappa (Pakistan) (Meadow *et al.* 1998), three seed beads were recovered in a pot together with some precious stone beads. This discovery suggests the possible use of organic and inorganic beads in the same jewellery item, probably due to the different symbolic values of the raw materials employed (Kenoyer 2005).

The observation of present indigenous communities can provide significant insights into the variety and role of ornamental assemblages used during prehistory. Personal ornaments worn by native groups can be considered expressions of their collective tribal ties to the land where they live and to the surrounding natural resources. In these communities, the frequent use of botanical materials as body ornaments underlines, even more, their connection with nature.

The choice of these communities to select specific categories of botanical raw materials (nuts, beans, seeds, wood, bamboo, etc.) is usually conditioned by their ease of availability. However, the aesthetic aspect and/or symbolic value can influence the preference for certain materials. The colour and shape of the ornaments can express a universal value or be strictly dependent on a distinct cultural or ethnic group. For example, Mary's bean beads, produced by a beach vine (Convolvulaceae) in Central America, are used to ward off evil spirits and as an auspicious sign to assure pregnant women of an easy delivery (Orchard 1975). *Prunus cerasoides* kernels are chosen by some Himalayan tribes to create religious rosaries, while *Prunus mahaleb* kernels are particularly appreciated by Hindu women for their scent (Mehra *et al.* 1975).

Similar considerations are possible for the prehistoric ornaments. Among ancient societies, they may have had multiple meanings that changed over time. The botanical beads from La Marmotta can be considered objects with layered meanings linked to identities, culture, productivity, as well as physical and spiritual well-being. Therefore, botanical ornaments must be interpreted as a reflection of an individual's integration in the environment, and their meaning is closely related to nature and its daily challenges.

Note

1 We are very grateful to Mauro Rottoli for his scientific contribution to the analysis of the botanical remains. We also thank Elisabetta Starnini for her comments and suggestions.

9

Lithic tools analysis

9.1. Flaked stone tools

Denis Guilbeau, Bernard Gassin, Juan F. Gibaja and Niccolò Mazzucco

Raw material

The flaked stone tool industry is abundant (n=12,139 registered so far). No important spatial or chronological differences are perceived in the industry. Many chipped stones are altered by fire-exposure, but at the same time, and thanks to the lacustrine context, there are almost no post-depositional fractures and no patina, except the lacustrine patina.

This industry is made primarily of flint (83.98%) (Table 9.1.1). Twelve different types can be differentiated by macroscopic discrimination with the naked eye (texture, translucency, inclusions, colour). Their provenance still has to be studied in detail but most are probably of local/regional origin. However, a significant amount may come from the Gargano flint outcrops, about 280–300 km to the south-east of the site. Obsidian is quite well represented (11.5%). The first determinations performed on 326 obsidian artefacts have shown that it comes mostly from Palmarola Island (n=268), about 140 km from the site and, in a smaller proportion, from Lipari (n=58), about 475 km from La Marmotta (De Francesco *et al.* 2012). Among the non-silicified or undetermined raw materials (4.52%), the presence of rock crystal is noteworthy (n=13).

Morpho-technological analysis

The different varieties of flint and obsidian were mostly introduced in the form of small blocks or nodules from primary outcrops. Most of the knapping was carried out on-site is quite simple *chaînes opératoires*.

A preliminary technological analysis has been carried out on a sample of 1370 pieces (Tables 9.1.2 and 9.1.3). The aim of *debitage* was first to produce blades: 65.2% of flint and 71.7% of the obsidian artefacts are blades or blade fragments. The detailed analysis of 928 flint and 442 obsidian chipped artefacts has enabled definition of the knapping sequence.

Evidence of knapping activities at the site are abundant for all raw materials but not for all the blanks. The local production of flakes was quite marginal, especially in the case of obsidian. The shaping of the blade cores in flint and obsidian exploited the natural regularity of the blocks (Fig. 9.1.1). The knappers did not seek to optimise production in terms of quantity and quality. Most of the time, blade knapping was performed in a plain or semi-rotational mode, but never a fully rotational mode. The blade cores are quadrangular or cylindrical but never conical or 'bullet-shaped'.

The butt of the blades is always thick, most of the time facetted, always prepared on the flaking surface and the overhang is always preserved. The size of the blades varies: about 10 mm wide on average but larger blades are quite frequent. The largest blades, especially those made on flint from the Gargano, were probably produced elsewhere and introduced as blanks. The morphology of the blades is not very standardised, with a low frequency of blades with a trapezoidal section and, among them, of those following a specific *debitage* pattern. They were knapped using different techniques. Rare blades detached by direct percussion correspond to blanks from the phases of preparation, resharpening

Table 9.1.1. Raw materials of the chipped stone industry.

Material	*No.*	*% of assemblage*
Flint	10,194	83.98
Obsidian	1396	11.50
Not silicified or undetermined	549	4.52
Total	12,139	100

Table 9.1.2. Flint and obsidian industry technological breakdown (preliminary morpho-technological analysis).

Debitage	*Flint*	*Obsidian*
Blocks	2	1
Debris	56	49
Cortical flakes	16	0
Flakes with partial cortical surface	36	10
Shaping flakes	9	9
Flake cores	9	3
Blade cores	17	12
Crested blades	5	0
Undercrested blades	13	0
Technical blades	11	12
Lateral blades	105	62
Central blades	513	243
Rejuvenation flakes	13	16
Flakes from blade cores	9	12
Reshaping flakes	2	5
Undetermined flakes	112	8
Total	928	442

Table 9.1.3. Lithic toolkit.

Object/retouch	*Flint*	*Obsidian*	*Total*	*%*
Lateral retouch	697	35	732	27.79
Geometric	543	3	546	20.73
Truncation	467	10	477	18.11
Notch	192	27	219	8.31
Lateral R+truncation	196	7	203	7.71
Indeterminate retouch	105	5	110	4.18
Borer	100	6	106	4.02
Sidescraper	98	3	101	3.83
Endscraper	70	2	72	2.73
Microburin	27	1	28	1.06
Denticulate	13	–	13	0.49
Backed	13	–	13	0.49
Burin	9	–	9	0.34
Point	3	–	3	0.11
Bifacial	1	–	1	0.04
Scaled pieces	1	–	1	0.04
Total	2,535	99	2634	100

or recycling of the blade cores. Quite regular blades with a regular thickness, but marked ripples detached by indirect percussion. Most of the blades are very regular, with parallel edges and arrises, a straight profile, a thin section, a constant thickness and a high and short bulb. They were detached with by pressure flaking. Their dimensions correspond to different modes of this technique (Pelegrin 1988; 2012), from pressure in the hand (mode 1) to pressure in a standing position with a long crutch (mode 4). Several fragments of very large and regular blades may correspond to blanks detached by the pressure technique with the help of a lever (mode 5). The largest obsidian pressure blades were detached with a short crutch in a standing position (mode 3) or a long crutch in a standing position (mode 4).

There is no strict correlation between the raw materials and the toolkit (Table 9.1.3, for the whole assemblage), except for obsidian, which was never used for the manufacture of sickle inserts. In the obsidian toolkit, some blades display direct retouch or abrasion on one edge and an inverse retouch or abrasion on the other edge of the proximal part (n=56 of the 243 blades studied).

The flint toolkit is characterised first by blanks used after a lateral retouch (n=2535) (Fig. 9.1.2 and 9.1.3). Many flint blades were worked into small segments by one or two truncations (n=477). The use of the microburin technique to break the blades is very rarely attested. The blanks used as tools are not very standardised, even if those segmented with truncations are considered. There are 546 geometrics, if we exclude those used as sickle inserts and the very long bitruncations. There are two different types: isosceles trapezium and scalene trapezium with a concave base. Other types, like triangles, are very rare. The sickle inserts, also very frequent (n=502), are fragments of blades which may or may not be modified by retouch (truncations, lateral retouch). They are about 20–30 mm long, and 10–12 mm wide on average. They were hafted obliquely. Only a handful was used several times after being unhafted and rehafted. Among the other tools, borers are numerous (n=106). Most are made on blades. There are 72 endscrapers, 42 made on blades and 30 on flakes. All but one of the 13 backed pieces are made on blades. Burins are especially rare (n=9). The flakes, which are scarce in the assemblage, are better represented in such category as scrapers or denticulates. The flint and obsidian tools were not intensively used. Most were rejected well before their edges were worn and resharpening is attested on only a handful.

The general technological and typological characteristics of the assemblage find close parallels in the central part of the Italian Peninsula. Raw material procurement is comparable, with the use of local or regional flint types, the presence of exogenous flint from the Gargano (Tarantini and Galiberti 2011), and the presence of obsidian from Palmarola and Lipari (Radi and Petrinelli 2018). The predominance of blades made by pressure flaking and indirect

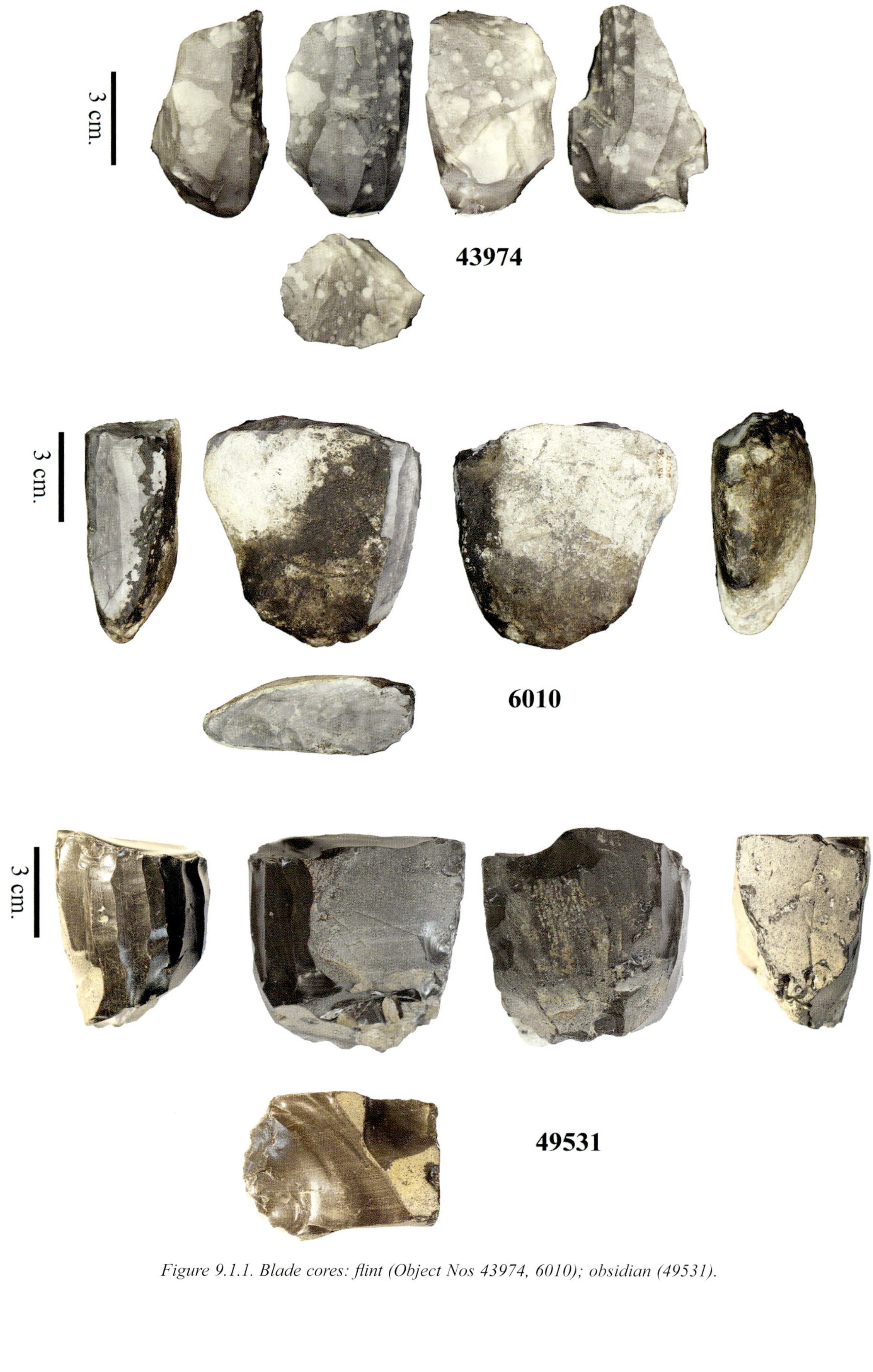

Figure 9.1.1. Blade cores: flint (Object Nos 43974, 6010); obsidian (49531).

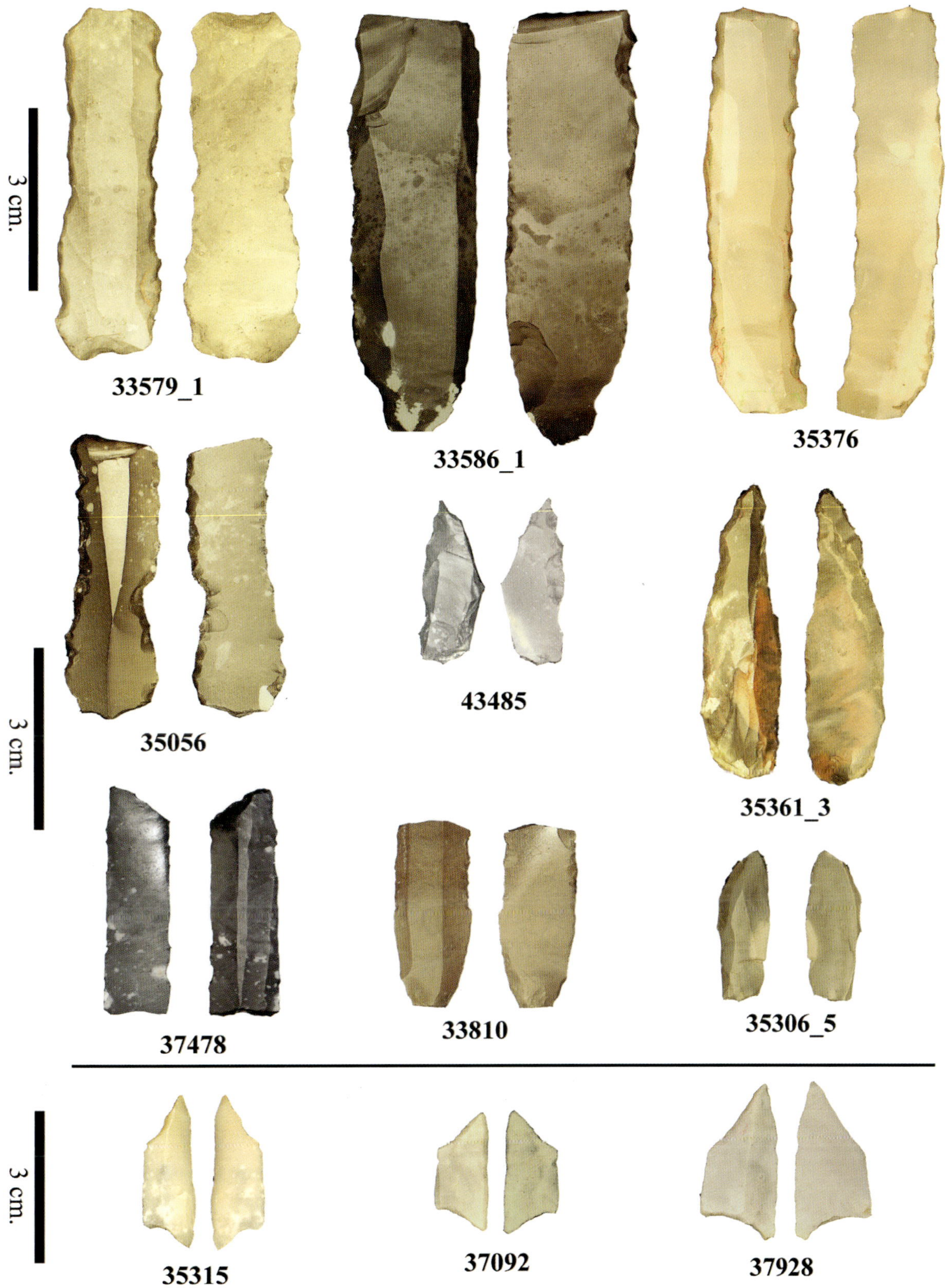

Figure 9.1.2. Toolkit on flint: blades with lateral retouch (Object Nos 33579_1; 33586_1, 35376, 35056); borers (Object Nos 43485, 35361_3); sickle inserts (Object Nos 37478, 33810, 35306_5); geometric trapezes: Object Nos 35315, 37092, 37928).

Figure 9.1.3. Toolkit on obsidian: 1–2: blades with lateral retouch (Object Nos 23645, 49699); 3: blade with truncation (Object No. 28471); 4: blade with lateral notches (Object No. 20873); 5: borer (Object No. 41348).

percussion and with a thick butt, among other features, is observed elsewhere, for instance at Catignano (Tozzi and Zamagni 2003; Guilbeau 2010). Such characteristics are also typical of blade knapping in Castelnovian sites. The probable presence of pressure-flaked blades in Gargano flint is typical of industries in the southern part of the peninsula. The only difference observed at La Marmotta is that the Gargano flint blades found are quite often made by indirect percussion and their butt is thick, with the overhang preserved, while in the southern part of the peninsula these blades are usually detached by the pressure technique and their butt is plain, very small and accurately prepared with the removal of the overhang.

The toolkit can also be compared with contemporary sites in the frequency of geometrics and sickle inserts hafted obliquely, for instance as at Catignano and Colle Santo Stefano in Abruzzo (Ciccone 2003). However, at the same time it shows specific features, like the scarcity of triangles attested for instance at Colle Santo Stefano (see Radi and Ronchitelli 2002) and the low number of burins, unlike sites in the eastern part of the peninsula, such as Passo di Corvo or Villa Comunale in Puglia (Ronchitelli 1983; Simone 1977–1982 respectively) and Maddalena di Muccia in the Marche (Silvestrini and Pignocchi 1998). The use of the microburin technique, very rarely attested at La Marmotta, is very frequent elsewhere, especially in the north of Italy, at Fagnigola for instance (Biagi 1975; Bagolini *et al.* 1994; Guilbeau obs. pers.).

Use-wear analysis

A pilot use-wear analysis conducted on a small sample of tools from the 2003 excavation season has obtained the first insights into the function of the stone tools at La Marmotta and into the economic and craft activities carried out in the area of the site excavated in that year. A total of 821 items were recorded during the 2003 excavation; of these, 233 items (28.38%) have been studied as part of this pilot study. The 2003 campaign is particularly interesting because it is associated with the excavation of House 7. Although the dendrochronological analyses are relatively old and should be revised in the light of new analytical techniques, based on the available data this house is probably one of the earliest structures at the site.

Our methodology has been based on both a macro- and microscopic approach, by integrating a BMS stereoscopic microscope, up to 60× magnification, and an Olympus BH2 reflected-light microscope equipped with 50×, 100× and 200× lenses (Vaughan 1985; Van Gijn 1989; González and Ibáñez 1994; Gassin 1996; Gibaja 2003). The state of preservation of the tools is variable. Some of the observed artefacts are in good condition, but others possess altered surfaces that impeded a corrected diagnostic of their use. Among the most common alterations we can cite the presence of soil lustres and areas with 'G' polish (or bright spots) produced by the friction between lithics. Thermal alterations are also very common (thermal lustres and fractures, and fire-cracked pieces), while some other artefacts are affected by the presence of metal-like striations caused when being drawn. Finally, some items bear a black patination of possible organic origin caused by deposition in the organic-rich layers that characterise the La Marmotta deposit. In conclusion, a series of post-depositional and post-excavation agents have caused mechanical and/or chemical alterations to the archaeological items. Nonetheless, whenever use traces are well developed, they are still easily recognisable and interpretable.

Table 9.1.4. Number of analysed tools. Total numbers of tools and of active zones (AZ).

No. Active Zones	*No. artefacts*	
1 AZ	82	
2 AZ	34	
3 AZ	5	133
4 AZ	10	
5 AZ	1	
7 AZ	1	
No traces	69	69
Not analysable	31	31
Total	233	233

Of the 233 analysed items, 133 present use related modifications, while the remaining 100 were not used or are too altered to be correctly interpreted. In total, 217 active zones (AZ) have been identified on the 133 tools. This means that a significant percentage of tools were used with different edges (Table 9.1.4).

Most of the utilised artefacts were employed to work with vegetal materials. As can be seen in Table 9.1.5 and Figure 9.1.4 the largest number of tools were used for cereal harvesting, for cutting/scraping vegetal fibres and for scraping wood. Other activities are represented by projectile points for hunting and tools used to work with animal and

Table 9.1.5. Working activities and number of Active Zones recorded for each.

Activity/material	*Longitudinal*	*Transversal*	*Long+trans*	*Rotatory*	*Impact*	*Indet.*
Butchering	10	–	–	–	–	–
Bone	–	2	–	–	–	–
Hide (indet)	–	1	1	–	–	–
Hide (dry)	–	4	–	1	–	–
Cereals	41	–	–	–	–	–
Plants indet.	11	21	–	–	–	1
Wood	1	45	–	–	–	–
Plants or wood	–	9	–	–	–	–
Hide or mineral	–	4	–	–	–	–
Hide or plants	–	5	–	–	–	–
Plants or mineral	–	1	–		–	–
Mineral	3	4	–	2		–
Projectile	–	–	–	–	15	–
Indet. Hard	–	11	–	–	–	–
Indet. Semi-hard	4	10	–	1	–	–
Indet. Soft	3	2	–	1	–	–
Indet.	–	2	–	–	–	1

mineral substances: soft animal materials, hide, bone/antler, stone and pottery.

Most of these tools (n=125; 93.98%) are blades. Only eight (6.02%) are flakes. Although our sample is too small to draw any conclusion about form/functional issues, we can point out a few tendencies. Tools used for cereal harvesting normally exploit only one edge (one AZ). Only three sickle blades show double utilisation, on both sides. Sickle inserts are mostly blades, often shaped by distal or proximal truncations (Fig. 9.1.5: 3–4). Inserts often show marginal edge scarring caused by wear on the edge during the use of the tool. However, in some cases, deliberate edge resharpening must have been carried out to prolong the use-life of the tool. Looking at the distribution of the gloss and taking into account data in the study of the complete wooden sickles (Mazzucco *et al.* 2022a; Chapter 5.3), we know that sickle inserts were hafted diagonally inside the haft to form a coarsely serrated edge. This kind of sickle is typical of the Mediterranean Early Neolithic, from Greece to Portugal (Ibáñez *et al.* 2008; Gibaja *et al.* 2017; Mazzucco *et al.* 2020; 2022a; Caruso-Fermé *et al.* 2021). Tools used for working wood are often characterised by several active zones. Most of the used tools are blades (n=14), retouched on both lateral edges. The others are four unretouched blades and six flakes, two of them retouched. It is sometimes difficult to distinguish between retouching and use removals; some of these edges probably show a combination of both types of removals.

Finally, it is not always easy to distinguish between wood and non-woody plants. Factors such as the development of the use-wear and the state of preservation of the surfaces influence our interpretation capability. In any case, those tools were used to craft wooden artefacts or to work vegetal fibres to make baskets/ropes/textiles, confirming that most of the craft processes associated with the spectacular artefacts found at La Marmotta were carried out locally and that stone tools participated in some phases of the production process.

Tools used to work non-ligneous plants are also mainly represented by retouched blades (n=14). Unretouched blanks are used only occasionally, (blades n=5; flakes n=1) (Fig. 9.1.5: 1). Most of the active edges for working wood and plants were used in negative-rake cutting, that is to say with a rake angle close to 90°. This scraping method does not allow deep penetration into the wood and raises fine and regular shavings (Fig. 9.1.5: 2). It is particularly suitable for finishing work, to obtain smooth surfaces. A smaller number were used in positive-rake cutting, with a rake angle greater than 90°: these tools can remove thicker chips, penetrate further into the wood, and can participate more in the shaping of objects. The traces are more ambiguous for some of the active zones, for which the rake angle cannot be precisely determined. The rake face (the one that lifts the chip) is a little more frequently the upper face than the lower face, but this is not systematic, which indicates certain flexibility in the use of the tools.

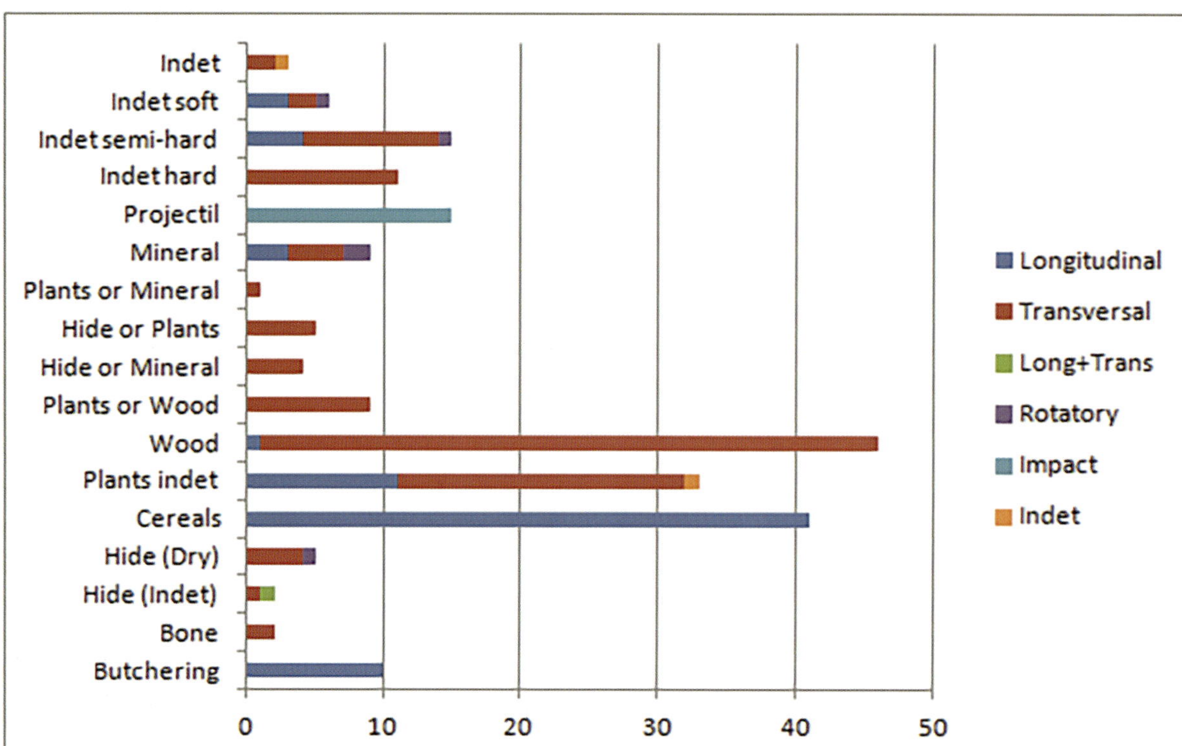

Figure 9.1.4. Use-wear analysis: examples of use-wear traces from working different materials.

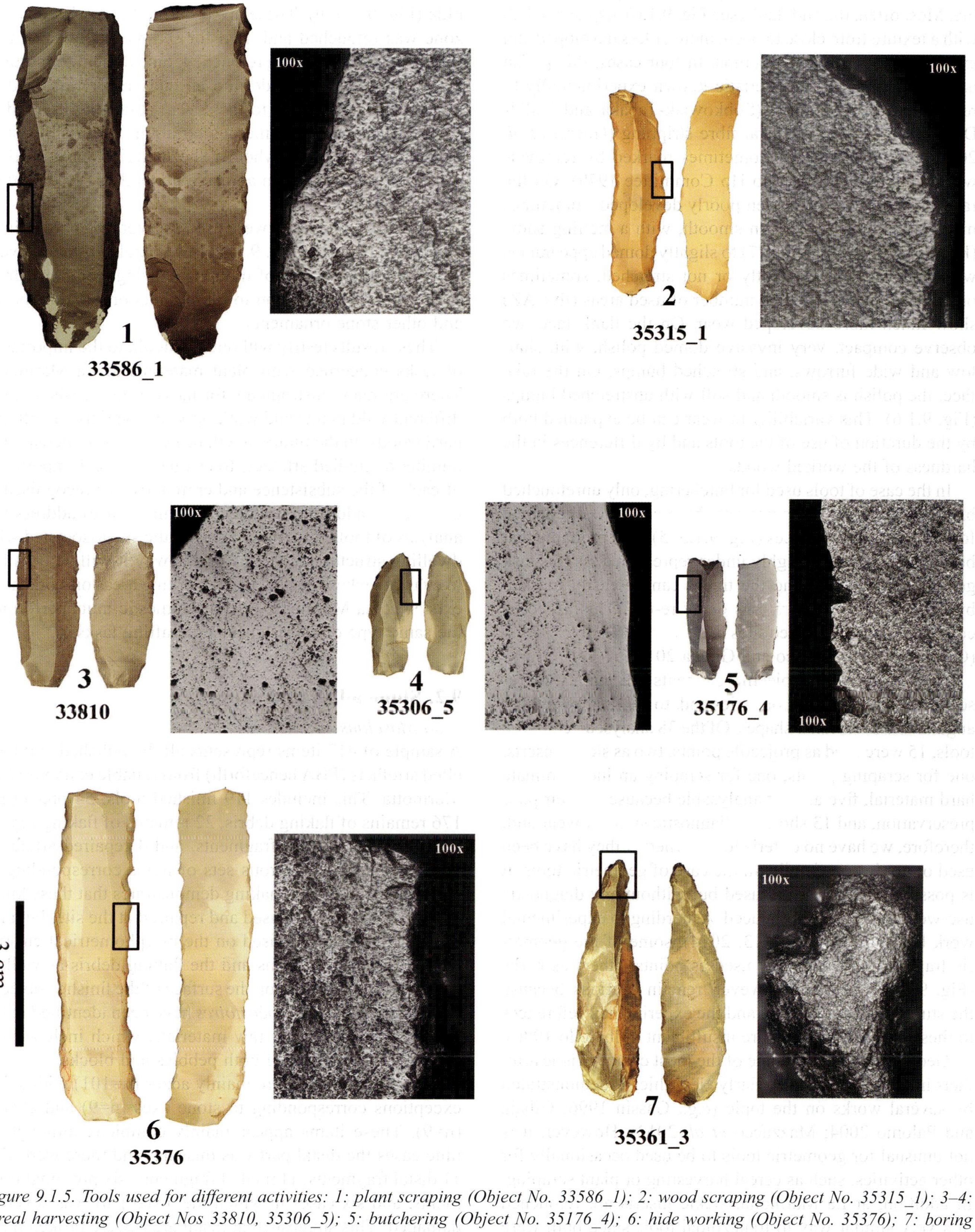

Figure 9.1.5. Tools used for different activities: 1: plant scraping (Object No. 33586_1); 2: wood scraping (Object No. 35315_1); 3–4: cereal harvesting (Object Nos 33810, 35306_5); 5: butchering (Object No. 35176_4); 6: hide working (Object No. 35376); 7: boring abrasive material (dry hide or mineral) (Object No. 35361_3).

The observed wear for wood/plant working is quite variable. Most often, the end flank (see Fig. 9.1.6) displays polish with a texture from close to open, more or less developed and extensive, with stretched bumps. In four cases, this polish is quite striated, a characteristic known experimentally to result from root scraping (Sobkowiak-Tabaka and Kufel-Diakowska 2019) or vegetal fibre stripping (Guéret *et al.* 2014). The flank face is sometimes marked by removals with bending initiation (Ho Ho Committee 1979). On the rake face, the polish is often poorly developed, sometimes more pronounced: it is then smooth, with a melting-snow (Keeley and Newcomer 1977) to slightly domed appearance, with bumps that are slightly or not stretched, sometimes oriented obliquely. A small number of used areas (five AZ) show much more developed wear. On the flank face, we observe compact, very invasive domed polish, with shallow and wide furrows, and stretched bumps. On the rake face, the polish is smooth and soft with unstretched bumps (Fig. 9.1.6). This variability in wear can be explained both by the duration of use of the tools and by differences in the hardness of the worked woods.

In the case of tools used for butchering, only unretouched blades were used. Tools possess sharp edges, well-adapted for cutting soft substances (Fig. 9.1.5: 5). It is probable that butchering traces are highly under-represented, as this task generates little wear and the traces can be easily masked by post-deposition alterations or by re-use. This aspect is common to other analysed sites in the Central Mediterranean (Gibaja 2003; Mazzucco and Gibaja 2018).

At La Marmotta projectile elements are mainly represented by trapezoidal geometrics and, to a lesser extent, triangular and semi-lunar shapes. Of the 38 analysed geometric tools, 15 were used as projectile points, two as sickle inserts, one for scraping plants, one for scraping an indeterminate hard material, five are not analysable because of their poor preservation, and 13 show no diagnostic signs of wear and, therefore, we have no criteria to say whether they have been used or not in a projectile. In the case of geometric tools, it is possible that they were used but without any diagnostic use-wear traces being produced. According to experimental work by L. Chesnaux (2013; 2014), some of the geometric trapezes were probably used as points, others as barbs (Fig. 9.1.7). We must, however, remain cautious because the studied sample is small and the experimental references to these types of trapezes are insufficient (Albarello 1986).

Geometric tools are some of the most characteristic artefacts in the Mediterranean Early Neolithic, as demonstrated by several works on the topic (*e.g.*, Gassin 1996; Gibaja and Palomo 2004; Mazzucco *et al.* 2012). However, it is not unusual for geometric tools to be used occasionally for other activities, such as cereal harvesting or plant scraping. In addition, at La Marmotta, sickle inserts are retouched in a very similar way to trapezoidal tools since both were shaped with two opposed truncations.

A small number of the artefacts were used to work with hide (Fig. 9.1.5: 6). These are usually blades whose active zone was retouched and used for scraping. However, two were used without being retouched; one of them for cutting. Only a single flake made into an endscraper was used in a scraping task. Owing to the severe abrasion observed in some polish, where numerous striations are visible, it is difficult to determine whether the material being worked was hide treated with an abrasive mineral or some kind of mineral itself.

Finally, some blades were used for working hard animal or mineral material (Fig. 9.1.5: 7). Mineral substances were worked with a variety of motions (sawing, scraping, drilling), probably in relation to the production of stone beads and other stone ornaments.

These results testify without any doubt to the importance of tasks concerned with plant materials at La Marmotta. There are many instruments for harvesting cereals, cutting different wild plants and working with a variety of soft and hard woods. In the future, it will be necessary to increase the number of studied artefacts to evaluate the real importance of each of the subsistence and craft activities recognised at the site. In addition, it would be important to address the analysis of tools from other areas of the site associated with dwelling structures. Perhaps in this way it will be possible to evaluate whether specialised working areas or workshops existed at La Marmotta, or if all domestic units performed the same type of subsistence and crafting tasks.

9.2. Stone adzes and axes

Alba Masclans

A sample of 417 items represents all the polished and bevelled artefacts (PBA henceforth) from reliable contexts at La Marmotta. This includes 119 finished tools, 54 pre-forms, 176 remains of flaking debris, 22 remains of flaking/repairing debris, 42 broken fragments, and 4 repaired artefacts. The presence of numerous sets of items corresponding to all the stages of PBA-making demonstrates that these kinds of tools were not only used and repaired at the site, but also manufactured there. Based on the morphometrical characteristics of the pre-forms and the flaking debris as well as technological evidence on the surface of the finished objects, two different *chaînes opératoires* have been identified in the artefacts made of local raw materials, which included the flaking and polishing of both pebbles and blocks.

The finished items are mainly adzes (n=101) with a few exceptions corresponding to stone axes (n=9) and chisels (n=9). These items appear mainly complete, although in nine cases the distal part was missing, and there were also 11 distal fragments, 11 medial fragments, six proximal fragments, and six cases in which the distal part was severely damaged. This suggests that distal areas were broken more often than any other part of the tools and they only rarely

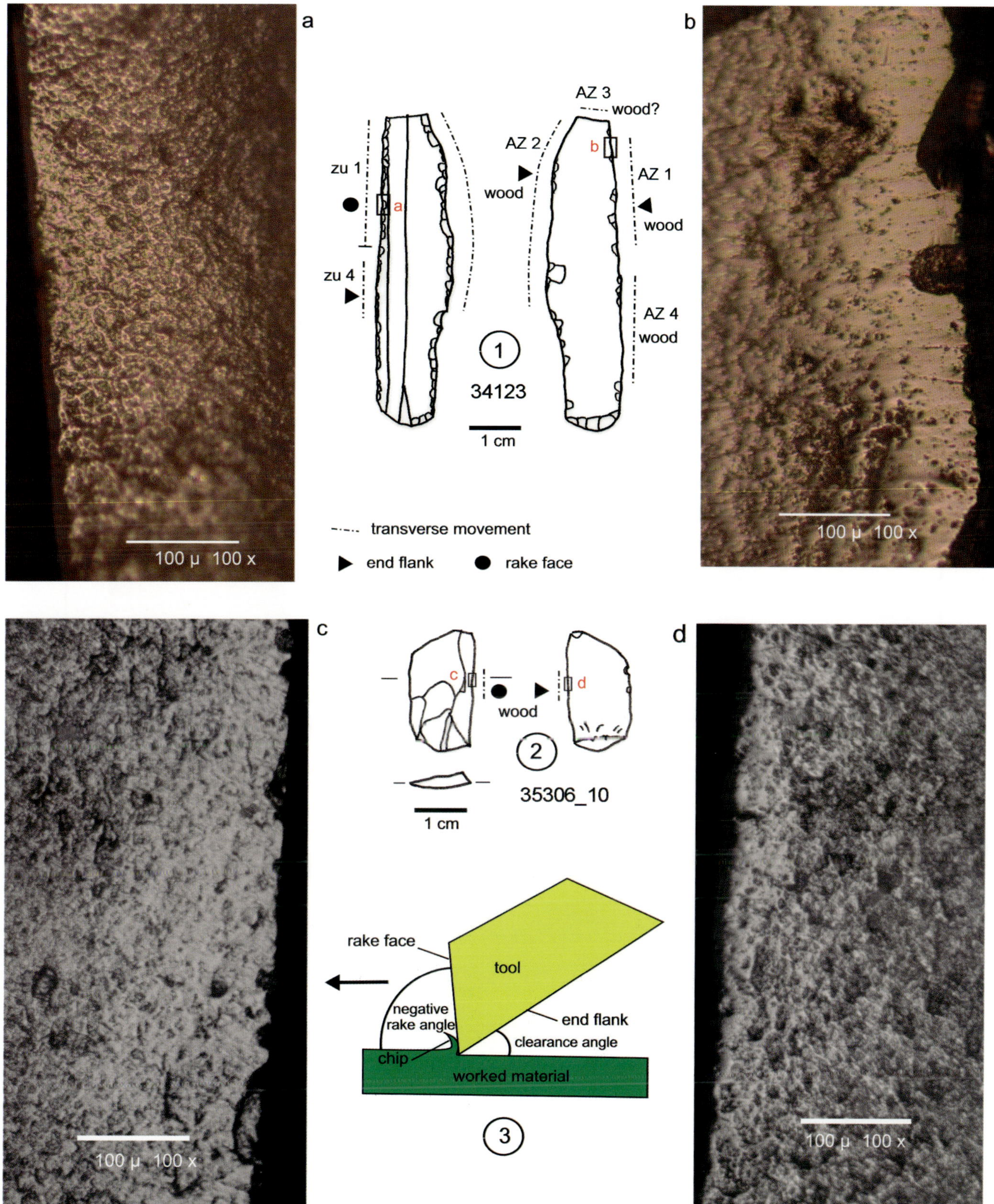

Figure 9.1.6. Active Zones identified on stone tools. 1: Blade: AZ 1, 2, 3, 4: scraping wood; 3, 4: negative rake cutting. 1, 2: positive or negative rake cutting. a: AZ 1, rake face. b: AZ 1, end flank. 2: Flake. right edge: scraping wood with a negative rake cutting angle. c: rake face. d: end flank. 3: vocabulary used to describe the mode of operation for the transverse motions.

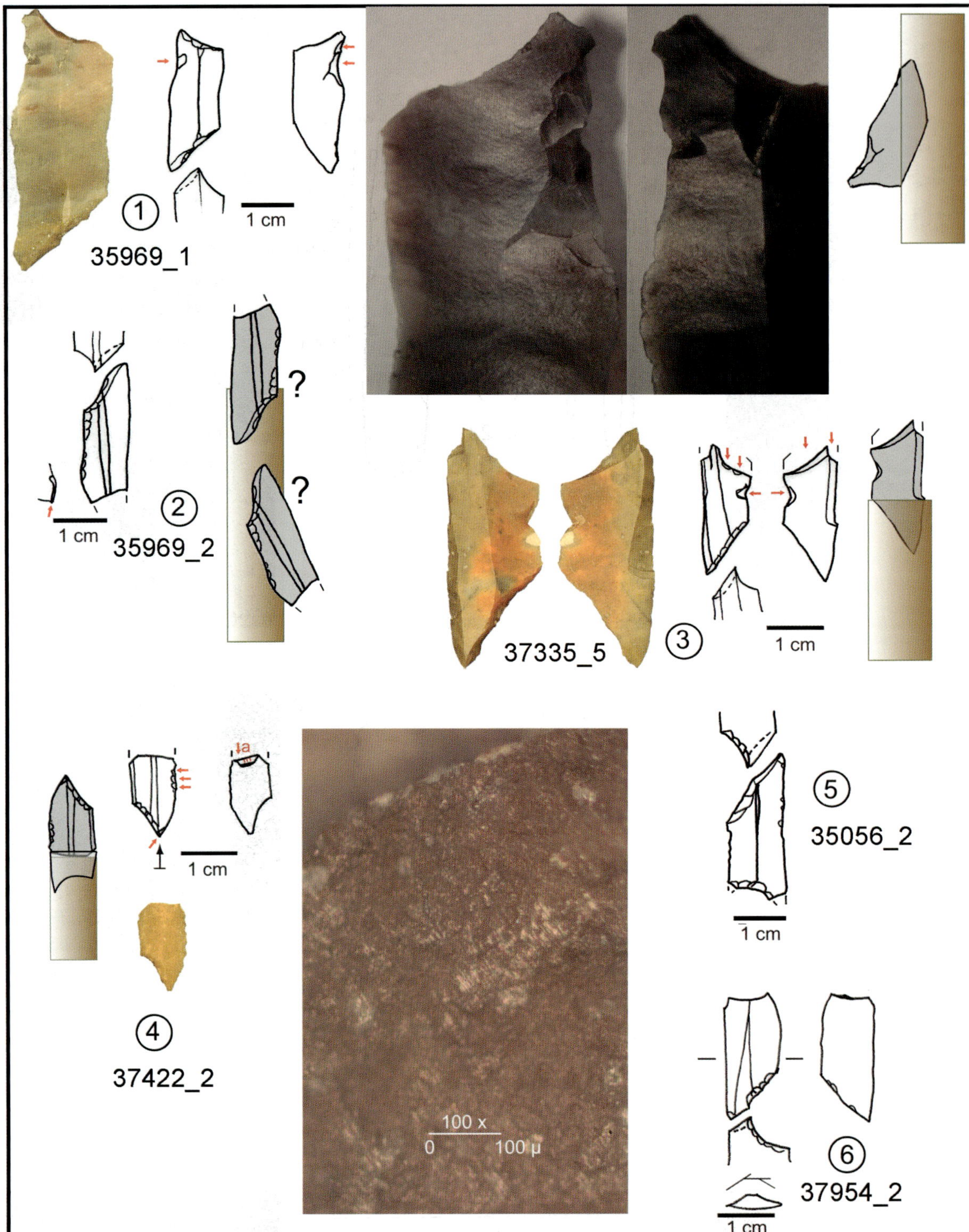

Figure 9.1.7. All geometric trapezes, except No. 4, with remains of the piquant-trièdre. A piquant-trièdre is "the trace visible on the extremity of a blade or bladelet when part of it has been removed by the microburin blow technique"(Inizan et al. 1999, p. 83, 149). 1. Lateral inverse bending scars, with a direct spin-off. Spin-off are secondary scars with cone initiation which initiate from a previous bending fracture (Fischer et al. 1984). Possible use as barb; 2. proximal transverse bending fracture and lateral spin-off (burin-like, length 4.5 mm). Possible use as a point or barb; 3. Bending transverse fracture with short spin-off scars on upper face and long spin-off on left side; scars on right side. Probable use as a point; 4. Bending fracture with a step terminating tongue (length 2.2 mm) and impact striae, bending scars on large base, short (length 1.5 mm) hinge terminating proximal fracture. Probable use as a point; 5. No diagnostic fractures; 6. No fracture.

display any trace of repair arrangements. However, the presence of three adzes whose distal area displayed evidence of flaking indicates that, when possible, PBA were subjected to repair by means of reshaping the active bevel.

The main hafting system seen in the sample is one in which the stone blade (in this case an adze displaying an asymmetric active bevel) is fixed perpendicularly to the haft. This evidence matches the data from the wooden handles (see Chapter 5.3); elbow-shapes, consisting of a platform where the adze was attached forming an angle with the haft, are predominant over ones where the blade (in this case an axe displaying a symmetric active bevel) was attached parallel to the handle.

Raw material

Most of the PBA were shaped from fine-grained, isotropic local raw materials of a volcanic and metamorphic origin (formed from sedimentary rocks). In this assemblage, however, ten finished artefacts corresponding to three adzes, four axes, a chisel and a broken fragment were made from different kinds of jadeite and eclogite from the Alps, suggesting the existence of long-distance exchanges with other Neolithic communities. Significantly, four of the nine axes at La Marmotta were not produced at the site, which re-inforces the idea of a very standardised hafting technology.

Morpho-technological analysis

Even though the PBA assemblage at La Marmotta depicts a quite uniform hafting tradition, the stone blades were morphologically heterogeneous. In order to perform a preliminarily exploration of the morphometric variability at the site, the maximum length, thickness and width of complete finished artefacts were used to achieve a general description of their shape. Two different approaches were then applied: the 'height-breadth-index' (HBI) to distinguish slim high adzes from broad flat ones, and a K-means Cluster analysis to evaluate the length/width ratio variability.

The XY graph displaying the PBA's length and width values indicates a varied set formed by tools with minimum/maximum lengths and widths of 28.5/196 mm and 6.5/83 mm respectively (Fig. 9.2.1: A). The K-means Cluster analysis reveals the presence of three main morphometric groups (Fig. 9.2.1: B): Group 1, formed by the smallest items (6.5/34 × 28.5/70 mm) including the chisels; Group 2, integrated exclusively by medium-sized adzes (35/65 × 40/80 mm); and Group 3, which aggregates the biggest tools (30/65 × 90/196 mm) including most of the axes.

According to Ramminger's (2007) typological classification based on the 'height-breadth-index' calculated as (thickness/width)*100, there are three types of tools at the site: Type 1, which includes all the chisels and the smaller and narrower (<20 mm width) adzes; Type 2, the flat adzes with a HBI of between 19 and 49 and absolute widths between 22 mm and 62 mm; and Type 3, the medium-high blades with a HBI of between 50 and 85 and absolute widths between 22 mm and 83 mm (Fig. 9.2.2). The presence of stone axes with distinct metric values stands out among Types 2 and 3 since they display larger widths and higher HBI indexes in both cases (Figs 9.2.3 and 9.2.4). The absence of high adzes (type 4) is noteworthy because they are emblematic tools in central European Early Neolithic contexts.

Given this significant morphometric variability, it is to be expected that specialised tools related to different kinds of activities are present in the assemblage. Polished and bevelled tools such as axes and adzes have been inventoried and repeatedly referred to as a technological innovation linked to the development of agrarian societies and as a votive object in the funerary record during the Neolithic. These kinds of tools have traditionally been associated with wood procurement and processing, but new studies based on use-wear analysis have broadened this perspective to include a wider range of activities, such as hide-processing, mining, land clearing, butchering and the infliction of violence (Wentink *et al.* 2011; Yerkes and Barkai 2013; Masclans 2020; Roy 2020).

Use-wear analysis

A preliminary use-wear study of 20 artefacts (23% of the total) was conducted according to the methodological criteria established by Masclans (2020). The results of the analysis indicate a broad spectrum of PBA uses including woodwork (three tools), contact with hide/leather (one tool), and meat (one tool). Additionally, two PBAs were employed with soft substances, one with an abrasive matter and one was used in direct percussion against a hard material but did not display enough evidence to determine the specific contact matter. The remaining eight items were not analysable due to the poor preservation of their active surfaces, which is common among the La Marmotta PBAs made of the less metamorphosed raw materials such as schist or calcareous rocks, which often exhibit evidence of surface alteration.

Attending to this preliminary data the predominant contact matter is wood, which is represented by object nos 40781, 32454 and 28881, where a shiny and undulating micro-polish typical of wood wear is well-developed on the active area matrix, combined with fresh factures that indicate continual exposure to a percussive activity against a hard material (Fig. 9.2.4). More data are still required to explore the different woodworking practices and to be able to discriminate between artefacts used for specific functions, such as chopping trees, cutting firewood, or various types of carpentry from building houses to small object carving.

9.3. Grinding tools for plant processing and food production in La Marmotta

Caroline Hamon and Marta Portillo

Literature on grinding technologies highlights their importance in food practices and social organisation worldwide (*e.g.* Searcy 2011; Hamon and Le Gall 2013; Alonso 2014).

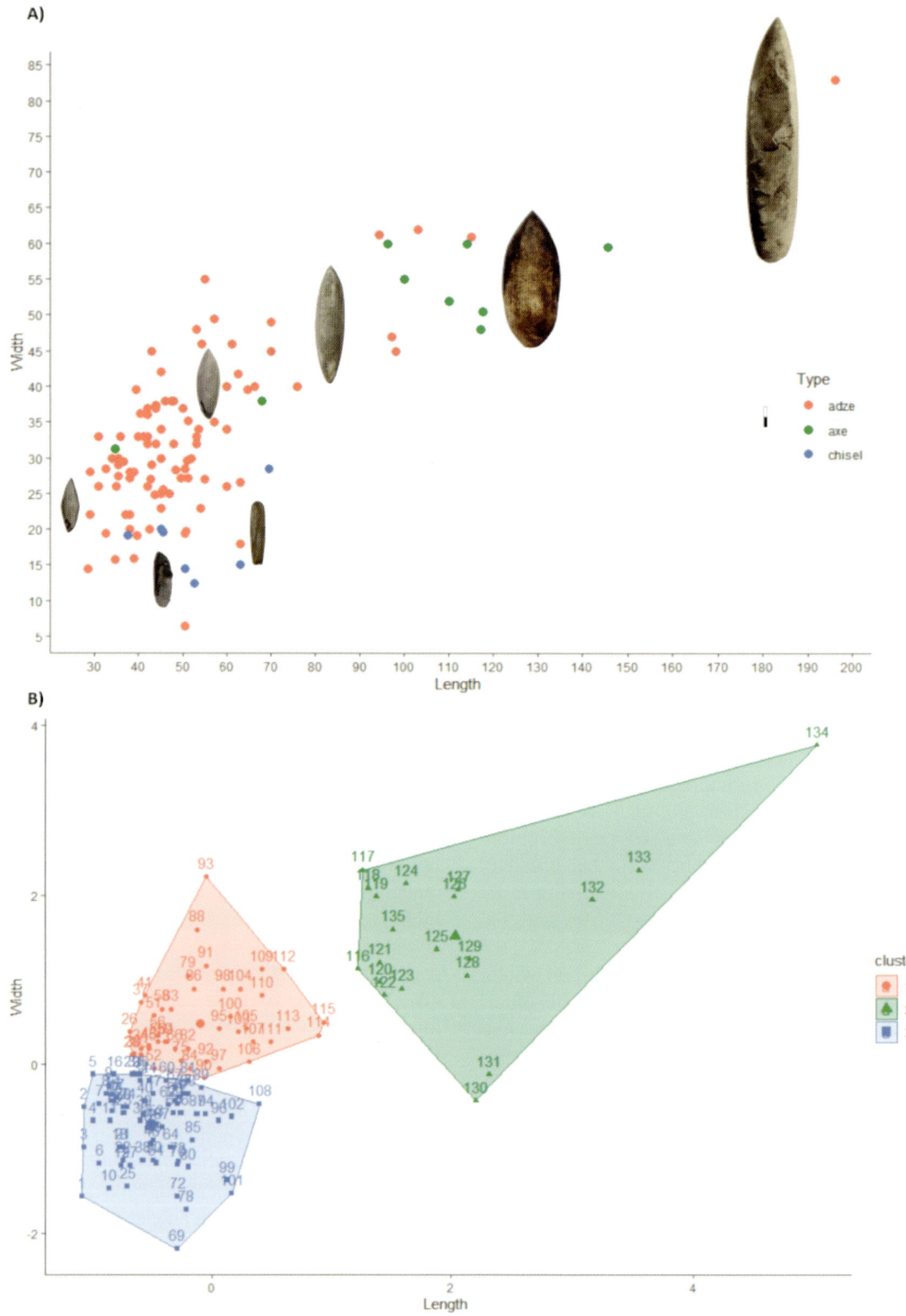

Figure 9.2.1. A) XY graph displaying the PBA length and width values according to the type of tool (adze, axe and chisel); B) K-means Cluster analysis.

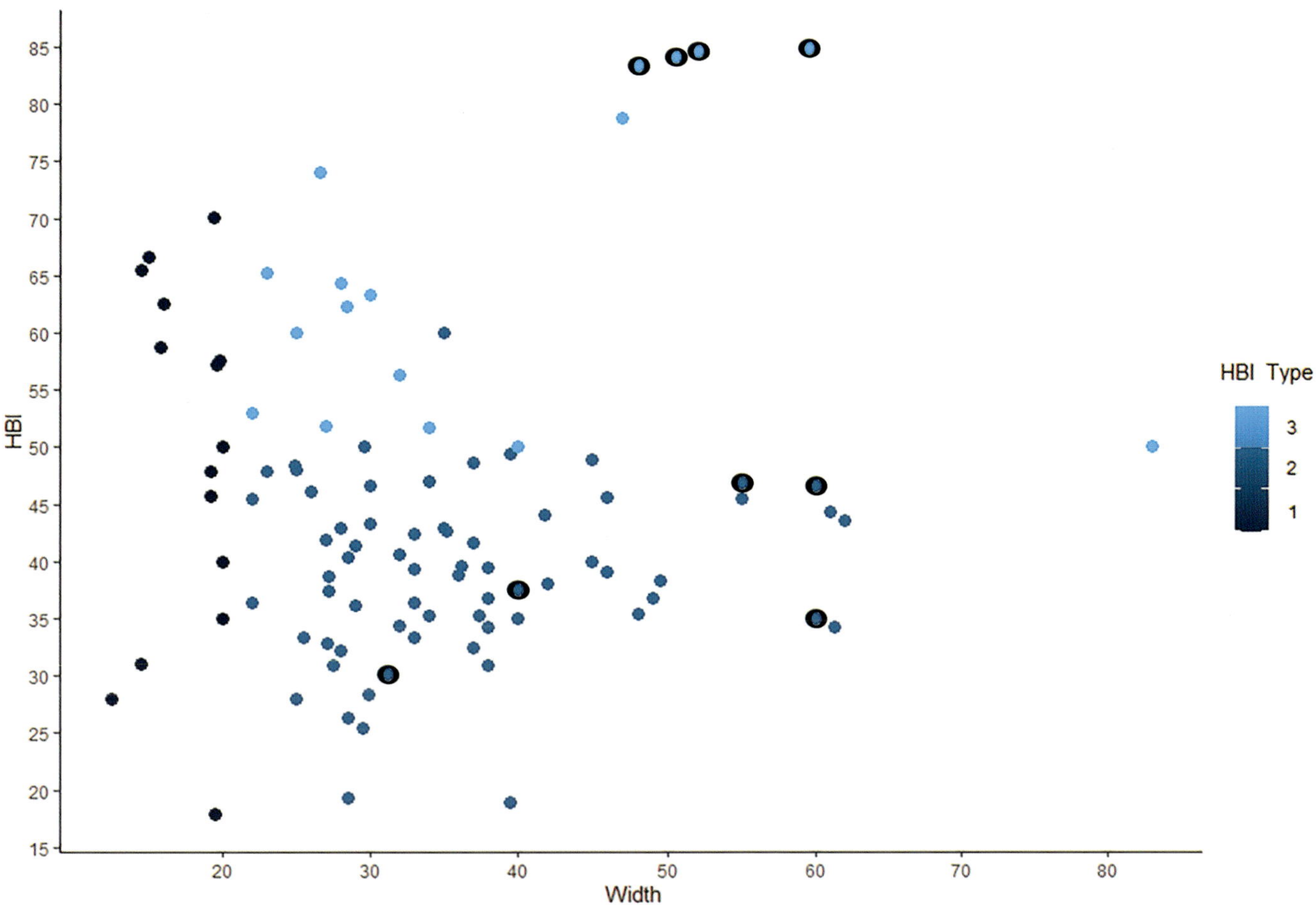

Figure 9.2.2. PBA metrical classification according to Ramminger's (2007) 'height-breadth-index'. Stone axes appear encircled.

Intensification in their daily use went hand-in-hand with the introduction of agriculture and a sedentary lifestyle, in a broader context of important changes in dietary habits and the massive introduction of cereals (*e.g.*, wheat, barley, millet, rice, sorghum, maize) and pulses (*e.g.*, peas, lentils) depending on the region of the world. In agricultural populations, grinding is known to be strongly gendered and is mostly performed by women, who are responsible for the food supply in general. Grinding tools are passed down from generation to generation among women and are part of inheritance rules and dowries in many ways. They generally occupy a central place in domestic activities. The organisation of grinding activities in some cases reflects the structure of the family unit and the social groups that make up the villages.

Archaeological research has demonstrated the widespread distribution and cultural value of grinding tools in Neolithic settlements across Europe from the 7th and 6th millennia onwards (Hamon 2021 and references therein). It is now well established that their technological properties, together with the production of pottery, flint and bone, contribute to the definition of cultural groups, cultural transmission and exchange. Current methodological issues focus on different aspects of the study of grinding tools. Raw material studies aim to define sourcing strategies over short and long distances, focusing on the mechanical properties of granite, basalt or sandstone blanks. Typological analyses based on morphological and dimensional criteria lead to the definition of different grinding systems that co-exist or compete with each other. The analysis of use-wear and residues allows us to determine the way in which cereals and plants were prepared and treated before consumption and to establish what exactly was ground and how. It seems particularly important to determine the family of plants that were ground, as well as the treatments (dehusking, soaking, roasting) prior grinding into flour and the importance of cereals in the diet.

Early Neolithic grinding tools in the Western Mediterranean

In the Western Mediterranean, few studies are available to allow us to define the grinding systems used by the Impressed and Cardial Ware peoples. For the Impressa complex, the use

Figure 9.2.3. PBA 'height-breadth-index' types.

of small, circular grinding systems made of cobblestones has been demonstrated in Pendimoun (France), which could be associated with the processing of hulled cereals (Binder *et al.* 2020). In Cardial culture, the co-existence of small circular tools and massive square grinding tools used with a reciprocal (back-and-forth) motion has been emphasised (Hamon 2021). The Early Neolithic in the Western Mediterranean is characterised by the association of small portable grinding tools with massive querns and grinders, and by the co-existence of two different motions: reciprocal and circular. Several hypotheses can explain this co-existence, such as the wish to preserve certain things or the quality of the final products. The nature, duration, seasonality and function of the sites themselves could also explain the differences. In the case of the Impressa complex, the small grinding tools suggest greater mobility and a less important role of grinding tools

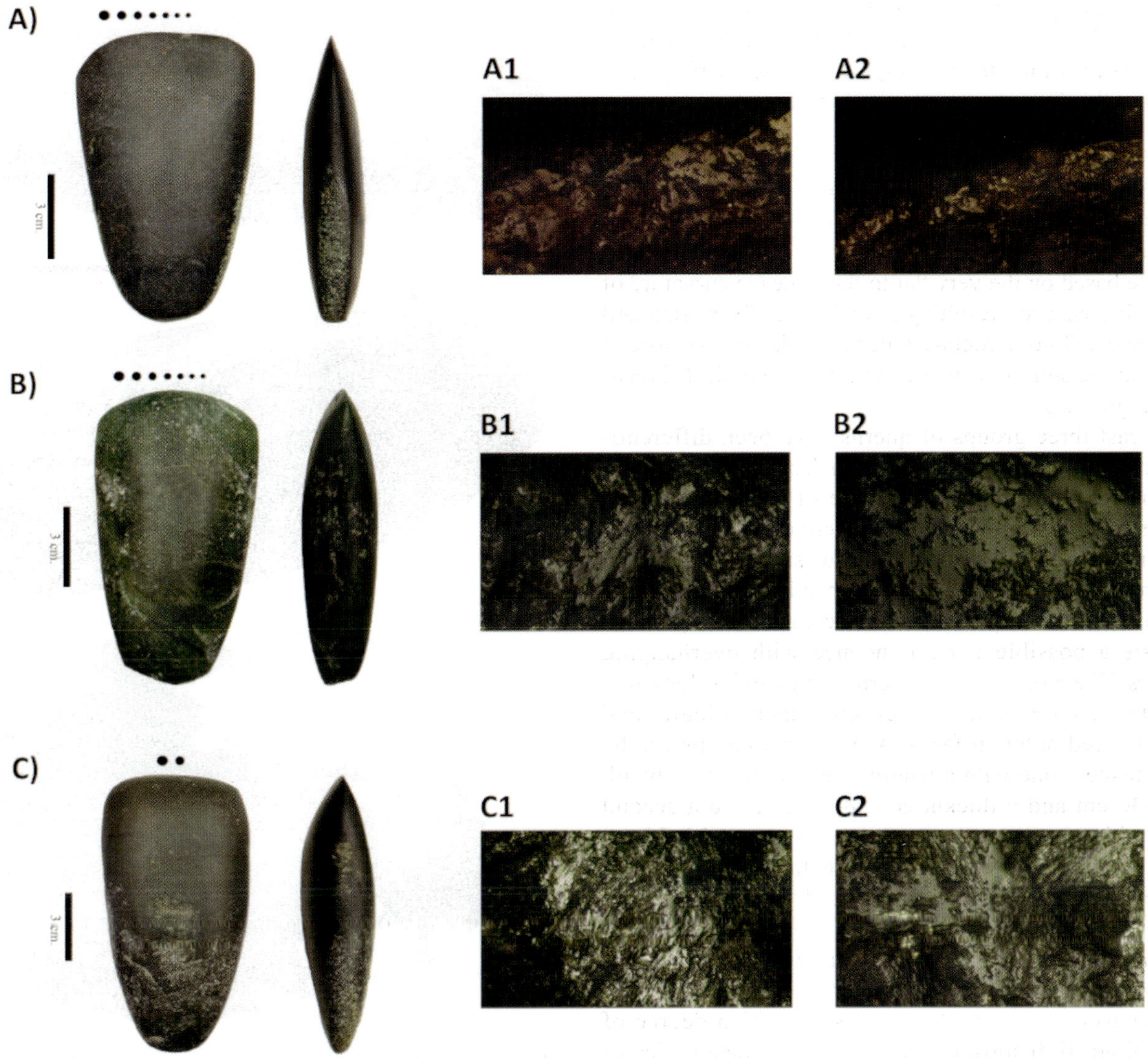

Figure 9.2.4. Stone adzes and axes displaying use-wear evidence of woodworking. A) Object No. 32454; A1–2) 200×; B) Object No. 40781; B1–2) 200×; C) Object No. 28881; C1–2) 200×.

in the less structured domestic environment. Instead, it is assumed that they were primarily utilitarian items that were relatively short-lived compared to other Neolithic contexts. In the Cardial culture, the great variety of tool types, both in terms of size and grinding style used, indicates that a wide range of plants were processed and an extensive array of foods prepared in the permanent settlements.

Grinding tools of La Marmotta

The large number of tools discovered at La Marmotta is a rare opportunity to make a first overview of the main features of the grinding systems. Vesicular basalt was mostly chosen for the querns and andesitic rocks for the grinders, although this was not systematic. In any case, the choice of these rocks indicates a supra-local supply oriented towards a high degree of surface roughness, which is considered the most important mechanical property for grinding work. The origin of these rocks is not known, although the geological context points to a volcanic area to the north-east of the site, on the opposite shore of Lake Bracciano. The grinding tools from the site of La Marmotta appear in a great diversity of types which could indicate a wide range of functions.

Technological and functional analysis of grinding systems

Grinding tools were recorded according to standard criteria of technological analysis, such as raw material, morphology, dimensions and shaping characteristics (Hamon 2006). Use-wear analysis on the active surface of a sample of tools was carried out by low-power observation of the tools with a stereomicroscope (Olympus SZ-PT 45×) at the Museo delle Civiltà in Rome, combined with high-power observation of PVS peels with a metallographic microscope (Olympus BX51) in the Trajectoires laboratory in Paris.

Reciprocal grinding system

The reciprocal grinding system (Querns n=32; Grinders n=65 analysed) is characterised by very different sizes and morphologies of querns and grinders. Their common features are based on the very flat to flat-concave curvature of their active surfaces, resulting from the use of very standard flat grinders. Two particular types of tools deserve special attention: the solid transversal type and the typical 'bread-shaped' grinders.

At least three groups of querns have been differentiated based on their size (Fig. 9.3.1). These querns represent the result of opportunistic use of natural boulders, formed by chipping only on their active surface and less frequently on their sides. A group of small querns is 20 cm long, 13 cm wide and 5–10 cm thick. These querns are characterised by their extreme narrowness, which suggests a possible correspondence with overhanging grinders. The most massive querns (up to 40 kg) look like very simple tools, with very different morphologies and little-changed outer surfaces. At least two groups can be distinguished: one with a length of about 40 cm, a width of 25–30 cm and a thickness of 8–14 cm, and a second group with a length of over 50 cm, a width of 30–35 cm and a thickness of over 22 cm. These dimensions indicate different possible working positions, from semi-standing to kneeling, and in any case a long run of the grinder. Due to the great morphological variety of the blanks and their general instability, they must have been set in an earth or wooden frame. In any case, the high degree of morphological distortion of the natural surface indicates at least a high intensity and probably a long period of use. The considerable dimensions of these tools therefore also raise some social questions. How were these boulders transported to the site: were they naturally present in the area or were they brought to the village by part of the community? Are these large tools an answer to problems related to feeding a large number of people on a domestic or village scale? Were they shared by families or even by several households at the neighbourhood level?

At least two types of standardised and well-formed grinders have been identified (Fig. 9.3.2). They are all very regular in shape and proportions. Their dimensions are equally regular: 16–24 cm long, 12–18 cm wide and 4–9 cm thick. All these grinding tools indicate a high degree of standardisation in their manufacture and also in their use. A square type has a narrow, concave grinding surface with a raised, flattened lip at each end (Fig. 9.3.2: b). The second type has a very regular ovoid shape and a semi-circular to triangular cross-section, which earned it the nickname of

Figure 9.3.1. Different types of massive querns at La Mamotta: a. flat quern used in reciprocal motion (Object No. CII 534); b. massive quern used in reciprocal motion with active surface orientated at 45° (Object No. 38743); c. basin slab used in circular and multi-directional motion probably with short circular grinder (Object No. 7623). Photographs: C. Hamon.

'bread-shaped' grinder (Figure 9.3.2: a). These are characterised by a pronounced shaping of the back and sides which have been intensively worked to create a uniform curvature and ensure comfortable handling of the tool back. Some display an extremely smooth back due to the long use. Their active surface sometimes has very dense grooves indicating an irregular lower surface or the grinding of a hard material.

Among the ten grinders analysed from a use-wear perspective: six are directly connected to cereal processing; one suggests participation also in deshusking actions; and two others were preferably used for plant transformation. In two cases, grinders were used or re-used for

Figure 9.3.2. Grinders used in back-and-forth motion with details of the morphology and shaping by fine regular pecking: left: 'bread-shaped' type (Object No. 37720) with cereal grinding use-wear at high magnification (100×; right: overhanging type (Object No. 37721). Photographs: C. Hamon.

the processing of other substances than plant food, such as mineral matter.

The contrast between poorly shaped lower grinding tools and highly standardised grinders is striking and raises the question of whether they were used in the same or a different paired grinding system. In fact, the easily recognisable features of these bread-shaped grinders open up the possibility of tracing them across the entire range of the Cardial complex if we consider them as possible cultural markers.

Circular grinding systems

The system of circular grinding (plates n=4; grinders n=8) is evidenced by basin plates, hand grinders and grinding hammerstones that were used in a circular motion. Tools that have hammering zones on their sides may have been used for combined actions of crushing and grinding. A few basin slabs are characterised by very deep and concave active surfaces of circular to ovoid shape (Fig. 9.3.1: a). They bear a very clear and pronounced smoothing of the grinding surface in their centre. Small hand grinders are generally ovoid to circular, with average diameters of *c.* 7–10 cm; they generally show intensive use.

Pestles and pounding activity

Due to the specificity of the archaeological context and underwater preservation, La Marmotta offers a rare opportunity to discuss the complementarity (or non-complementarity) of stone grinding tools and wooden tools (mortars/pans) for food preparation. Although no mortars have been identified at the site, some rare large and small pestles testify to pounding activities. These pestles were made from cylindrical or elongated cobbles of two sizes (22 × 9 cm and 8 × 5 cm).

Phytolith assemblages

Phytolith samples were extracted from the active surfaces of stone tools found in different areas of excavation by pippeting and brushing with distilled water. Both grinders (n=8) and querns (n=13) were sampled. Comparative sediment samples were obtained from their non-active surfaces and served as reference or control samples (coded as C; samples n=22). Phytolith extraction and quantitative analyses followed the methods of Katz *et al.* (2010). An aliquot of *c.* 40 mg of sample was treated with 50 µl of a

Table 9.3.1. Description of samples and main quantitative phytolith results obtained from grinders and querns. C: Control sample.

Sample No.	*Object No.*	*No. phytoliths/ 1 g sediment*	*Grass phytoliths (%)*	*Dicotyledonous phytoliths (%)*	*Weathered phytoliths (%)*	*Multicelled phytoliths (%)*	*Sample type*
1	37721	58,000	78.7	1.3	20	0	C
2		900,000	69.9	5.3	24.8	0	Grinder
3	35887	24,000	60	23.3	16.7	0	C
4		330,000	75.2	11.5	13.3	6.7	Grinder
5	37720	56,000	83.3	8.3	8.3	8.3	C
6		840,000	67.1	11.4	21.5	1.9	Grinder
7	34711	210,000	85.2	6.6	8.2	4.9	C
8		300,000	48	4	48	2.7	Grinder
9	34435	150,000	76.8	4.3	18.9	27	C
10		1,730,000	67.8	8.1	24.1	42.6	Grinder
11	37785	42,000	52.7	1.8	45.5	18.2	C
12		300,000	79.6	2.5	17.9	42.9	Grinder
13	36204	30,000	70	5	25	0	C
14		520,000	75	6.3	18.8	2.5	Grinder
15	35883	300,000	86.7	6.4	6.9	36.8	C
16		640,000	82.7	7	10.3	6.2	Grinder
17	7623	105,000	59.3	20	20.7	10.3	C
18		330,000	70.8	16.4	12.8	1.2	Quern
19	40301	17,000	80	0	20	20	C
20		7,000	100	0	0	0	Quern
21	42404	160,000	76.6	1.5	22	24.4	C
22		35,000	70	5	25	12.5	Quern
23	30617	370,000	89	3.1	7.8	29.4	C
24		400,000	84.8	6.6	8.6	67.2	Quern
25		190,000	84.9	4.9	10.2	12.2	C
26		1,400,000	72.2	6	21.9	17.9	Quern
27	7173	130,000	80	3.9	16.1	3.2	C
28		320,000	69.1	3.7	27.2	18.5	Quern
29		160,000	84.8	4.3	10.9	8.7	Quern
30	12806	190,000	89.8	6.1	4.1	73.5	C
31		840,000	87.3	5	7.7	6.7	Quern
32	37243	34,000	88.9	0	11.1	55.6	C
33		390,000	86.8	6.1	7.1	23.5	Quern
34	49480	85,000	72.2	16.7	11.1	72.2	C
35		590,000	82.2	5.3	12.5	34.2	Quern
36	7523	110,000	88.4	1.1	10.5	57.9	C
37		620,000	75.7	11.5	12.8	22.7	Quern
38	35687	0,000	83.6	1	15.4	46.1	C
39		135,000	81.9	2.4	15.7	22.9	Quern
40	30663	80,000	90	0.9	9.1	36.4	C
41		540,000	84.9	5.4	9.6	2.6	Quern

(Continued)

Table 9.3.1. (Continued)

Sample No.	*Object No.*	*No. phytoliths/ 1 g sediment*	*Grass phytoliths (%)*	*Dicotyledonous phytoliths (%)*	*Weathered phytoliths (%)*	*Multicelled phytoliths (%)*	*Sample type*
42	38743	150,000	88	3.1	8.9	64.4	C
43		560,000	79	9.9	11.1	15.2	Quern

volume solution of 6N HCl and 450 µl 2.4 g/ml of sodium polytungstate (Na6(H2W12O40)). Microscope slides were mounted with aliquots of 50 µl of sample. Slides were examined using an Olympus B, 43× optical microscope. A minimum of 200 phytoliths with diagnostic morphologies were counted whenever possible at 200× and 400×. Morphological identification was based on modern plant reference collections (Tsartsidou *et al.* 2007; Albert *et al.* 2008; 2016; Portillo *et al.* 2014) and standard literature (Piperno 2006 and references therein). The terms used to describe phytolith morphotypes follow the International Code for Phytolith Nomenclature, ICPN v. 2.0 (Neumann *et al.* 2019).

In contrast to the general lower phytolith amounts noted in the control sediment samples, the active tool surfaces of both grinders and querns show high concentrations of grass phytoliths, especially the vesicular basaltic surfaces, where the processed remains usually remain embedded. The morphological results indicate that phytolith records are dominated by grasses, mostly from the Pooideae subfamily, including major cereals such as barley and wheat. These are consistent with the macrobotanical records at the site: mainly hulled barley (*Hordeum vulgare*), einkorn (*Triticum monococcum*) and emmer (*T. dicoccum*), along with free-threshing wheat. Further, dicotyledonous phytoliths are also noted, but to a lesser extent, in addition to weathered morphotypes, *i.e.* altered phytolith morphologies that are not identifiable due to dissolution, likely due to water immersion. The anatomical origin of the grass phytoliths points to diagnostic morphotypes from the leaves and stems (such as bulliforms) and their inflorescences (mainly elongate dendritics and *papillates*; Fig. 9.3.3: a–b), in addition to short cells which are produced in both plant parts and are also informative to grass subfamily level. The short cell morphotypes belong mainly to Pooideae grasses (polylobates and rondels), whereas Panicoids (bilobates) have been observed in lesser amounts (Fig. 9.3.3: c–d). Of particular note are the differences in the proportions of multicelled or anatomically connected grass phytoliths (Table 9.3.1). These multicellullar phytoliths are relatively abundant on grinders and querns linked to both back-and-forth and circular motion, but here again specially on vesicular basaltic raw materials.

Function of the tools and the La Marmotta economy

The function of most of these tools was related to the processing of plants for food consumption. Use-wear analysis demonstrates that most of the bread-shaped grinders were used for cereal-grinding; this indicates a kind of specialisation of these tools for food preparation. In contrast, circular systems of grinding show different use-wear traces: they could have been used for a specific step in cereal processing or, possibly, for the processing of other plants as well. We must also highlight cases of re-use of these grinding tools for completely different purposes, especially for the processing of red colouring matter well known throughout the Impresso-Cardial complex in the Western Mediterranean.

This study also provides direct microfossil evidence for plant processing from grindstones in La Marmotta. The phytolith assemblages further support the processing of grasses, with an important input of cereals, such as hulled barley, einkorn and emmer, and free-threshing wheat, according to the macrobotanical records at the site. Furthermore, the phytolith records also point to the presence of panicoids that may be related to wild/weed grasses that may have been brought into food processing areas at the site unintentionally together with the crops. Also of significance are the variable amounts of multicelled or anatomically connected phytoliths from the floral part of grasses, pointing towards flour-based ground products possibly linked to the preparation of bread-like items, in addition to the remains of dehusking by-products and grain cleaning. Phytoliths are particularly resistant to forms of mechanical degradation, including those produced by cleaning, dehusking and grinding, in addition to other post-depositional processes, as demonstrated quantitatively through experimentally produced records obtained by processing hulled cereals such as einkorn and barley (Portillo *et al.* 2013; 2017).

These results, combining technological, use-wear and phytolith analyses, highlight the complementarity of 'kitchen' equipment for vegetal food transformation in Cardial contexts, and their importance in the domestic units of La Marmotta more widely.

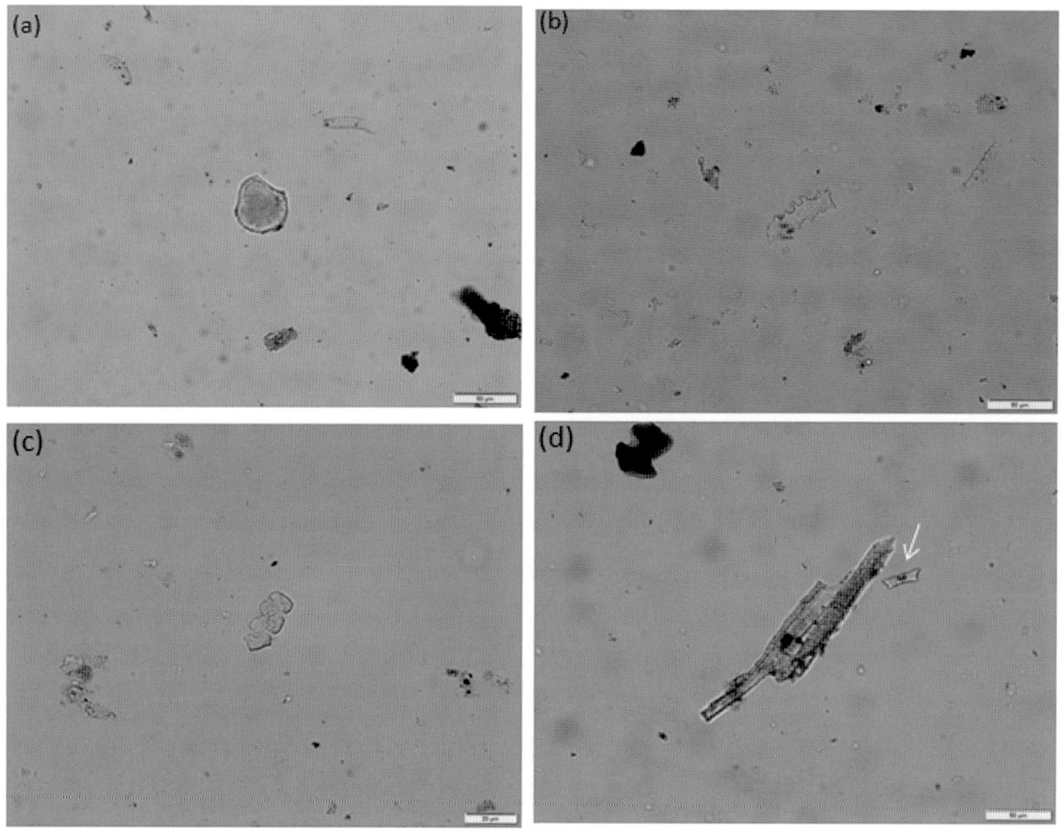

Figure 9.3.3. Photomicrographs of phytoliths identified in the samples (200× or 400×): (a) bulliform, sample 10 (grinder, Object No. 34435); (b) dendritic, sample 41 (quern, Object No. 30663); c) short cell polylobate, sample 8 (grinder, Object No. 34711); d) multicellular elongate phytoliths from grass leaves/culms and short cell rondel (arrow), sample 4 (grinder, Object No.35887). Photographs: M. Portillo.

10

Restoration of wooden and textiles artefacts at La Marmotta

Mario Mineo

The Neolithic settlement of La Marmotta, under the water of Lake Bracciano, is an archaeological record of exceptional quality because of the potential environmental, biological and cultural data it can provide (Bondioli *et al*. 2000; Fugazzola and Mineo 2000). The excellent state of preservation of the organic remains demands multi-disciplinary research and a precise reconstruction of the socio-economic structure of the Neolithic community that lived there.

All archaeological remains, both organic and inorganic (wood, bone, horn, pottery, seeds, cereal ears, etc.), submerged in water for a long time, are exposed to processes of chemical, physical and biological degradation. In some cases these cause major changes in their structure. The alterations depend on the nature of the object, the time it is in the water, the environmental conditions (pH, presence of pollutants, nature of the sediment), etc.

Organic items particularly require a precise protocol for their treatment immediately after being taken out of the water. These operations are aimed at their disinfection, restoration and conservation. One very important factor in the decomposition of wooden objects is the action of aerobic and non-aerobic micro-organisms. As the cells metabolise, bacteria make part of the components soluble and these generally dissolve in the surrounding environment by hydrolosis. This first causes the disappearance of sugary components and, in time, everything else, in particular for wood, the hemicellulose and cellulose. For this reason, when organic remains like wood and plant fibres are taken out of water, conservation work is vital. The aim, especially in the case of wood, is to avoid a reduction in its volume and the appearance of cracks and deformations.

Depending on the nature of the object, the treatment should wash away any residue of silt, algae or any other element that hinders the penetration of the solution used to conserve and consolidate it. In the case of La Marmotta, as explained below, this involved the slow and gradual impregnation of a polyethylene glycol (PEG) solution with the correct molecular weight. As seen throughout this book, the organic artefacts found at the site include wooden remains of very different sizes: from small utensils like the spindles and the medium-sized bows and sickles to the huge dugout canoes, several metres long.

All the conservation work was carried out in the facilities of the restoration laboratory in the former National Prehistory-Ethnography Museum L. Pigorini. The work was initially co-ordinated by Dr Maria Santa Montanari and later by Dr Luciana Rossi, with the collaboration of the restorer Francesca Quarato and the anthropologists Luca Bondioli and Roberto Macchiarelli. In the case of the first four pirogues, the *Giovanni Morigi e figlio S.N.C.* company took part because of their wide experience in the restoration of large wooden artefacts.

Canoe Marmotta 1

The work carried out (partly experimental) on the pirogue Marmotta I was particularly useful for the restoration of the first four canoes that were recovered. The model of procedure was a guide to the restoration of the others.

Canoe Marmotta 1 was not easy to restore. Its large size and the limited literature on the matter meant that it was difficult to decide on the best method. Therefore, the restoration was carried out in a series of phases under continuous monitoring. The restoration tasks began in late 1994 and finished in 2000 when the totally restored and consolidated canoe was placed in a specially monitored glass case. The impregnation procedure followed for its stabilisation, as described below, was designed by the company *Giovanni Morigi e figlio S.N.C.*

Phase 1

During the first phase of the restoration work, the canoe was washed by spraying water and using soft brushes. The remains of sediment adhered to it were gradually removed.

Later it was disinfected with 3% benzalkonium chloride in water. The aim was to avoid the growth of micro-organisms and eliminate small algae adhered to the wood fibres.

To maintain the wood in optimal conditions, a humidification system was installed with a PVC tube at the side of the canoe. Ten nebulisers fitted at a distance of about 1 m maintained the humidity of the whole surface of the canoe. This humidification process was carried out every 5 minutes for 2 hours in 3 months. The rapid evaporation of the water was avoided by use of an impermeable cloth. Finally, once every 24 hours, a dispenser injected a dosage of benzalkonium chloride in the water to continue disinfecting the wood.

Phase 2

The second phase of the restoration consisted of transporting the canoe on a wheeled platform to the museum room where the treatment could continue. A made-to-measure glass fibre consolidation tank had been designed by a specialised laboratory. The fragments of the canoe were kept in this tank and, after being washed, they were joined together in a space with almost complete weightlessness. The wooden fragments were joined by carbon fibre pins. During the long process of the consolidation of the canoe, the impregnation of PEG had acted as a kind of adhesive. This meant that the cracks became smaller so that they are now almost invisible. In any case, the gaps were filled with a mix of wax and aggregates (a technique used successfully by the same company to restore the wooden throne from Verucchio).

Phase 3

In this third phase, the pre-impregnation work began by immersing the whole canoe in a tank with a 10% solution of polyethylene glycol 400 mw (liquid PEG 400) at room temperature. Later, gradually over 14 months, the PEG percentage was increased to 45% under a temperature of about 40º. During this preliminary impregnation phase, the impregnation with high molecular weight glycol began (10% of PEG 4000 mw, solid PEG4000). The solution was increased gradually to reach a percentage of 80–100%, as the temperature was also increased to 60º for another 14 months.

Disinfection of micro-organisms

In addition to the normal disinfection with benzalkonium chloride or with borax and boric acid, 'pasteurisation' was attempted by the sudden heating of the solution to +40º (a treatment carried out successfully by Ya'acov Kahanov in the Maritime Study Centre at the University of Haifa for the 'Ma'agan Michael' ship). A special glass case to control the ambient conditions was created for the definitive conservation of the canoe. This avoided the wood cracking, deforming or breaking as a consequence of excessively dry conditions or changes in the relative humidity. This protection also impeded the development and proliferation of micro-organisms. Moreover, the canoe was exhibited with low lighting without ultra-violet radiation. Although the glass case with the first three canoes was moved to the second floor of the museum in 2011, they are now exhibited in separate cases in a room devoted exclusively to La Marmotta. The canoes are placed as if they were lying on a beach.

Canoes Marmotta 2, 3 and 4

The restoration of the canoes Marmotta 2, 3 and 4 was equally assigned to the company *Giovanni Morigi e figlio S.N.C.* The procedure followed was similar:

1. elimination of the very fine silt and algae adhered to their surface. This allowed them to be manipulated, washed and impregnated with benzalkonium chloride;
2. consolidation of the fractures;
3. storage in a glass fibre support and impregnation with a 48% polyethylene glycol solution (PEG). The PEG was a mixture of 4000mw=80%, 400mw=20%;
4. maintenance of the temperature between 38 and 40º.

The canoe Marmotta 5

The restoration process of the canoe Marmotta 5 was different. When it was excavated in 2005 its state of preservation was excellent. The marks left by stone axes when it was carved were still visible. As the restoration and consolidation work could not be carried out, the canoe was left in a tank full of water in municipal premises in Anguillara Sabazia. It remained there from 2005 to 2020, when the director and team at the museum determined that its conservation was a matter of urgency. The remains of the canoe had decayed badly owing to biodeteriogens that had penetrated inside the wood fibres. Algae had grown, threatening the fragility of the structure and its consequent fragmentation.

Although the water tank had stopped the total deterioration of the pirogue, it did not prevent exposure to two major factors causing degradation: prolonged contact with oxygen in the water and exposure to light in the room where it was stored. This led to the wood losing consistency and the development of colonies of aquatic micro-organisms.

The restoration of this last canoe, perhaps the most complete of the five, was due to the interest of the then director of the Museo delle Civiltà, Filippo Maria Gambari, and the archaeologist Mario Mineo. Since 2011 they had never ceased endeavouring to solve all the problems arising with the different municipal administrations regarding the conservation of the canoe. The decisive moment came in October 2020, when the two of them, together with Professor Marco Fioravanti, an expert in the restoration of waterlogged wood at the University of Florence, met the Mayor, Antonio Pizzigallo, to address its definitive restoration and public exhibition. The company *Conservación y Restauración de Ilaria Bianca Perticucci* was then hired to restore the canoe. After a first phase of impregnation with polyethylene glycol 4000, the lyophilisation and its later storage was started in September 2022 (Fig. 10.1).

Figure 10.1. Restoration of the canoe, Marmotta 5.

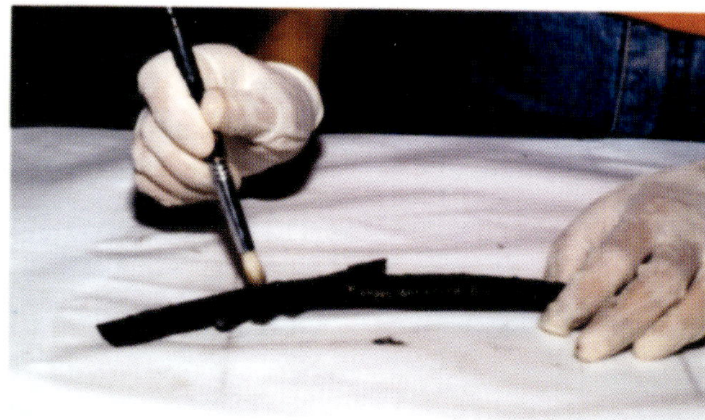

Figure 10.2. Restoration of a wooden sickle during its manual cleaning in the laboratory.

Small wooden objects

The treatment to revitalise and consolidate small and medium-sized wooden objects, and artefacts made from plant fibres, was all carried out in the Restoration Laboratory of the former Superintendence of the National Museum Prehistoric Etnographic Luigi Pigorini (now merged into the Museo delle Civiltà) from 1992 to 2009.

As the cellular structure of wood is highly permeable to water, over time this enters into its cavities. This water needs to be eliminated not naturally but by very controlled drying, otherwise the volume of the object would decrease because of evaporation with consequent contraction and the appearance of cracks and deformations. The process is so risky that, if it is not done correctly, in certain cases the weakest parts of the wood might disintegrate. Most of the remains possessed an average water content of between 550% and 650% and, therefore, the consolidation procedure aimed to replace the water with another material with a high capacity of penetration inside the cell cavities that would solidify at room temperature (Fig. 10.2).

When wooden artefacts were found at the site they were kept in polythene bags or containers for their initial storage and transport to the Restoration Laboratory in the Museo delle Civiltà. There, the first step was to clean them carefully and delicately with a soft brush and continual changes of water to remove remains of silt and algae. It was not always easy to eliminate the algae because they had penetrated into the wood. It had to be done extremely carefully or the objects might break up. After they had been cleaned, the remains were kept in water with a solution of quaternary ammonium salts.

Several factors influenced the choice of procedure: the number of objects to be treated, their degree of decay, the equipment available in the laboratory and, last but not least, the quality that could be attained. After these considerations, it was decided to consolidate the artefacts with polyethylene glycol (PEG) mw 400 in concentrations that increased from 10% to 90%. The increase in concentration was accompanied by a gradual rise in the temperature to 60±2°. This favoured penetration of the polymer and the evaporation of the internal water. At the end of the treatment, the remains were taken from the solution and dried slowly. As it dried, the wood achieved a good consistency.

The validity of the treatment was assessed *a posteriori* by comparing the size of the objects before and after the process and after a certain period of time. It was observed that they had been stabilised correctly, without deformations, contractions or fractures.

Textiles

The textile fragments were also taken to the Restoration Laboratory at the Museo delle Civiltà in a container together with lake water. The greatest difficulty was to clean the fragments, which were generally very fragile, dry them and consolidate them. After measuring the pH of the lake water, they were washed with boiled distilled water so as not to alter too much the slightly acidic conditions that had been recorded.

After they had been washed, the textiles were cleaned manually while observing the process with a stereomicroscope. The material was sprayed with distilled water and cleaned with a soft brush. Where it was possible to move the fibres without any risk, tweezers were used to remove fragments of algae tangled in the textile.

Although initially the cloth had been treated by dehydration and consolidation with hydro-alcoholic solutions, this method was abandoned because a thin whitish patina was forming. Therefore, it was decided to deposit the material in a space where the humidity could be monitored and then decrease it gradually. This slow drying out did not cause alterations to the structure of the different pieces. When totally dry, the textile fragments were consolidated with a 1% solution of paraloid B-72 in trichloroethanol.

11

Conclusions and future perspectives

Niccolò Mazzucco, Mario Mineo and Juan F. Gibaja

This volume has aimed to present an updated view of the submerged lakeshore site of La Marmotta. Far from pretending to provide a comprehensive and complete description and interpretation of the site and its many and varied archaeological features, we wanted to offer new insights into La Marmotta's material culture, especially artefacts made from vegetal and wooden raw materials, unpublished until now and practically unknown to the scientific community. Only a few of those finds had been published previously and most of the materials studied in the previous chapters have never been presented in any publication.

From the year 2016, in the framework of a collaboration agreement between the Museo delle Civiltà (Italy) and the Consejo Superior de Investigaciones Científicas CSIC (Spain), and thanks to several research projects, it became possible to start new research on the La Marmotta materials. Agricultural implements, and in particular stone tools and wooden sickles, were studied initially but gradually our research was enlarged to cover a larger set of materials and problematics.

During the last few years, our work has been largely focused on the recording, cataloguing and description of all available evidence and information from the site's excavations. The review and digitalisation of the excavation and artefactual data (plans, photos, etc.) was the basis to start a more detailed study of the archaeological materials. The number of remains is huge, impressively huge for a Mediterranean Early Neolithic site, and the work needed to examine and check all the archaeological materials stored at the Museo delle Civiltà (Rome, Italy) has been an unexpectedly large task. Most of the data created by M. A. Fugazzola and her team are extremely detailed and this has favoured our work enormously. Despite that, between the data produced during the early fieldwork in the 1980s and the last seasons in the 2000s, some differences exist in the quality and the type of available information. Our aim has been to compare and homogenise data, to avoid duplicates and erroneous attributions. This work is still ongoing but it is fundamental to guarantee the correct conservation and preservation of the site and of all associated data.

We are aware that we are here only scratching the surface of a much larger story and La Marmotta deserves a much deeper and comprehensive understanding of the overall site organisation, subsistence practices and craft productions. Such a goal will not be quickly or easily achieved as the remaining tasks to be fulfilled are numerous, the number of studies to be completed is huge, and many research possibilities are yet to be explored. The uniqueness and variety of the La Marmotta archaeological record, and its privileged preservation conditions, offers (and requires) the opportunity of conducting innovative research, of exploring new possibilities furnished by recent cutting-edge analytical methods and of setting up pilot studies to create a reference framework for the study of both wet and dry sites. All of this requires time, funds and people. Nevertheless, it was important to restart publishing research on this exceptional site and slowly open up new avenues of study.

After the intense research activity propelled by M.A. Fugazzola and her colleagues during the 1990s and the first decade of the 2000s, the site had gradually fallen into partial oblivion. Between 2005 and 2022 there were few publications relating to the site or its archaeological record. Although cataloguing, conservation and dissemination activities about the site were being carried out by the Museo delle Civiltà, research activities slowed down.

Once our team, originating from an encounter between Mario Mineo, former conservator of the prehistoric collections at the Museo delle Civiltà, and Niccolò Mazzucco and Juan F. Gibaja, both researchers focused on the Mediterranean Early Neolithic, started working together, our attention was naturally attracted to the wooden and vegetal materials. Despite being some of the most exceptional finds at the site, those materials had largely remained unstudied. Sickles, adzes, ropes, spoons, baskets and a broad array of enigmatic wooden tools were conserved in the museum storerooms and most of the research work was yet to be done. The chapters of this book provide an overview and a detailed account of those materials by presenting all available information on woodworking, basketry, rope-making, textiles, and stone tools associated with plant-working activities.

Woodworking is probably the most amazing aspect of La Marmotta, not only because of the exceptional preservation of the materials, but because of the diversity of wooden artefacts recovered. Good examples are the five dugout canoes that are presented in this book for the first time. They are among the most important discoveries at the site and in the entire Mediterranean Neolithic. Despite the preliminary nature of our results, we have succeeded in demonstrating that all five canoes are dated between *c.* 5620 and 5045 cal BC, coinciding with the lifespan of the village, as determined by radiocarbon and dendrochronology. Our study suggests that dugout canoes were probably part of a more complex navigation system, as can be hypothesised by the presence of several objects that can be linked to the fixation of a possible sail, or to fasten other nautical attachments such as an outrigger, or even to attach another vessel, forming a double-hulled canoe. While more work is needed to understand which of these hypotheses might be the most likely, the evidence provides fresh data for a better understanding of the nautical technology of Neolithic people, which until now has been certainly under-estimated. Most models and simulations concerning Neolithic navigation in the Mediterranean consider that single dugout canoes were used for pilotage (Zilhão 2014). More complex navigation systems, including sails, stabilisers and/or double-canoes, were thought to be in use for the colonisation of Cyprus, to achieve open-sea journeys of about 70–100 km (Vigne 2009; Bar-Yosef Mayer *et al.* 2015). La Marmotta data suggest that more complex navigation systems were most likely also in use in the Central Mediterranean. In addition, the presence of canoes of different sizes supports the hypothesis that various types of boats were used, possibly depending on the sailing environment (*e.g.*, sea, rivers, lakes), the length of the journey and the reasons for the expedition (*e.g.*, transportation of people, animals, materials, provisions, etc.).

Wood crafts and woodworking at La Marmotta are not limited to navigation. All spheres of the village life at La Marmotta appear to have been closely tied to the use of wood: dwellings, domestic and cooking equipment, agriculture, vegetal fibres and textile production, hunting, etc. The assemblage includes more than 40 bows; a huge diversity of textiles, cordage, wooden bowls, and other utensils associated with vegetal fibres processing and basket production; several handles for adzes/axes; and a possible wooden mace. Timber was used also for the houses and to build the main structure, but also to create pavements and drainage surfaces. For many of those artefacts there are almost no comparable objects, neither from dryland sites nor from contemporary wetland locations.

Wooden sickles are among the most exceptional finds at La Marmotta. Few sites in the world have yielded such an abundance and variety of harvesting tools. On the basis of the shape of the handle, it has been possible to define two main types of sickles: one sabre-shaped and the other with a hinged handle. However, several subtypes can be defined based on both the shape and size of the tool, suggesting handles were possibly specifically adapted and designed for each harvester. Our previous study (Mazzucco *et al.* 2022a) successfully demonstrated that sickles were used to harvest both barley and emmer, probably in small patches of cereal fields located not far from the lake and the site. The presence of decorations and a fine surface polish on these tools suggests that their value went beyond a purely utilitarian function. One of them in particular was probably used to collect a genus of aquatic plants, *Oenanthe*, that possesses pharmacological and psychoactive properties. Another good example of how harvesting tools were probably also associated with non-utilitarian behaviour is the presence of one small sickle made of clay. This artefact, despite being fragmentary (only a mesial portion of the tool is preserved), is extremely rare and no comparisons exist in the entire Mediterranean. The tool appears extremely fragile; it might represent a sort of miniaturist clay model of the wooden sickles. However, it bears a lithic insert with clearly distinguishable gloss on its edge, and so the question of whether this little clay sickle was actually used or not can legitimately be raised.

Beyond this specific aspect, what is of greater significance is the presence at La Marmotta of a huge artefactual diversity, which is not only limited to wooden artefacts, but all categories and raw materials, including pottery and clay artefacts, chipped lithics and polished and ground stones, objects made from vegetal fibres, etc. The artefactual diversity and richness are surprising but the most interesting thing is that all these artefacts are in some way related to each other; all part of interconnected *chaînes opératoires*, whose complexity is still to be fully decrypted.

This volume has tried to present a first summary of this material richness by presenting an overview of almost all categories of artefacts. In this sense, La Marmotta opens a window to an unexpected past, demonstrating that the technological capacity and the craft skills of Early Neolithic communities were much more advanced that often thought based on the archaeological record from dryland sites. Publishing the materials from La Marmotta was a first, necessary, step to make visible to the scientific and non-scientific community the archaeological wealth of this exceptional site. There is still much to do, a lot to catalogue, to analyse, and to interpret. All this will only be only possible through the involvement of several research institutions integrating competences and technologies, under the guidance of the Museo delle Civiltà. La Marmotta deserves it.

Bibliography

Albarello, B. (1986) Sur l'usage des microlithes comme armatures de projectiles/The use of microliths to frame projectile. *Revue archéologique du Centre de la France* 25 (2), 127–143.

Albert, R.M., Ruiz, J.A. and Sans, A. (2016) PhytCore ODB: a new tool to improve efficiency in the management and exchange of information on phytoliths. *Journal of Archaeological Science* 68, 98-105.

Albert, R.M., Shahack-Gross, R., Cabanes, D., Gilboa, A., Lev-Yadun, S., Portillo, M., Sharon, I., Boaretto, E. and Weiner, S. (2008) Phytolith-rich layers from the Late Bronze and Iron Ages at Tel Dor (Israel): Mode of formation and archaeological significance. *Journal of Archaeological Science* 35, 57–75.

Alfaro, C. (2012) Textiles from the Pre-pottery Neolithic site of Tell Halula (Euphrates valley, Syria). *Paléorient* 38 (1–2), 41–54.

Allen, J.R.M., Watts, W.A., McGee, E. and Huntley, B. (2002) Holocene environmental variability – the record from Lago Grande di Monticchio, Italy. *Quaternary International* 88, 69–80.

Alonso Martinez, N. (2014) Etnoarqueología del proceso de molienda manual de cereales: grañones, sémolas y harinas. *Revista d'arqueologia de Ponent* 24, 113–136.

Álvarez-Fernández, E. (2002) Ejemplares perforados del gasterópodo Homalopoma sanguineum en Europa occidental durante el Paleolítico superior. *Cypsela* 14, 43–54.

Ambrose, S.H. (1984) Introduction to pastoral adaptations to the highlands of East Africa. In J.D. Clark and S.A. Brandt (eds) *From Hunters to Farmers*, 212–239. Berkeley CA, University of California Press.

Andersen, S.H. (1986) Mesolithic dug-outs and paddles from Tybrind Vig, Denmark. *Acta Archaeologica* 57, 87-106.

Andersen, S.H. (1994) New finds of Mesolithic logboats in Denmark. In C. Westerdahl (ed). *International Symposium on Boat and Ship Archaeology 6*, 1–10. Oxford: Oxbow Books.

Andersen, S.T. (1979) Identification of wild grass and cereal pollen. In B. Aaby (ed.) Årbog 1978, *Danmarks Geologiske Undersøgelse*, 69–92.

Anderson, P.C. and Formenti, F. (1996) Fonctionnement de « faucilles » en céramique de Tell el Oueili. Rapport sur de nouvelles expériences et tentatives d'analyse de traces d'utilisation. In J.L. Huot (ed.) *Les travaux de 1987 et 1989 à Tell el Oueili*, 373–380. Paris, ERC.

Angelucci, D.E., Boschian, G., Fontanals, M., Pedrotti, A. and Vergès, J.M. (2009) Shepherds and karst: the use of caves and rock-shelters in the Mediterranean region during the Neolithic. *World Archaeology* 41(2), 191–214. [https://doi.org/10.1080/00438240902843659]

Aniol R.W. (1983) Tree-ring analysis using CATRAS. *Dendrochronologia* 1, 45–53.

Aniol, R.W. (1987) A new device for computer assisted measurement of tree-ring widths. *Dendrochronologia* 5, 135–141.

Antolín, F., Martínez-Grau, H., Steiner, B. L., Follmann, F., Soters, R., Häberle, S., Prats, G., Schäfer, M., Mainberger, M., Hajdas, I. and Banchieri, D.G. (2022) Neolithic occupations (c. 5200–3400 cal BC) at Isolino Virginia (Lake Varese, Italy) and the onset of pile-dwelling phenomenon around the Alps. *Journal of Archaeological Science: Report* 42, 103375. [https://doi.org/10.1016/j.jasrep.2022.103375]

Arranz-Otaegui, A., Gonzalez Carretero, L., Ramsey, M., Fuller, D.Q. and Richter, T. (2018) Archaeobotanical evidence reveals the origins of bread 14,400 ago in northeastern Jordan. *Proceedings of the National Academy of Sciences* 115 (31), 7925–7930. [https://doi.org/10.1073/pnas.1801071111]

Arnold, B. (1995) *Pirogues monoxyles d'Europe centrale: Construction, typologie, evolution*. Neuchâtel, Archéologie Neuchâteloise 20–21.

Arnold, B. (2014) Transports lacustres et fluviaux pendant la Préhistoire. *Archäologie und Geschichte*, 13–17.

Asouti, E. (2006) Beyond the Pre-Pottery Neolithic B interaction sphere. *Journal of World Prehistory* 20, 87–126. [https://doi.org/10.1007/s10963-007-9008-1]

Asouti, E. and Kabukcu, C. (2012) Catalhoyuk Anthracology Archive Report 2012, compiled by Burcu Tung, 238–246. Cambridge, unpublished Catalhoyuk archive report.

Attenbrow, V., Fullagar, R. and Szpak, C. (1998) Stone files and shell fishhooks in southeastern Australia. In R. Fullagar (ed.) *A Closer Look: recent Australian studies of stone tools*, 127–148. Sydney, Archaeological Computing Laboratory, University of Sydney.

Aura, J.E., Pérez, G., Carrión, Y., Seguí, J.R., Jordá, J.F., Miret, C. and Verdasco, C. (2019) Cordage, basketry and containers at the Pleistocene–Holocene boundary in southwest Europe. Evidence from Coves de Santa Maira (Valencian region, Spain). *Vegetation History and Archaeobotany* 29, 581–594. [https://doi.org/10.1007/s0033 4-019-00758-x]

Bagolini, B., Barfield, L.H., Broglio, A. (1973) Notizie preliminary delle ricerche sull'insediamento neolitico di Fimon-Molino Casarotto (Vicenza). *Rivista di scienze preistoriche* 28 (1), 161–215.

Bagolini, B., Ferrari A., Grillo A, Pessina A., Tonon M. (1994) Il villaggio neolitico di Fagnigola (scavi 1979) e gli ultimi dati dal territorio. In *Preistoria e Protostoria del Friuli-Venezia Giulia e dell'Istria. Atti della XXIX Riunione scientifica (28–30 settembre 1990). Istituto Italiano di Preistoria e Protostoria*, 185–200. Firenze, Istituto Italiano di Preistoria e Protostoria.

Bakels, C., Constantin, C. and Hauzeur, A. (1992) Utilisation des graines de pavot comme degraissant dans un vase du groupe de Blicquy. *Archäologisches Korrespondenzblatt* 22 (4), 473–479.

Bar-Yosef Mayer, D.E. (2015) Nassarius shells: Preferred beads of the Palaeolithic. *Quaternary International* 390, 79–84. [https://doi.org/10.1016/j.quaint.2015.05.042]

Bar-Yosef, O. (2019) The '8200 cal BP Cold Event' in the Levant. In A Marciniak (ed.) *Concluding the Neolithic: The Near East in the Second Half of the Seventh Millennium BCE*, 17–40. Atlanta, Lockwood Press.

Bar-Yosef, O. and Alon, D. (1988) Nahal Hemar cave. The excavations. *Atiqot 18*, 1–30

Bar-Yosef Mayer, D.E., Kahanov, Y., Roskin, J. and Gildor, H. (2015) Neolithic voyages to Cyprus: Wind patterns, routes, and mechanisms. *Journal of Island and Coastal Archaeology* 10 (3), 412–435.

Baysal, E. (2019) *Personal Ornaments in Prehistory*. Oxford, Oxbow Books.

Bazzanella, M., Mayr, A., Moser, L. and Rast-Eicher, A. (2003) *Textiles. Intrecci e tessuti dalla preistoria europea*. Trento, Servizio Beni Culturali. Provincia Autonoma di Trento.

Benco, N.L. (1992) Manufacture and use of clay sickles from the Uruk Mound, Abu Salabikh, Iraq. *Paléorient* 18(1),119–134. [https://doi.org/10.3406/paleo.1992.4569]

Berihuete-Azorín, M., Girbal, J., Piquè, R., Palomo, A. and Terradas, X. (2018) Punk's not dead. Fungi for tinder at the Neolithic site of La Draga (NE Iberia). *Plos One* 13 (4), e0195846. [https://doi.org10.1371/journal.pone.0195846]

Bernicchia, A., Fugazzola Delpino, M.A., Gemelli, V., Mantovani, B., Lucchetti, A. Cesari, M. and Speroni, F. (2006) DNA recovered and sequenced from an almost 7000 y-old Neolitic polypore, *Daedaleopsis tricolor*. *Mycological Research* 110, 14–17.

Bertagnini, A., Carrara, C., Cremaschi, M., Dai Pra, G., De Rita, D., Follieri, M., Funiciello, R., Giardini, M., Girotti, O., Landi, P., Magri, D., Narcisi, B., Piccardi, E., Rosa, C. and Sadiru, L. (1993) Field excursion guide book. *INQUA – SEQS Symposium 'Quaternary stratigraphy in volcanic areas', September 20–22, 1993*. Rome, International Union of Quaternary Research.

Beug, H.-J. (2004) *Leitfaden der Pollenbestimmung für Mitteleuropa und angrenzende Gebiete*. München, Pfeil.

Biagi, P. (1975) Stazione neolitica a Fagnigola (Azzano Decimo–Pordenone). Relazione preliminare della scavo 1974. *Annali dell'Università di Ferrara, Sezione XV, Paleontologia umana e paletnologia* 2 (6), 247–269.

Bigazzi, G., Oddone, M. and Radi, G. (2005) The Italian obsidian sources. *Archeometriai Műhely* 1, 1–12.

Binder, D., Lanos, P., Angeli, L., Gomart, L., Guilaine, J., Manen, C., Maggi, R., Muntoni, I. M., Panelli, C., Radi, G., Tozzi, C., Arobba, D., Battentier, J., Brandaglia, M., Bouby, L., Briois, F., Carré, A., Delhon, C., Gourichon, L., Marinval, P., Nisbet, R., Rossi, S., Rowley-Conwy, P. and Thiébault, S. (2017) Modelling the earliest north-western dispersal of Mediterranean Impressed Wares: New dates and Bayesian chronological model. *Documenta Praehistorica* 44, 54–77. [https://doi.org/10.4312/dp.44.4]

Binder, D., Battentier, J., Bouby, L., Brochier, J.E., Carré, A., Cucchi, T., Delhon, C., De Stefanis, C., Drieu, L., Evin, A., Girdland Flink, L., Goude, G., Gourichon, L., Guillon, S., Hamon, C. and Thiébault, S. (2020) Earliest farming in north-western Mediterranean: Evidences from Castellar, 'Pendimoun during the 6th millennium BCE'. In K. Gron, L. Sorensen and P. Rowley-Conwy (eds) *Farmers at the Frontier: a pan-european perspective on Neolithisation*, 145–160. Oxford, Oxbow Books.

Bocquet, A. and Berretrot, F. (1988) Le travail des fibres textiles au Néolithique récent à Charavines (Isère). In *IXe rencontres internationales d'archéologie et d'histoire,* 113–128. Juan-les-Pins, APDCA.

Bocquet, A. and Noël, M. (1985) The Neolithic or wood age. *Endeavour* 9 (1), 34–41. [https://doi.org/10.1016/0160-9327(85)90007-9]

Bondioli, L., Macchiarelli, R., Mineo, M., Morigi, G., Montanari, M. and Rossi, L. (2000) Il restauro dei manufatti lignei provenienti da siti umidi. In *Schutz des Kulturerbes unter Wasser. Beitrage zum Internationalen Kongress fur Unterwasserarchaeologie (IKUWA '99)*, 475–480. Mecklenburg, Beitrage zur Ur- und Frugeschichte Mecklenburg-Vorpommerns 35.

Bosch, A., Chinchilla, J. and Tarrús, J. (2000) *El poblat lacustre neolític de la Draga. Excavacions de 1990–1998*. Girona, Monografies del CASC 2.

Bosch, A., Chinchilla, J., Tarrús, J. and Piqué, R. (2006) Els objectes de fusta i fibres vegetals. In A. Bosch, J. Chinchilla and J. Tarrús (eds) *Els objectes de fusta del poblat neolític de la Draga. Excavacions de 1995–2005*, 27–126. Girona, Monografies del CASC 6.

Bottema, S. (1992) Cereal-type pollen in the Near East as indicators of wild or domestic crops. In P.C. Anderson (ed.) *Préhistoire de l'agriculture: nouvelles approches expérimentales et ethnographiques*, 95–106. Paris, CRA.

Bouby, L., Marinval, P., Durand, F., Figueiral, I., Briois, F., Martzluff, M., Perrin, T., Valdeyron, N., Vaquer, J., Guilaine, J. and Manen, C. (2020) Early Neolithic (ca. 5850–4500 cal BC) agricultural diffusion in the Western Mediterranean: An update of archaeobotanical data in SW France. *PlosOne* April, 1–26. https://doi.org/10.1371/journal.pone.0230731

Bouzouggar, A., Barton, N., Vanhaeren, M., d'Errico, F., Collcutt, S., Higham, T., Hodge, E., Parfitt, S., Rhodes, E., Schwenninger, J.-L., Stringer, C., Turner, E., Ward, S., Moutmir, A. and Stambouli, A. (2007) 82,000Year-old shell beads from North Africa and implications for the origins of modern human behavior. *Proceedings of the National Academy of Sciences* 104 (24), 9964–9969. [https://doi.org/10.1073/pnas.0703877104]

Breuil, H. (1955) Découverte par M. l'abbé Glory de débris de corde paléolithique à la grotte de Lascaux (Dordogne). *Comptes rendus des séances de l'Académie des Inscriptions et Belles-Lettres* 2, 194.

Brizzi, V. (2002) Dinamica dell'arco e balistica della freccia nel cacciatore primitivo. *Catene Operative dell'Arco Preistorico*, 20–64. Fiavé, Comano Terme (Treno).

Bronk Ramsey, C. (2021) OxCal v4. 4.4. [https://c14. arch. ox. ac. uk/oxcal.html]

Bulgarelli, G. and Flamigni, S. (2010) *Le piante tossiche e velenose*. Milan, Hoepli.

Buxó, R. (2007) Crop evolution: New evidence from the Neolithic of west Mediterranean Europe. In S. Colledge and J. Conolly (eds) *The Origins andSspread of Domestic Plants in Southwest Asia and Europe*, 155–171. Walnut Creek CA, Left Coast Press.

Cacho, C., Papí, C., Sánchez-Barriga, A. and Alonso, F. (1996) La cestería decorada de la Cueva de Los Murciélagos (Albuñol, Granada). *Complutum* 6 (1), 105–122.

Cameron, J. and Guoping, S. (2022) Textile production and craft specialisation at Tianluoshan in the lower Yangzi Valley. *Antiquity* 96 (389), 1124–1141. [https://doi.org/10.15184/aqy.2022.104]

Caramiello, R. and Arobba, D. (2003) Analisi palinologiche. In R. Caramiello and D. Arobba (eds) *Manuale di Archeobotanica. Metodiche di recupero e studio*, 67–113. Milan, Franco Angeli.

Caruso-Fermé, L., Mineo, M., Ntinou, M., Remolins, G., Mazzucco, N. and Gibaja, J.F. (2021) Woodworking technology during the Early Neolithic: First results at the site of La Marmotta (Italy). *Quaternary International* 593–594, 399–406. [https://doi.org/10.1016/j.quaint.2020.10.067].

Cassoli, P.F. and Tagliacozzo, A. (1993) Analisi preliminare delle faune. *Bulletino di Paletnologia Italiana* 84, 323–337.

Cauvin, M.-C. (1983) Les Faucilles préhistoriques du Proche-Orient. Données morphologiques et fonctionnelles. *Paléorient* 9 (1), 63–79. [https://doi.org /10.3406/paleo.1983.4332]

Cesari, J., Courtaud, P., Leandri, F., Perrin, T. and Manen, C. (2012) Le site de Campu Stefanu. Une occupation du Mésolithique et du Néolithique ancien dans le contexte corso-sarde. *Stantari* 29, 14–17.

Chesnaux, L. (2013) Les microlithes du 62 rue Henry-Farman à Paris (15e arrondissement): des flèches diverses pour différents gibiers abattus en des lieux distincts ? In B. Valentin, B. Souffi, T. Ducrocq, J.-P. Fagnart, F. Séara and C. Verjux (eds) *Palethnographie du Mésolithique: recherches sur les habitats de plein air entre Loire et Neckar. Actes de la table ronde internationale de Paris (26–27 novembre 2010)*, 119–132. Paris, Société préhistorique française (Séances de la Société préhistorique française 2-1).

Chesnaux, L. (2014) *Réflexion sur le microlithisme en France au cours du premier Mésolithique (Xe–VIIIe millénaires avant J.-C. Approches technologique, expérimentale et fonctionnelle*. Paris, Université de Paris I Panthéon-Sorbonne.

Chiquet, P., Rachez, E. and Petrequin, P. (1997) Les défenses de sanglier. In P. Petrequin (ed.) *Les sites littoraux néolithiques de Clairvaux-les-Lacs et de Chalain (Jura), III: Chalain station 3, 3200–2900 av. J.-C*, 511–521. Paris, Éditions la Maison des Sciences de l'Homme.

Ciccone, A. (2003) L'industria litica di Colle Santo Stefano. In *Atti della XXXVI Riunione Scientifica, Preistoria e Protostoria dell'Abruzzo, Chieti–Celano (27–30 Settembre 2001)*, 615–618. Firenze, Istituto Italiano di Preistoria e Protostoria.

Ciuffarella, L. (1996) Studio palinologico di una lunga sequenza di Valle di Baccano (Complesso vulcanico Sabatino, Italia centrale). Unpublished PhD thesis in Botanical Sciences, VIII Cycle, Università 'La Sapienza', Roma.

Cole, S. (1954) The Prehistory of East Africa. *American Anthropologist* 56, 1026–1050. [https://doi.org/10.1525/aa.1954.56.6.02a00060]

Cornaggia, O. and Calegari, G. (1978) Le piroghe monossili italiane. Nuova tassonomia – Aggiornamenti – Iconografia. *Preistoria Alpina* 14, 163–172.

Crema, E.R. and Bevan, A. (2021) Inference from large sets of radiocarbon dates. Software and methods. *Radiocarbon* 63(1), 23–39. [http://doi.org/10.1017/RDC.2020.95]

Cristiani, E. and Boric, D. (2020) Appearance and function of harpoons in northeastern Italy. In J.F. Gibaja, I. Clemente, N. Mazzucco and J. Marreiros (eds) *Hunter-gatherers Tool-kit: A functional perspective*, 1–27. Newcastle-upon-Tyne, Cambridge Scholars Publishing.

Cristiani, E., Farbstein, R. and Miracle, P. (2014) Ornamental traditions in the eastern Adriatic: The Upper Palaeolithic and Mesolithic personal adornments from Vela Spila (Croatia). *Journal of Anthropological Archaeology* 36, 21–31. [https://doi.org/10.1016/j.jaa.2014.06.009]

Curti, L. (ed.) (1992) *Herbarium, un'inedita collezione di piante del XVIII secolo conservata presso l'orto Botanico dell'Università di Padova*. Padova, Signum Verde Limena.

Debono Spiteri, C., Gillis, R. E., Roffet-Salque, M., Castells Navarro, L., Guilaine, J., Manen, C. and Evershed, R.P. (2016) Regional asynchronicity in dairy production and processing in early farming communities of the northern Mediterranean. *Proceedings of the National Academy of Sciences* 113(48), 13594–13599. [https://doi.org/10.1073/pnas.1607810113]

Degasperi, N. and Steffè, G. (2019) *Il villaggio neolitico di Lugo di Romagna-Fornace Gattelli: strutture, ambiente, culture*. Firenze, Istituto Italiano di Preistoria e Protostoria.

Delpino, C. (2020) Il Neolitico antico dell'areale medio-tirrenico: gli aspetti della ceramica impressa e della ceramica lineare nel Lazio e nel territorio di Roma. In A.P. Anzidei and G. Carboni (eds.) *Roma prima del mito abitati e necropoli dal Neolítico alla Prima Eta' dei Metalli nel territorio di Roma (VI–III Millennio A.C.)*, 3–24. Oxford: Archaeopress Archaeology.

Dreschner-Schneider, R., de Beaulieu, J.L., Magny, M., Walter-Simonnet, A.V., Bossuet, G., Millet, L., Brugiapaglia, E. and Drescher, A. (2007) Vegetation history, climate and human impact over the last 15,000 years at Lago dell'Accesa (Tuscany, Central Italy). *Vegetation History and Archaeobotany* 16, 279–299.

D'Amico, C. (2000) La pietra levigata neolítica in Italia settentrionale e in Europa. Litologia, produziones e circozalione. In A. Pessina and G. Muscio (eds.) *La neolitizzazione tra Oriente e Occidente*, 67–80. Udine, Comune di Udine.

D'Amico, C., Starnini, E., Gasparotto, G. and Ghedini, M. (2004) Eclogites, jades and other HP-metaophiolites employed for prehistoric polished stone implements in Italy and Europe. *Periodico di Mineralogia* 73, 17–42.

D'Errico, F., Backwell, L., Villa, P., Degano, I., Lucejko, J.J., Bamford, M.K., Higham, T.F.G., Colombini, M.P. and Beaumont P.-B. (2012) Reply to Evans: Use of poison remains the most parsimonious explanation for Border Cave castor bean extract. *Proceedings of the National Academy of Science* 109 (48), E3291-E3292. [doi: 10.1073/pnas.1214711109]

De Francesco, A.M., Bocci, M., Mirocle-Crisci, G. and Francaviglia, V. (2012) Obsidian provenance at several Italian and Corsican archaeological sites using the non-destructive

X-ray Fluorescence method. In C. Stevenson and I. Liritzis (eds) *Obsidian and Ancient Manufactured Glasses*, 115–129., Albuquerque NM, University of New Mexico Press.

De Rita, D., Funiciello, R., Corda, L., Sposato, A. and Rossi, U. (1993) Volcanic units. In M. Di Filippo (ed.) *Sabatini Volcanic Complex*, 33–79. Roma, CNR, Quaderni de 'La Ricerca Scientifica' 114 (11).

Efstratiou, N. (2014) Microhistories of transition in the Aegean islands. The cases of Cyprus and Crete. In C. Manen, T. Perrin and J. Guilaine (eds) *La transition néolithique en Méditerranée. Comment des chasseurs devinrent agriculteur*, 169–187. Toulouse, Errance.

Efstratiou, N., Biagi, P. and Starnini, E. (2014) The Epipalaeolithic site of Ouriakos on the island of Lemnos and its place in the Late Pleistocene peopling of the East Mediterranean region. *Adalya* 17, 1–23.

Egloff, M. (1987) Emmanchements du Néolithique à l'Âge du Bronze dans les palafittes d'Auvernier (lac de Neuchâtel). In D. Stordeur (ed.) *La Main et l'Outil. Manches et emmanchements préhistoriques*, 229–245. Paris, Table Ronde CNRS. Travaux de la Maison de l'Orient.

Erič, M. and Kavur, B. (2012) Late Mesolithic logboat from Hotiza. In A. Gaspari and M. Eric (eds) *Potopljena Preteklost*, 405–408. Ljubljana, Didakta.

Fábregas, R. (2001) *Los petroglifos y su contexto: un ejemplo de la Galicia meridional*. Vigo, Instituto de Estudios Vigueses.

Falci, C.G., Cuisin, J. Delpuech, A., Van Gijn, A. and Hofman, C.L. (2019) New insights into use-wear development in bodily ornaments through the study of ethnographic collections. *Journal of Archaeological Method and Theory* 26, 755–805. [https://doi.org/10.1007/s10816-018-9389-8]

Fiore, I., Fuggazzola, M.A. and Tagriacozzo, A. (2006) L'utilizzo dei canini di suino nel villaggio neolítico de 'La Marmotta' (Anguillara Sabazia – Roma). In *Atti della XXXIX Riunione Scientifica, Firenze 25-27 novembre 2004,* 964–969. Firenze, Istituto italiano di preistoria e protostoria.

Fischer, A. (1985) *På jagt med stenalder-våben. Foesog med fortiden 3*. Lejre, Historisk-Arkeologisk Forsogcenter 6.

Fischer A., Vemming Hansen P. and Rasmussen P. (1984) Macro and Micro Wear Traces on Lithic Projectile Points. Experimental Results and Prehistoric Examples. *Journal of Danish Archeology* 3, 19–46.

Fontanals-Coll, M., Subirà, M.E., Marín-Moratalla, N., Ruiz, J. and Gibaja, J.F. (2014) From Sado Valley to Europe: Mesolithic dietary practices through different geographic distributions. *Journal of Archaeological Science* 50, 539–550.

Fort, J. (2022) Dispersal distances and cultural effects in the spread of the Neolithic along the northern Mediterranean coast. *Archaeological and Anthropological Science* 14, 153. [https://doi.org/10.1007/s12520-022-01619-x]

Forte, V. and Lemorini, C. (2017) Traceological analysis applied to textile implements: an assessment of the method through the case study of the 1st millennium BCE ceramic tools in central Italy. *Origini* 40, 165–182.

Fowler, B. (2000) *Uncovering the Life and Times of Prehistoric Man Found in an Alpine Glacier*. New York: Random House.

Fugazzola, M.A. (1996) *Un tufo nel passato. 8000 anni fa nel lago Bracianno*. Roma, Sopraintendenza SMNPE, «Luigi Pigorini».

Fugazzola, M.A. (2000–2001) La piccola 'dea Madre' del lago di Bracciano. *Bulletino di Paletnologia Italiana* 91–92, 27–45.

Fugazzola, M.A. (2002) La Marmotta, Lazio. In M.A. Fugazzola, A. Pessina and V. Tiné (eds) *Le ceramiche impresse nel Neolitico antico. Italia e Mediterraneo*, 373–395. Roma, Istituto Poligrafico e Zecca dello Stato, Studi di Paletnologia 1.

Fugazzola, M.A. (2004a) Su alcuni funghi rinvenuti nel villaggio neolítico de 'La Marmotta' (Anguillara Sabazia, Roma). Considerazioni preliminari. *Bulletino di Paletnologia Italiana* 95, 1–20.

Fugazzola, M.A. (2004b) Il villaggio de La Marmotta. In M.A. Fugazzola, A. Pessina and V. Tinè (eds) *Civiltà dell'argilla. Le prime comunità del Neolitico*, 157–169. Roma, Catalogo della mostra, Museo Nazionale Preistorico Etnografico Luigi Pigorini (7 dicembre 2002–30 marzo 2003), Caserta.

Fuggazzola, M.A. (2019) Modellini di natanti neolitici: possibili lucerne? In A. Asta, G. Caniato, D. Gnola and S. Medas (eds) *Atti del III Convegno Nazionale dell'Istituto Italiano di Archeologia e Etnologia Navale, 15-16 aprile 2016*, 17–23. Padova, Navis, Rassegna di studi di archeologia, etnologia e storia navale 6.

Fugazzola, M.A. and Mauro, N. (2014) La seconda imbarcazione monossile del villaggio neolitico de La Marmotta. In *Atti del II Convegno nazionale, 13–14 Aprile 2012*, 125–132. Padova. Navis 5, Archeologia, storia, etnologia navale.

Fugazzola, M.A. and Mineo, M. (1995) La piroga neolitica del lago di Bracciano («La Marmotta 1»). *Bulletino di Paletnologia Italiana*, 86, 197–266.

Fugazzola, M.A. and Mineo, M. (2000). Die fruhneolithische Siedlung 'La Marmotta' (Italien) als Spiegelbild mittelmeerischer Kulturkontakte. In *Schutz des Kulturerbes unter Wasser. Beitrage zum Internationalen Kongress fur Unterwasserarchaeologie (IKUWA '99)*, 121–6. Mecklenburg, Beitrage zur Ur- und Frugeschichte Mecklenburg-Vorpommerns 35.

Fugazzola, M.A. and Tinazzi, O. (2010) Dati di cronologia da un villaggio del Neolitico Antico. Le indagini dendrocronologiche condotte sui legni de La Marmotta (lago di Bracciano, Roma). In *Miscellanea in ricordo di Francesco Nicosia*, 1–10. Pisa-Roma, Studia Erudita, Fabrizio Serra Editore.

Fugazzola, M.A., D'Eugenio, G. and Pesina, A. (1993) «La Marmotta» (Anguillara Sabazia, RM). Scavi 1989. Un abitato perilacustre di età neolitica. *Bulletino di Paletnologia Italiana* 84, 183–315.

Fugazzola, M.A, Calandra, G., Fiore, I., Fois, G., Pregagnoli, S. and Tagliacozzo, A. (2002) La Marmotta (Anguillara Sabazia - RM). In C. Peretto (ed.) *Analisi informatizzata e trattamento dati delle strutture di abitato di età preistorica e protostorica in Italia, Atti del Convegno (Ferrara 26-27 Novembre 2001)*, 217–232. Firenze, Origines Progetti 1.

Fugazzola, M.A., Manfredini, A., Martini, F., Radi, G., Sarti, L. and Silvestrini, M. (2003) Insediamenti e strutture neolitiche ed eneolitiche dell'Italia Centrale. In *Le comunità della preistoria italiana. Studi e ricerche sul Neolitico e le età dei metalli. Atti della XXXV Riunione Scientifica dell'I.I.P.P. (Lipari 2–7 giugno 2000)*, 93–112, Firenze, l'Istituto Italiano di Preihistoria e Protohistoria.

Furholt, M. (2016) Settlement layout and social organisation in the earliest European Neolithic. *Antiquity* 90 (353), 1196–1212. [https://doi:10.15184/aqy.2016.170]

Gabriele, M., Convertini, F., Vérati, C., Gratuze, B., Jacomet, S., Boschian, G. and Binder, D. (2019) Long-distance mobility in the North-Western Mediterranean during the Neolithic transition using high resolution pottery sourcing. *Journal of Archaeological Science: Reports* 28, 102050. [https://doi.org/10.1016/j.jasrep.2019.102050]

Gassin, B. (1996) *Évolution socio-économique dans le Chasséen de la grotte de l'église supérieure (Var). L'apport de l'analyse fonctionnelle des industries lithiques*. Paris, CNRS éditions, Monographie du CRA 17.

Giagkoulis, T.S. (2020) The pile-field of the Neolithic lakeside settlement Anarghiri IXb (Amindeon, western Macedonia, Greece) and the non-residential wooden structures on the periphery of the habitation. In A. Hafner, E. Dolbunova, A. Mazurkevich, E. Pranckenaite and M. Hinz (eds) *Settling Waterscapes in Europe: The archaeology of Neolithic & Bronze Age pile-dwellings*, 137–155. Heidelberg, Heidelberg University Library.

Giardini, M. (2007) Late Quaternary vegetation history at Stracciacappa (Rome, central Italy). *Vegetation History and Archaeobotany* 16, 301–316.

Gibaja, J.F. (2003) *Comunidades Neolíticas del Noreste de la Península ibérica. Una aproximación socio-económica a partir del estudio de la función de los útiles líticos*. Oxford, British Archaeological Report S1140.

Gibaja, J.F. and Palomo, A. (2004) Geométricos usados como proyectiles. Implicaciones económicas, sociales e ideológicas en sociedades neolíticas del VI–IV milenio cal BC en el noreste de la Península Ibérica. *Trabajos de Prehistoria* 61 (1), 81–97. [https://doi.org/10.3989/tp.2004.v61.i1.30]

Gibaja, J.F., Subirà, M.E., Terradas, X., Santos, F.J., Agulló, L., Gómez-Martínez, I., Allièse, F. and Fernández-López de Pablo, J. (2015) The emergence of Mesolithic cemeteries in SW Europe: Insights from the El Collado (Oliva, Valencia, Spain) radiocarbon record. *Plos One*. [https://doi.org/10.1371/journal.pone.0115505]

Gibaja, J.F., Ibáñez, J.-J., Nielsen, E., Kienholz, A., van Willigen, S. and Linton, J. (2016) The Neolithic reaping knives from Egolzwil 3: A Mediterranean technical tradition in the Late 5th millennium Swiss Neolithic. *Quaternary International* 427, 158–174.

Gibaja, J.F., Mazzucco, N., Ibáñez, J.J., Mineo, M., Rodríguez, A., Gassin, B., Perales, U., Martín, I. and López, C. (2017) Reconociendo el camino seguido por las primeras comunidades neolíticas cas asentadas en el Mediterráneo centro-occidental a través del análisis de sus hoces. *Arkeogazte* 7, 5–24.

Gleba, M. and Harris, S. (2018) The first plant bast fibre technology: identifying splicing in archaeological textiles. *Archaeological and Anthropological Sciences* 11, 2329–2346. [https://doi.org/10.1007/s12520-018-0677-8]

Gómez, J. (1982) Une pirogue monoxyle néolithique dans le lit de la Charente. *Bulletin de la Societé Préhistorique Française* 79 (2), 61–63.

Góngora, M. (1868) *Antigüedades Prehistóricas de Andalucía, monumentos, inscripciones, armas, utensilios y otros importantes objetos pertenecientes a los tiempos más remotos de su población*. Madrid, C. Moro

González, J.E. and Ibáñez, J.J. (1994) *Metodología de análisis funcional de instrumentos tallados en sílex*. Bilbao, Universidad de Deusto, Cuadernos de Arqueología 14.

Gonzalez Carretero, L., Wollstonecroft, M. and Fuller, D. (2017) A methodological approach to the study of archaeological cereal meals: A case study at Çatalhöyük East (Turkey). *Vegetation History and Archaeobotany* 26, 415–432.

Grabundžija, A., Schlichtherle, H., Leuzinger, U., Schier, W. and Karg, S. (2021) The interaction of distant technologies: Bridging Central Europe using a techno-typological comparison of spindle whorls. *Antiquity* 95 (381), 627–647. [https://doi.org/10.15184/aqy.2021.6]

Gramsch, B. (1992) Friesack Mesolithic wetlands. In B. Coles (ed.) *The Wetland Revolution in Prehistory*, 65–72. London, University of Exeter and The Prehistoric Society.

Grömer, K. (2018) Late Neolithic weaving tools from Melk-Spielberg in Austria: Experiments with crescent-shaped weights. In M. Siennicka, L. Rahmstorf and A. Ulanowska (eds) *First Textiles: The beginnings of textile manufacture in Europe and the Meidterranean*, 117–128. Oxford, Ancient Textiles 32.

Gronenborn, D. (2003) Migration, acculturation and culture change in western temperate Eurasia, 6500–5000 cal. BC. *Documenta Praehistorica* 30, 79–91.

Gronenborn, D. (2009) Climate fluctuations and trajectories to complexity in the Neolithic towards a theory. *Documenta Praehistorica* 36, 97–110.

Guéret, C., Gassin, B., Jacquier, J. and Marchand, G. (2014) Traces of plant working in the Mesolithic shell midden of Beg-an-Dorchenn (Plomeur, France). *Mesolithic Miscellany* 22 (3), 3–15.

Guerra Doce, E. (2006) Evidence for drug-taking in prehistoric Europe. *Trastornos Adictivos* 8 (1), 53–61.

Guerra Doce, E. and Lopez Sáez, J.A. (2006) El registre arqueobotânico de plantas psicoactivas en la prehistoria de la Peninsula Ibérica. Uni aproximacion etnobotânica y fitoqmmica a la interpretaciôn de la evidencia. *Complutum* 17, 7–24.

Guerrero, V.M. (2006) Comer antes que viajar. Pesca y barcas de base monóxila en la prehistoria occidental. *Mayurqa* 31, 7–56.

Guilaine, J. (2000–2001) La diffusion de l'agriculture en Europe: une hypothese arythmique. *Zephyrus* 53–54, 267–272.

Guilaine, J. (2017) The Neolithic transition: From the eastern to the western Mediterranean. In O. García-Puchol and D. Salazar-García (eds) *Times of Neolithic Transition along the Western Mediterranean*, 15–31. Cham, Springer Fundamental Issues in Archaeology. [https://doi.org/10.1007/978-3-319-52939-4_2]

Guilaine, J. and Briois, F. (2005) Shillourokambos et la neolithisation de chypre: quelques Reflexions. *Mayurqa* 30, 13–32.

Guilbeau, D. (2010) Les grandes lames et les lames par pression au levier du Néolithique et de l'Énéolithique en Itali. Unpublished thesis, Université Paris Ouest.

Haddon, A.C. (1937) *The Canoes of Melanesia, Queensland and New Guinea*. Honolulu, Bishop Museum Special Publication 28.

Hafner, A., Rey, F., Hostettler, M., Laabs, J., Bolliger, M. Brombacher, C., Francuz, J., Gobet, E., Häberle, S., Rentzel, P., Schäfer, M., Schibler, J., Wey, O. and Tinner, W. (2020) Archaeological and palaeoecological investigations at Burgäschisee (Swiss Plateau): New interdisciplinary insights in Neolithic settlement, land use and vegetation dynamics. In A Hafner, E. Dolbunova, A. Mazurkevich, E. Pranckenaite and M. Hinz (eds) *Settling Waterscapes in Europe: The archaeology of Neolithic & Bronze Age pile-dwellings*, 173–274. Heidelberg, Heidelberg University Library.

Hall, V.A. (1988) The role of harvesting techniques in the dispersal of pollen grains of Cerealia. *Pollen et Spores* 30 (2), 265–270.

Halstead, P. (2000) Land use in postglacial Greece: Cultural causes and environmental effects. In P. Halstead and C. Frederick (eds) *Landscape and Land use in Postglacial Greece*, 110–130. Sheffield, Sheffield Studies in Aegen Archaeology.

Hamon, C. (2006) *Broyage et abrasion au Néolithique ancien. Caractérisation technique et fonctionnelle des outillages en grès du Bassin parisien*. Oxford, British Archaeological Report S1551.

Hamon, C. (2021) A revolution in food preparation. Grinding and pounding plants in the first farming communities of Western Europe and the Mediterranean region. *Food History* 19 (1–2), 271–294.

Hamon, C. and Le Gall, V. (2013) Millet and sauce: The uses and functions of querns among the Minyanka (Mali). *Journal of Anthropological Archaeology* 32, 109–121.

Heer, O. (1865) *Die Pflanzen der Pfahlbauten* 68. Zürich, Druck von Zürcher und Furrer.

Heiss, A.G., Pouget, N., Wiethold, J., Delor-Ahu, A. and Le Goff, I. (2015) Tissue-based analysis of a charred flat bread (galette) from a Roman cemetery at Saint- Memmie (Dept Marne, Champagne-Ardenne, north-eastern France). *Journal of Archaeological Science* 55, 71–82.

Heiss, A.G., Antolín, F., Bleicher, N., Harb, C., Jacomet, S., Kühn, M., Marinova, E., Stika, H.P. and Valamoti, S.M. (2017) State of the art. Analytical approaches in the investigation of components and production traits of archaeological bread-like objects, applied to two finds from the Neolithic lakeshore settlement Parkhaus Opéra (Zürich, Switzerland). *Plos One* 12 (8), e0182401.[https:/doi.org/10.1371/journal.pone.0182401]

Heiss, A. G., Antolín, F., Berihuete Azorín, M., Biederer, B., Erlach, R., Gail, N., Griebl, M., Linke, R., Lochner M., Marinova, E., Oberndorfer D., Stika, H.P. and Valamoti S.M. (2019) The Hoard of the Rings. 'Odd' annular bread-like objects as a case study for cereal-product diversity at the Late Bronze Age hillfort site of Stillfried (Lower Austria). *Plos One* 14 (6), e0216907. [https://doi.org/10.1371/journal.pone.0216907]

Heiss, A. G., Azorín, M. B., Antolín, F., Kubiak-Martens, L., Marinova, E., Arendt, E. K., Biliaderis, C.G., Kretschmer, H., Lazaridou, A., Stika, H.-P., Zarnkow, M., Baba, M., Bleicher, N., Ciałowicz, K.M., Chłodnicki, M., Matuschik, I., Schlichtherle H. and Valamoti, M.S. (2020) Mashes to mashes, crust to crust. Presenting a novel microstructural marker for malting in the archaeological record. *Plos One* 15(5), e0231696. [https://doi.org/10.1371/journal.pone.0231696]

Hellmund, M. (2008) The Neolithic records of *Onopordum acanthium*, *Agrostemma githago*, *Adonis* cf. *aestivalis* and *Claviceps purpurea* in Sachsen-Anhalt, Germany. *Vegetation History and Archaeobotany* 17, S123–S130.

Henry, A.G., Hudson, H.F. and Piperno, D.R. (2009) Changes in starch grain morphologies from cooking. *Journal of Archaeological Science* 36 (3), 915–922.

Henshilwood, C, d'Errico, F, Vanhaeren, M, van Niekerk, K. and Jacobs, Z. (2004) Middle Stone Age shell beads from South Africa. *Science* 304 (5669), 404. [https://www.science.org/doi/10.1126/science.1095905]

Henshilwood, C., d'Errico, F., Yates, R., Jacobs, Z, Tribolo, C., Duller, G.A.T., Mercier, N., Sealy, J.C., Valladas, H., Watts, I., and Wintle, A.G. (2002) Emergence of modern human behaviour: Middle Stone Age engravings from South Africa. *Science* 295, 1278–1280. [https://www.science.org/doi/10.1126/science.1067575]

Heron, C., Habu, J., Katayama Owens, M., Ito, Y., Eley, Y., Lucquin, A., Radini, A., Saul, H., Debono Spiteri, C. and Craig, O.E. (2016) Molecular and isotopic investigations of pottery and 'charred remains' from Sannai Maruyama and Sannai Maruyama No. 9, Aomori Prefecture, Japan. *Japanese Journal of Archeology* 4, 29–52.

Hickman, C.N. (ed.) (1947) *Archery: The technical side*. Milwaukee WI, National Field Archery Association.

Ho Ho Committee (1979) The Ho Ho classification and nomenclature committee report. In B. Hayden (dir) *Lithic Use-Wear Analysis*. Academic Press, New York.

Hodder, J. (2011) Human-thing entanglement: towards an integrated archaeological perspective. *Journal of the Royal Anthropological Institute* 17, 154–77.

Horejs, B. (2019) Long and short revolutions towards the Neolithic in western Anatolia and Aegean. *Documenta Praehistorica* 46, 68–83. [https://doi.org/10.4312/dp.46.5]

Hourmouziadis, G.X. (1996) *The Prehistoric Lakeside Ssettlement of Dispilio (Kastoria)*. Thessaloniki, Codex.

Hourmouziadis, G.X. (ed.) (2002) *Dispilio: 7500 years later*. Thessaloniki: University Studio Press (in Greek).

Huet, T., Cubas, M., Gibaja, J.F., Oms, F.X. and Mazzucco, N. (2022) NeoNet Dataset. Radiocarbon dates for the Late Mesolithic/Early Neolithic transition in the north Central-Western Mediterranean basin. *Journal of Open Archaeology Data*, 10 (3) [http://doi.org/10.5334/joad.87]

Ibáñez, J.J., González-Urquijo, J., Teira-Mayolini, L.C. and Lazuén, T. (2018) The emergence of the Neolithic in the Near East: A protracted and multi-regional model. *Quaternary International* 470, 226–252. [https://doi.org/10.1016/j.quaint.2017.09.040]

Ibáñez, J.J., Clemente, I., Gassin, G., Gibaja, J.E, González, J.E., Márquez, B., Philibert, S. and Rodríguez, A. (2008). Harvesting technology during the Neolithic in South-West Europe. In L. Long and N. Skakun (eds) *'Prehistoric Technology' 40 Years Later: Functional studies and the Russian legacy. Proceedings of the International Congress Verona (Italy, 2005)*, 183–196. Oxford, British Archaeological Report S1783.

Inizan M.-L., Reduron-Ballinger M., Roche H. and Tixier J. (1999) *Technology and terminology of knapped stone* (Vol. 5). Cercle de Recherches et d'Etudes Préhistoriques, Nanterre.

Ivanova, M., De Cupere, B., Ethier, J. and Marinova, E. (2018) Pioneer farming in southeast Europe during the early sixth millennium BC: Climate-related adaptations in the exploitation of plants and animals. *PLoS One* 13(5), e0197225. [https://doi.org/10.1371/journal.pone.0197225]

Jesus, A., Bonhomme, V., Evin, A., Ivorra, S., Soteras, R., Salavert, A., Antolín, F. and Bouby L. (2021) A morphometric approach to track opium poppy domestication. *Scientific Reports* 11, 9778. [http://doi.org/10.1038/s41598-021-88964-4]

Joly, C., Barillé, L., Barreau, M., Mancheron, A. and Visset, L. (2007) Grain and annulus diameter as criteria for distinguishing pollen grains of cereals from wild grasses. *Review of Palaeobotany and Palynology* 146, 221–233.

Junkmanns, J. (2013) *Pfeil und Bogen: von der Altsteinzeit bis zum Mittelalter*. Tübingen, Angelika Hörnig.

Kabaciński, J. and Terberger, T. (2015) Features and finds of the Stone Age sites Dąbki 9 and 10. In J. Kabaciński, S. Hartz, D.C.M. Raemaekers and T. Terberger (eds) *The Dąbki Site in Pomerania and the Neolithisation of the North European Lowlands (*c. *5000–3000 cal BC)*, 137–155. Rahden/Westfahlen, Archaeology and History of the Baltic 8.

Kadereit, J. (1988) Sectional affinities and geographical distribution in the genus *Papaver* L. (Papaveraceae). *Beiträge zur Biologie der Pflanzen* 63, 139–156.

Kapitän, G. (1987) Records of native craft in Sri Lanka-I: The single outrigger fishing canoe oruwa – Part 1. Sailing oru. *International Journal of Nautical Archaeology and Underwater Exploration* 16 (2), 135–147.

Katz, O., Cabanes, D., Weiner, S., Maeir, A., Boaretto, E. and Shahack-Gross, R. (2010) Rapid phytolith extraction for analysis of phytolith concentrations and assemblages during an excavation: An application at Tell es-Safi/Gath, Israel. *Journal of Archaeological Science* 37, 1557–1563.

Keeley, L.H. and Newcomer, M.H. (1977) Microwear analysis of experimental flint tools: a test case, *Journal of archaeological science* 4 (1), 29–62.

Keller, F. (1866) *The Lake Dwellings of Switzerland and Other Parts of Europe*. London, Longmans, Green & Co.

Kelly, M.G. and Huntley, B. (1991) An 11000-year record of vegetation and environment from Lago di Martignano, Latium, Italy. *Journal of Quaternary Science* 6 (3), 209–224.

Kenoyer, J.M. (2005) Bead technologies at Harappa, 3300–1900 BC: A comparison of tools, techniques and finished beads from the Ravi to the Late Harappan Period. In C. Jarrige and V. Lefèvre (eds) *The Global Perspective of Beads and Beadwork: History, Manufacture, Trade, and Adornment*, 1–12. Istanbul, Kadir Has University.

Khan, R., Ahmad, M., Zafar, M. and Ullah, A. (2017) Scanning electron and light microscopy of foliar epidermal characters: A tool for plant taxonomists in the identification of grasses. *Microscopy Research Technique* 80, 1123–1140.

Klooss, S. and Lübke, H. (2009) The terminal Mesolithic and Early Neolithic logboats of Stralsund-Mischwasserspeicher, evidence of early waterborne transport on the German southern Baltic coast. In R. Bockius (ed.) *Between the Seas. Transfer and Exchange in Nautical Technology. Proceedings of the Eleventh International Symposium on Boat and Ship Archaeology*, 97–105. Mainz. Römisch-Germanischen Zentralmuseums.

Knapp, A.B. (2010) Cyprus's earliest Prehistory: Seafarers, foragers and settlers. *Journal of World Prehistory* 23, 79–120.

Kollmann, J. and Grubb, P.J. (2002) *Viburnum lantana* L. and *Viburnum opulus* L. (*V. lobatum* Lam., *Opulus vulgaris* Borkh.). *Journal of Ecology* 90 (6), 1044–1070.

Kooi, B.W. and Bergman, C.A. (1997) An approach to the study of ancient archery using mathematical modelling. *Antiquity* 71 (271), 124–134.

Krauß, R., Marinova, E., De Brue, H. and Weninger, B. (2018) The rapid spread of early farming from the Aegean into the Balkans via the Sub-Mediterranean-Aegean Vegetation Zone. *Quaternary International* 496, 24–41. [https://doi.org/10.1016/j.quaint.2017.01.019]

Kreisel, H. and Ansorge, J. (2009) Subfossile Baumschwämme aus dem Quartär Vorpommerns. *Zeitschrift für Mykologie* 75 (1), 33–50.

Kubiak-Martens, L., Brinkkemper, O. and Oudemans, T.F.M. (2015) What's for dinner? Processed food in the coastal area of the northern Netherlands in the Late Neolithic. *Vegetation History and Archaeobotany* 24, 47–62.

Kuhn, S.L. and Stiner M.C. (2007) Body ornamentation as information technology: towards and understanding of the significance of early beads. In P. Mellars, K. Boyle, O. Bar-Yosef and C. Stringer (eds) *Rethinking the Human Revolution: New Behavioural and biological perspectives on the origin and dispersal of modern humans*, 45–54. Cambridge, McDonald Institute Monographs, University of Cambridge.

Kvavadze, E., Bar-Yosef, O., Belfer-Cohen, A., Boaretto, E., Jakeli, N., Matskevich, Z. and Meshveliani, T. (2009) 30 000-year-old wild flax fibers. *Science* 325 (5946), 1359. [https://doi.org/10.1126/science.1175404]

Lagerås, P. (1996) Long-term history of land-use and vegetation at Femtingagölen – a small lake in the Småland Uplands, southern Sweden. *Vegetation History and Archaeobotany* 5, 215–228.

Lanting, J.N. (2000) Dates for origin and diffusion of the European longboat. *Palaeohistoria* 39–40, 627–650.

Lo Vetro, D. and Martini, F. (2016) Mesolithic in central southern Italy: Overview of lithic productions. *Quaternary International* 423, 279–302.

Loi, C. (2012) Le corde di lino per archi fra etnografia e sperimentazione archeologica. *Tiro con l'arco tradizionale* 1, 82–85.

Long, D.J., Milburn, P., Bunting, M.J., Tipping, R. and Holden, T.G. (1999) Black henbane (*Hyoscyamus niger* L.) in the Scottish Neolithic: A re-evaluation of palynological findings from Grooved Ware pottery at Balfarg Riding School and henge, Fife. *Journal of Archaeological Science* 26 (1), 45–52.

Long, D.J., Tipping, R., Holden, T.G., Bunting, M.J. and Milburn, P. (2000) The use of henbane (*Hyoscyamus niger* L.) as a hallucinogen at Neolithic 'ritual' sites: A re-evaluation. *Antiquity* 74 (283), 49–53.

Lowe, J.J., Accorsi, C.A., Bandini Mazzanti, M., Bishop, A., Van Der Kaars, S., Forlani, L., Mercuri, A.M., Rivalenti, C., Torri, P. and Watson, C. (1996) Pollen stratigraphy of sediment sequences from lakes Albano and Nemi (near Rome) and from the central Adriatic, spanning the interval from oxygen isotope Stage 2 to the present day. In P. Guilizzoni and F. Oldfield (eds) *Palaeoenvironmental Analysis of Italian Crater Lake and Adriatic Sediments*, Memorie dell'Istituto Italiano di Idrobiologia 55, 71–98.

Lozovski, V.L. and Lozovskaya, O.V. (2016) New evidence of the fishing economy of Stone Age waterlogged sites in central and north-western Russia: The example of Zamostje 2. In P. Uino and K. Nordqvist (eds) *New Sites, New Methods. Proceedings of the Finnish-Russian Archaeological Symposium, Helsinki 19–21 November 2014*, 85–100. Helsinki, Iskos 21.

Magri, D. (1999) Late-Quaternary vegetation history at Lagaccione near Lago di Bolsena (central Italy). *Review of Palaeobotany and Palynology* 106, 171–208.

Magri, D. and Sadori, L. (1999) Late Pleistocene and Holocene pollen stratigraphy at Lago di Vico, central Italy. *Vegetation History and Archaeobotany* 8, 247–260.

Magri, D., Celant, A. and Di Rita, F. (2019) The vanished *Alnus*-dominated forests along the Tyrrhenian coast. *Catena* 182, 104136. [https://doi.org/10.1016/j.catena.2019.104136]

Maniatis, Y. and Adaktylou, F. (2021) Revenia-Korinos: One of the earliest Neolithic settlements in north Greece as evidenced by radiocarbon dating. *Radiocarbon* 63(3), 1025–1051. [https://doi.org/10.1017/RDC.2021.26]

Maninnen, M. (2014) *Culture, Behaviour, and the 8200 cal BP Cold Event. Organisational Change and Culture-environment Dynamics in Late Mesolithic Northern Fennoscandia.* Helsinki, Monographs of the Archaeological Society of Finland 4.

Mantero, D. (1993) Rinvenimenti preistorici in località Arrone-La Torre, Anguillara Sabazia (RM): considerazioni su una stratigrafia lacustre del lago di Bracciano. *Origini* 17, 107–124.

Marangou, C. (1991) Maquettes d'embarcations: les débuts (Boat models: the beginnings of navigation). In R. Laffineur (ed.), *Thalassa. L'Egée préhistorique et la mer. Actes de la 3e Rencontre Internationale de l'Université de Liège, Calvi (Corse)*, 21–42, Liège, Aegaeum 7.

Marangou, C. (1996) Assembling, displaying, and dissembling Neolithic and Eneolithic figurines and models. *Journal of European Archaeology* 4(1), 177–202. [https://doi.org/10.1179/096576696800688169]

Marangou, C. (2001) Neolithic craft: Evidence about boat types and uses. In Y. Bassiakos, E. Aloupi and Y. Facorellis (eds) *Archaeometry Issues in Greek Prehistory and Antiquity.*, 737–751. Athens, Hellenic Society of Archaeometry.

Marciniak, A., Barański, M.Z., Bayliss, A., Czerniak, L., Goslar, T., Southon, J. and Taylor, R.E. (2015) Fragmenting times: Interpreting a Bayesian chronology for the Late Neolithic occupation of Çatalhöyük East, Turkey. *Antiquity* 89, 154–176. [https://doi.org/10.15184/aqy.2014.33]

Marinova, E. (2009) Archaeobotanical materials from the Neolithic site Ohoden-Valoga. Structure 1 and Grave 1. In G. Ganetsovski (ed.) *Ohoden. A Site from the Early Neolithic, Excavations 2002–2006*, 76–80. Sofia, Craft House Bulgaria.

Marinova, E. and Riehl, S. (2009) *Carthamus* species in the ancient Near East and south-eastern Europe: archaeobotanical evidence for their distribution and use as a source of oil. *Vegetation History and Archaeobotany* 18, 341–349. [https ://doi.org/10.1007/s00334-009-0212-z]

Marinova, E., Filipovic, D., Obradović, D. and Allué, E. (2013) Wild plant resources and land use in Mesolithic and Early Neolithic south-east Europe Archaeobotanical evidence from the Danube Catchment of Bulgaria and Serbia. *Offa* 69/70, 467–478.

Märkle, T. and Rösch, M. (2008) Experiments on the effects of carbonization on some cultivated plant seeds. *Vegetation History and Archaeobotany* 1 (Suppl. 1), 257–263. [https://doi.org/10.1007/s00334-008-0165-7]

Marshall, D.M. (2005) Archaeological pollen: Extraction from ancient resins. 38th Annual Meeting American Association of Stratigraphic Palynologists. September 18–21, St. Louis, Missouri. Abstract 34.

Martí, M., Pou, R. and Carlús, X. (1997) *Excavacions a la Ronda Sud de Granollers, 1994. La necròpolis del neolític mitjà i les restes romanes del Camí de Can Grau (la Roca del Vallès, Vallès Oriental). Els jaciments de Cal Jardiner (Granollers, Vallès Oriental).* Barcelona, Generalitat de Catalunya. Departament de Cultura, Excavacions Arqueològiques a Catalunya 14.

Martin, L. (2015) Plant economy and territory exploitation in the Alps during the Neolithic (5000–4200 cal BC): First results of archaeobotanical studies in the Valais (Switzerland). *Vegetation History and Archaeobotany* 24, 63–73.

Martinelli, N. (1993) Indagini dendrocronologiche. Nota preliminare. *Bullettino di Paletnologia Italiana* 84 (2), 317–322.

Masclans, A. (2020) *Use-wear Analyses of Polished and Bevelled Stone Artefacts during the Sepulcres de Fossa/Pit Burials Horizon (NE Iberia, c. 4000–3400 cal B.C.).* Oxford, British Archaeological Report S2972.

Masclans, A., Palomo, A., Gibaja, J.F., Remolins, G. and Gómez, D. (2017) Use-wear analysis of Neolithic polished axes and adzes: The site of 'Bòbila Madurell- Can Gambús 1–2' (North east of the Iberian Peninsula). *Quaternary International* 427, 158–174.

Mazare, N.P. (2012) The Craft of Textile Production at the Neolithic and Eneolithic Communities in Transylvania. Unpublished PhD thesis, University of Alba Iulia.

Mazzucco, N. and Gibaja, J.F. (2018) A paleoeconomic perspective on the Early Neolithic lithic assemblages of the N-NE of the Iberian Peninsula. *Quaternary International* 472, 236–245. [https://doi.org/10.1016/j.quaint.2016.05.012]

Mazzucco, N., Gassin, B., Gibaja, J.F. and Palomo, A. (2012) Microliths use in western Mediterranean during VI-V millenium BC. *Rubricatum* 5, 129–136.

Mazzucco, N., Clemente-Conte, I., Gassiot, E. and Gibaja, J.F. (2015) Insights into the economic organization of the first agro-pastoral communities of the NE of the Iberian Peninsula: a traceological analysis of the Cueva de Chaves flaked stone assemblage. *Journal of Archaeological Science: Reports* 2, 353–366. [https://doi.org/10.1016/j.jasrep.2015.02.010]

Mazzucco, N., Ibáñez, J.J., Capuzzo, G., Gassin, B., Mineo, M. and Gibaja, J.F. (2020) Migration, adaptation, innovation: The spread of Neolithic harvesting technologies in the Mediterranean. *Plos One* 15 (4), e0232455. [https://doi.org/10.1371/journal.pone.0235874]

Mazzucco, N., Mineo, M., Arobba, D., Caramiello, R., Caruso, L., Gassin, B., Guilbeau, D., Ibáñez, J.J., Morandi, L.F., Mozota, M., Pichon, F., Portillo, M., Rageot, M., Remolins, G., Rottoli, M. and Gibaja, J.F. (2022a) Multiproxy study of 7500-year-old wooden sickles from the Lakeshore Village of La Marmotta, Italy. *Scientific Reports* 12, 14976. [https://doi.org/10.1038/s41598-022-18597-8]

Mazzucco, N., Sabanov, A., Antolín, F., Naumov, G., Fidanoski, L. and Gibaja, J.F. (2022b) The spread of agriculture in south-eastern Europe: New data from North Macedonia. *Antiquity* 96 (385), 15–33. [doi:10.15184/1qy.2021.32]

Meadow, R.H., Kenoyer, J.M. and Wright, R.P (1998) Harappa Archaeological Research Project: Harappa Excavations 1998. Karachi, unpublished report submitted to the Director General of Archaeology and Museums, Government of Pakistan, Karachi.

Médard, F. (2003) Vestiges textiles et activités de filage sur le site néolithique d'Arbon-Bleiche 3 (TG Suisse). *Bulletin de la Société préhistorique française* 100 (2), 375–391.

Mehra, K.L., Kanodia, K.C. and Srivastava, R.N. (1975) Folk uses of plants for adornment in India. *Economic Botany* 29, 39–46.

Meiklejohn, C., Roksandic, M., Jackes, M. and Lubell, D. (2009) Radiocarbon dating of the Mesolithic human remains in Portugal. *Mesolithic Miscellany* 20 (1), 4–16.

Mercuri, A.M., Accorsi, C.A. and Bandini Mazzanti, M. (2002) The long history of Cannabis and its cultivations by the Romans in central Italy, shows by pollen records from Lago Albano and Lago di Nemi. *Vegetation History and Archaeobotany* 11, 263–276.

Merino, J.M. (1986) *La pesca desde la prehistoria hasta nuestros días*. Vitoria, Servicio central de Publicaciones del Gobierno Vasco.

Micheli, R. (2021) Similarities and differences between Italian Early Neolithic groups: The role of personal ornaments. *Open Archaeology* 7 (1), 1274–1294. [https://doi.org/10.1515/opar-2020-0194]

Micheli, R., Bassetti, M., Degasperi, N., Fozzati, L., Martinelli, N. and Rottoli, M. (2018) Nuove ricerche al Palù di Livenza: lo scavo del Settore 3. In E. Borgna, P. Cassola Guida and S. Corazza (eds) *Preistoria e Protostoria del Caput Adriae, Studi di Preistoria e Protostoria* 5, 481–490. Firenze, IIPP.

Mineo, M. (2015) Monossili d'Europa. costruite anche per le rotte marine? Ubi minor… Le isole minori del Mediterraneo centrale dal Neolitico ai primi contatti coloniali, Convegno di Studi in ricordo di Giorgio Buchner, a 100 anni dalla nascita (1914–2014). *Scienze dell'Antichità* 22 (2), 453–473.

Mineo, M. (2018) Asentamientos neolíticos lacustres en el área mediterránea central y en la región alpina. In *La revolución neolítica: La Draga, el poblado de los prodigios*, 35-54. Madrid, Museo Arqueológico Regional.

Mineo, M. (2019) Tessiture e intrecci. In *Trame di storia. Metodi e strumenti dell'archeologia sperimentale. Archeofest 2017*, 119–146. Roma, E.S.S. Editorial Service System.

Moore, P.D., Webb, J.A. and Collinson, M.E. (1991) *Pollen Analysis* (2nd edn). Oxford, Blackwell.

Morandi, L.F. (2018) Parasite ova and cysts. In S. López-Varela (ed.) *The Encyclopedia of Archaeological Science*, 1–4. Chichester, Wiley.

Moutsiou, T, Reepmeyer, C., Kassianidou, V., Zomeni, Z. and Agapiou, A. (2021) Modelling the Pleistocene colonisation of Eastern Mediterranean islandscapes. *Plos One* 16(10), e0258370. [https://doi.org/10.1371/journal.pone.0258370]

Mozota, M. and Gibaja, J.F. (2015) 'For a few awls more'. Bone tools in northeastern Iberia Neolithic burials (4th–5th millennia cal BC). A morpho-technical and functional approach. *Journal of Archaeological Science Reports* 4, 65–77. [https://doi.org/10.1016/j.jasrep.2015.08.023]

Mueller Epstein, E. (2017) Games, exchange, and stone: Hunter-gatherer beads at home. In D. Bar-Yosef Mayer, C. Bonsall and A.M. Choyke (eds) *Not Just for Show: The archaeology of beads, beadwork and personal ornaments*, 81–94. Oxford, Oxbow Books.

Muntoni, I.M., Delluniversità, E., Allegretta, I., Terzano, R. and Eramo, G. (2021) Chert sources and Early to Middle Neolithic exploitation in the Tavoliere (northern Apulia, Italy). *Quaternary International* 615, 43–65. [doi.org/10.1016/j.quaint.2021.01.016]

Myking, T., Hertzerb, A. and Skrøppa, T. (2005) History, manufacture and properties of lime bast cordage in northern Europe. *Forestry* 78 (1), 65–71.

Nadel, D., Danin, A., Werker, E., Schick, T., Kislev, M.E. and Stewart, K. (1994) 19,000-year-old twisted fibers from Ohalo II. *Current Anthropology* 35, 451–457.

Nanoglou, S. (2009) Animal bodies and ontological discourse in the Greek Neolithic. *Journal of Archaeological Method and Theory* 16, 184–204. [https://doi.org/10.1007/s10816-009-9069-9]

Naumov, G. (2020) Neolithic wetland and lakeside settlements in the Balkans. In A Hafner, E. Dolbunova, A. Mazurkevich, E. Pranckenaite and M. Hinz (eds) *Settling Waterscapes in Europe: The archaeology of Neolithic & Bronze Age pile-dwellings*, 111–135. Heidelberg, Heidelberg University Library.

Neumann, K., Strömberg, A.E.C., Ball, T.B., Albert, R.M., Vrydaghs, L. and Scott-Cummings, L. (2019) International code for phytolith nomenclature (ICPN) 2.0. *Annals of Botany* 124 (2), 189–199.

Neuweiler, E. (1935) Nachträge urgeschichtlicher Pflanzen. *Vierteljahrsschrift der Naturfoschenden Gesellchaft Zürich* 80, 98–122.

Nilhamn, B., Astruc, L. and Gulon, A. (2009) White ware – Near Eastern plaster container. In L. Astruc, A. Gaulon, and L. Salanova (eds) *Méthodes d'approche des premières productions céramiques: étude de cas dans les Balkans et au Levant. Table-ronde de la Maison de l'Archéologie et de l'Ethnologie (Nanterre, France) 28 février 2006*, 63–72. Rahden/Westfahlen, Marie Leidorf.

Oeggl, K. (2009) The significance of the Tyrolean Iceman for the archaeobotany of Central Europe. *Vegetation History and Archaeobotany* 18(1), 1–11.

Oeggl, K. and Schoch, W. (2000) Dendrological analyses of artefacts and other remains. In S. Bortenschlager and K. Oeggl (eds) *The Iceman and his Natural Environment.*, 29–61. Vienna, Springer, The Man in the Ice 4 [https://doi.org/10.1007/978-3-7091-6758-8_4]

Orchard, W.C. (1975) *Beads and Beadwork of the American Indians.* New York, Museum of the American Indian, Heye Foundation. [https://doi.org/10.5479/sil.75634.39088016090508]

Özdogan, M. (2008) Westward expansion of the Neolithic way of life: Sorting the Neolithic Package into distinct packages. In P. Matthiae, F. Pinnock, L. Nigro and N. Marchett (eds) *Proceedings of the 6th International Congress on the Archaeology of the Ancient Near East, May 5th–10th, 2008*, 883–897. Wiesbaden Harrassowitz, Sapienza Università di Roma.

Palmisano, A., Bevan, A., Lawrence, D. and Shennan, S. (2022) The NERD Dataset: Near East radiocarbon dates between 15,000 and 1,500 cal. yr. BP. *Journal of Open Archaeology Data* 10, 2. [http://doi.org/10.5334/joad.90]

Palomo, A., Gibaja, J.F., Pique, R. and Bosch, A. (2011) Harvesting cereals and other plants in Neolithic Iberia: The assemblage from the lake settlement at La Draga. *Antiquity* 85, 759–771.

Paris, R.R. and Moyse, H. (1981) *Matière Médicale* Vol. 2. Paris, Masson.

Peintner, U., Poder, R. and Pumpel, T. (1998) The Iceman's fungi. *Mycological Research* 102, 1153–1162.

Pelegrin, J. (1988) Débitage expérimental par pression, 'du plus petit au plus grand'. In J. Tixier (ed.) *Technologie préhistorique*, 37–53. Paris. Éditions du CNRS, URA 28.

Pelegrin, J. (2012) New experimental observations for the characterization of pressure blade production techniques. In P.M. Desrosiers (ed.) *The Emergence of Pressure Blade Making. From Origin to Modern Experimentation*, 465–500. New York, Springer.

Peresani, M., Fiore, I., Gala, M., Romandini, M. and Tagliacozzo, A. (2011) Late Neandertals and the intentional removal of feathers as evidenced from bird bone taphonomy at Fumane Cave 44 ky B.P., Italy. *Proceedings of the National Academy of Science* 108 (10), 3888–3893. [https://doi.org/10.1073/pnas.1016212108]

Peresani, M., Vanhaeren, M., Quaggiotto, E., Queffelec, A. and d'Errico, F. (2013) An ochered fossil marine shell from the Mousterian of Fumane Cave, Italy. *PlosOne* 8, 7. [https://doi.org/10.1371/journal.pone.0068572]

Perini, R. (1987) *Scavi archeologici nella zona palafitticola di Fiavé-Carera. Parte II. Campagne 1969–1976.* Trento, Servizio Beni Culturali della Provinzia Autonoma di Trento.

Perlès, C. (1995) La transition Pléistocène/Holocène et le problème du Mésolithique en Grèce. In V. Villaverde (ed.) *Los últimos cazadores. Transformaciones culturales y económicas durante el Tardiglaciar y el inicio del Holoceno en el ámbito mediterráneo*, 179–209. Alicante, Instituto de Cultura Juan Gil-Albert, Diputación de Alicante.

Perlès, C. (2001) *The Early Neolithic in Greece*. Cambridge, Cambridge World Archaeology.

Perlès, C. (2005) From the Near East to Greece: Let's reverse the focus. Cultural elements that didn't transfer. In C. Lichter (ed.) *How did Farming Reach Europe? Anatolian–European Relations from the Second Half of the 7th through the First Half of the 6th Millennium cal BC*, 275–290. Istanbul, Ege Yayınları, BYZAS 2.

Perlès, C. (2018) *Ornaments and Other Ambiguous Artifacts from Franchthi. The Palaeolithic and the Mesolithic* 1. Bloomington IN, Indiana University Press.

Perrin, T. and Manen, C. (2021) Potential interactions between Mesolithic hunter-gatherers and Neolithic farmers in the Western Mediterranean: The geochronological data revisited. *PlosOne* 16(3), e0246964. [https://doi.org/10.1371/journal.pone.0246964]

Pessina, A. and Tiné, V. (2010) *Archeologia del Neolitico. L'Italia tra VI e IV milenio a.C.* Roma, Carocci.

Petrequin, P. and Petrequin, A.M. (1988) *Le Néolithique des Lacs. Préhistoire des lacs de Chalain et de Clairvaux (4000-2000 av. J.-C.)*. Paris, Editions Errance Collection des Hespérides.

Petrinelli Pannocchia, C. and Vassanelli, A. (2021) The first Italian farmers: The role of stone ornaments in tradition, innovation, and cultural change. *Open Archaeology* 7 (1), 1398–1424. [https://doi.org/10.1515/opar-2020-0175]

Pickard, C. and Bonsall, C. (2007) Late Mesolithic coastal fishing practices. The evidence from Tybrind Vig, Denmark. In K. Jennbert, B. Hårdh and D. Olausson (eds) *On the Road. Studies in honour of Lars Larsson*, 176–183. Lund, Almqvist & Wiksell.

Piezonka, H., Nedomolkina, N., Elberfeld, V., Heußner, K.-U., Kirleis, W., Lorenz, S. and Wieckowska-Lüth, M. (2020) Pile dwellers in the Sukhona basin? Wooden structures of the 4th and 3rd millennium cal BC at Veksa, Northern Russia. In A. Hafner, E. Dolbunova, A. Mazurkevich, E. Pranckenaite and M. Hinz (eds) *Settling Waterscapes in Europe: The archaeology of Neolithic & Bronze Age pile-dwellings*, 59–93. Heidelberg, Heidelberg University Library.

Pignatti, E., Pignatti, S., D'Angeli, D., De Nicola, C., Maffei, L., Testi, A. and Tinelli, A. (2015) The Laurisilva as a cultural heritage: Proposal for the protection of the relict of laurel forest near Ponte Renaro. *Rendiconti Lincei, Scienze Fisiche e Naturali* 26 (Suppl. 3), S643–S649.

Piličiauskas, G., Pranckenaite, E., Peseckas, K., Mazeika, J. and Matuzeviciute, S. (2020) Ancient logboats in Lithuania: New finds, wood taxa and chronology. *Radiocarbon* 62 (5), 1299–1315.

Piperno, D.R. (2006) *Phytoliths: A comprehensive guide for archaeologists and paleoecologists*. Lanham MD, Altamira Press.

Piqué, R., Revelles, J., Berihuete-Azorín, M., Lladó, J. G., Palomo, A. and Terradas, X. (2020) Use of fungi for tinder at the Early Neolithic settlement of La Draga (NE Iberia). *Quaternary International* 541, 152–161. [https://doi.org/10.1016/j.quaint.2019.12.002]

Piqué, R., Romero, S., Palomo, A., Tarrús, J., Terradas, X. and Bogdanovic, I. (2018) The production and use of cordage at the early Neolithic site of La Draga (Banyoles, Spain). *Quaternary International* 468, 262–270. [http://dx.doi.org/10.1016/j.quaint.2016.05.024]

Piqué, R., Palomo, A., Terradas, X., Tarrús, J., Buxó, R., Bosch, A., Chinchilla, J., Bodganovic, I., Lopez, O. and Saña, M. (2015) Characterizing prehistoric archery: technical and functional analyses of the Neolithic bows from La Draga (NE Iberian Peninsula). *Journal of Archaeological Science* 55, 166–173.

Popova, T. (2016) Bread remains in archaeological contexts. In K Bacvarov and R. Gleser (eds) *Southeast Europe and Anatolia in Prehistory. Essays in Honor of Vassil Nikolov on his 65th Anniversary*, 519–526. Bon, Habelt.

Portillo, M., Bofill, M., Molist, M. and Albert, R.M. (2013) Phytolith and usewear functional evidence for grinding stones from the Near East. In P.C. Anderson, C., Cheval, A. Durand (eds) *Regards croisés sur les outils liés au travail des végétaux. An interdisciplinary focus on plant working tools*, 161–174, Antibes, APDCA.

Portillo, M., Kadowaki, S., Nishiaki, Y. and Albert, R.M. (2014) Early Neolithic household behavior at Tell Seker al-Aheimar (Upper Khabur, Syria): A comparison to ethnoarchaeological study of phytoliths and dung spherulites. *Journal of Archaeological Science* 42, 107–118.

Portillo, M., Llergo, Y., Ferrer, A. and Albert, R.M. (2017) The impact of cereal-processing in phytoliths and pollen using an experimental approach. *Vegetation History and Archaeobotany* 26, 59–74.

Prendi, E. (2018) *The Prehistoric Settlement of Maliq*. Tirana, Academy of Albanological Studies, Institute of Archaeology.

Punt, W. (1984) Umbelliferae. *Review of Palaeobotany and Palynology* 42, 155–364.

Radi, G. and Danese, E. (2003) L'abitato di Colle Santo Stefano di Ortucchio (L'Aquila). In *Atti della XXXVI Riunione Scientifica IIPP, Preistoria e Protostoria dell'Abruzzo, Chieti-Celano, 27–30 settembre 2001 IIPP*, 145–161. Firenze, Istituto Italiano di Preistoria e Protostoria.

Radi, G. and Petrinelli, C.P. (2018) The beginning of the Neolithic era in Central Italy. *Quaternary International* 470, 270–284. [https://doi.org/10.1016/j.quaint.2017.06.063]

Radi, G. and Ronchitelli, A. (2002) Le industrie litiche. In M.A. Fugazzola Delpino, A. Pessina and V. Tiné (eds) *Le ceramiche impresse nel Neolitico antico, Italia e Mediterraneo*, 251–268. Roma, Istituto Poligrafico e Zecca dello Stato.

Ramminger, B. (2007) *Wirtschaftsarchäologische Untersuchungen zu alt- und mittelneolithischen Felsgesteingeräten in Mittel-und Nordhessen (Archäologie und Rohmaterialversorgung*. Rahden/ Westfahlen, Internationale Archäologie 102.

Ramseyer, D. (2000) *Muntelier/Fischergässli. Un habitat néolithique au bord du lac de Morat (3895 à 3820 av. J.C.)*. Fribourg, Archéologie fribourgeoise 15.

Rast-Eicher, A. (2005) Bast bfore wool: The first textiles. In P. Bichler, K. Grömer, R. Hofmann-de Keijzer, A. Kern and H. Reschreiter (eds) *Hallstatt Textiles: Technical analysis, scientific investigation and experiment on Iron Age textiles*, 117–131. Oxford, Archaeopress.

Rast-Eicher, A. (2016) *Fibres, Microscopy of Archaeological Textiles and Furs*. Budapest, Archaeolingua Alapitvany.

Rast-Eicher, A., Karg, S. and Jørgensen, L.B. (2021) The use of local fibres for textiles at Neolithic Çatalhöyük. *Antiquity* 95 (383), 1129–1144

Reimer, P.J., Austin, W.E., Bard, E., Bayliss, A., Blackwell, P.G., Ramsey, C. B. *et al*. (2020). The IntCal20 Northern Hemisphere radiocarbon age calibration curve (0–55 cal kBP). *Radiocarbon* 62 (4), 725–757.

Reingruber, A., Toufexis, G., Kyparissi-Apostolika, N., Anetakis, M., Maniatis, Y. and Facorellis, Y. (2017) Neolithic Thessaly: Radiocarbon dated periods and phases. *Documenta Praehistorica* 44, 34–53. [https://doi.org/10.4312/dp.44.3]

Riding, J.B. (2021) A guide to preparation protocols in palynology. *Palynology* 45 (1), 1–108.

Rieck, F. and Crumlin-Pedersen, O. (1988) *Bådc fra Danmarks oldtid*. Roskilde, Vikingeskibshallen.

Rivollat, M., Jeong, C., Schiffels, S., Küçükkalıpçı, İ., Pemonge, M.H., Rohrlach, A.B. and Haak, W. (2020) Ancient genome-wide DNA from France highlights the complexity of interactions between Mesolithic hunter-gatherers and Neolithic farmers. *Science advances* 6(22), eaaz5344. [https://doi.org/10.1126/sciadv.aaz5344]

Robinson, M. and Hubbard, R.N.L.B. (1977) The transport of pollen in the bracts of hulled cereals. *Journal of Archaeological Science* 4, 197–199.

Robson, H.K. (2018) The Star Carr fungi. In N. Milner, C. Conneller and B. Taylor (eds), *Star Carr Volume 2: Studies in Technology, Subsistence and Environmen*t, 437–445. York, White Rose University Press. [https://doi.org/10.22599/book2.q]

Romandini, M., Cristiani, E. and Peresani, E. (2014) A retouched bone shaft from the Late Mousterian at Fumane cave (Italy). Technological, experimental and micro-wear analysis. *Comptes Rendus Palevol* 14 (1), 63–72. [https://doi.org/10.1016/j.crpv.2014.08.001]

Romero, S., Herrero, M., Piqué, R., Rosillo, R., Terradas, X., López, O., Berrocal, A. and Palomo, A. (2021a) Los objetos elaborados con fibras vegetales del Neolítico Antiguo de Coves del Fem, Ulldemolins (Tarragona). *Munibe* 72, 43–56. [https://doi.org/10.21630/maa.2021.72.14]

Romero, S., Piqué, R. and Herrero, M. (2021b) The basketry at the early Neolithic site of La Draga (Banyoles, Spain). *Journal of Archaeological Science Reports* 35, 102692. [https://doi.org/10.1016/j.jasrep.2020.102692]

Ronchitelli, A.-M. (1983) L'industria litica dell'area β. In S. Tiné (ed.) *Passo di Corvo e la civilta neolitica del Tavoliere*, 101–122. Genova, Sagep Editrice.

Rottoli, M. (1993) 'La Marmotta', Anguillara Sabazia (RM). Scavi 1989, Analisi paletnobotaniche: prime risultanze. In M.A. Fugazzola Delpino, G.D'Eugenio and A. Pessina (eds) 'La Marmotta' (Anguillara Sabazia, RM). Scavi 1989. Un abitato perilacustre di età neolitica. *Bullettino di Paletnologia Italiana* Nuova Serie 2, 84, 305–315.

Rottoli, M. (2002) Zafferanone selvatico (*Carthamus lanatus*) e cardo della Madonna (*Silybum marianum*), piante raccolte o coltivate nel Neolitico antico a 'La Marmotta'?. *Bulletino di Paletnologia Italiana* 91–92, 41–61.

Rottoli, M. (2006) Alcuni aspetti dell'agricoltura neolitica nell'Italia settentrionale. *Atti della Societa dei Naturalisti e Matematici di Modena* 137, 243–254.

Rottoli, M. and Pessina, A. (2007) Neolithic agriculture in Italy: an update of archaeobotanical data with particular emphasis on northern settlements. In S. College and J. Conolly (eds.) *The Origins and Spread of Domestic Plants in Southwest Asia and Europe*, 141–153. Walnut Creek CA, Left Coast Press.

Roussel, B. (2005) *La production du feu par percussion de la pierre. Prehistoire, Ethnographie, Experimentation*. Montagnac, Editions Monique Mergoil.

Roy, A.S. (2020) The use and significance of Early Bronze Age stone battle-axes and axe-hammers from northern Britain and the Isle of Man. *Proceedings of the Prehistoric Society* 86, 237–260.

Sadori, L. (2018) The Lateglacial and Holocene vegetation and climate history of Lago di Mezzano (central Italy). *Quaternary Science Reviews* 202, 30–44.

Sadori, L., Jahns, S. and Peyron, O. (2011) Mid-Holocene vegetation history of the central Mediterranean. *The Holocene* 21 (1), 117–129.

Salavert, A. (2010) Le pavot (*Papaver somniferum*) à la fin du 6e millénaire av. J.-C. en Europe occidentale. *Anthropobotanica* 1, 3–16.

Salavert, A., Zazzo, A., Martin, L., Antolín, F., Gauthier, C., Thil, F., Tombret, O., Bouby, L., Manen, C., Mineo, M., Mueller-Bieniek, A., Piqué, R., Rottoli, M., Rovira, N., Toulemonde, F. and Vostrovská, I. (2020) Direct dating reveals the early history of opium poppy in western Europe. *Scientific Reports* 10(1), 20263. [https://doi.org/10.1038/s41598-020-76924-3]

Sampson, A. (2014) The Mesolithic of the Aegean Basin. In C. Manen, T. Perrin and J. Guilaine (eds) *La transition néolithique en Méditerranée. Comment des chasseurs devinrent agriculteur*, 189–207. Toulouse, Errance.

Sampson, A., Kaczanowska, M. and Kozłowski, J.K. (2012) Mesolithic occupations and environments on the island of Ikaria, Aegean, Greece. *Folia Quaternaria* 80, 5–40.

Samuel, D. (1996) Investigation of ancient Egyptian baking and brewing methods by correlative microscopy. *Science* 273, 488–490.

Scheuermeier, P. (1980) *Il lavoro dei contadini*. Milano, Longanesi.

Schick, T. (1986) Perishable remains from the Nahal Hemar Cave. *Israel Prehistoric Society* 1986, 95–97.

Schlichtherle, H., Hafner, A. and Borrello, M.A. (2013) Les villages préhistoriques des bords des lacs circumalpins entre le ve et le IVe millénaire av. J.-C. In. M.A. Borrello (ed.) *Les hommes préhistoriques et les Alpes*, 69–84. Oxford, British Archaeological Report S2476.

Searcy, M.T. (2011) *The Life-Giving Stone: Ethnoarchaeology of Maya Metates*. Tucson AZ, University of Arizona Press.

Shennan, S. (2018) *The First Farmers of Europe: An evolutionary perspective*. Cambridge, Cambridge World Archaeology

Sherratt, A.G. (1981) Plough and pastoralism: Aspects of the Secondary Products Revolution. In I. Hodder, G. Isaac and N. Hammond (eds) *Pattern of the Past*, 261–306. Cambridge, Cambridge University Press

Silvestrini, M. and Pignocchi, G. (1998) La neolitizzazione lungo l'Adriatico: le Marche. In A. Pessina and G. Muscio (eds) *Settemila anni fa il primo pane. Ambiente e culture delle società neolitiche*, 71–77. Udine, Comune di Udine, Museo Friulano di Storia Naturale.

Simmons, A. (2014) Akrotiri-Aetokremnos (Cyprus) 20 years later: An assessment of its significance. In A.J. Ammerman and T. Davis (eds) *An Island Archaeology and the Origins of Seafaring in the Eastern Mediterranean*, 139–156. *Eurasian Prehistory* 10 (1–2).

Simone, L. (1977–1982) Il villaggio neolitico della Villa Comunale di Foggia. *Origini* 11, 129–160.

Sobkowiak-Tabaka, I. and Kufel-Diakowska, B. (2019) The shining piece of the puzzle: Evidence of plant use in the Late Palaeolithic. *Archaeological and Anthropological Sciences* 11 (4), 1373–1389.

Sofronidou, M. (2008) The prehistoric lakeside settlement of Dispilio, Kastoria: A first introduction. *Anaskamma* 1, 10–25.

Spataro, M. (2002) *The First Farming Communities of the Adriatic: Pottery production and circulation in the Early and Middle Neolithic*. Trieste, Quaderni della Società per la preistoria e protostoria della regione Friuli-Venezia Giulia 9.

Spindler, K. (1995) *The Man in the Ice: the discovery of a 5.000-year-old body reveals the secrets of the Stone Age*. New York, Crown Publishers.

Stockmar, J. (1971) Tablets with spores used in absolute pollen analysis. *Pollen et Spores* 13 (4), 615–621.

Stoddart, S., Woodbridge, J., Palmisano, A., Mercuri, A.M., Mensing, S.A., Colomaroli, D., Sadori, L., Magri, D., Di Rita, F., Giardini, M., Mariotti, M., Montanari, C., Bellini, C., Florenzano, A., Torri, P., Bevan, A., Shennan, S., Fyfe, R. and Roberts, N. (2019) Tyrrenian central Italy: Holocene population and landscape ecology. *The Holocene* 29 (5), 761–775.

Tagliacozzo, A. (2005) Animal exploitation in the Early Neolithic in central-southern Italy. *Munibe* 57, 429–439.

Tarantini, M. and Galiberti, A. (2011) *Le miniere di selce del Gargano, VI–III millennio a.C. Alle origini della storia mineraria europea.* Borgo S. Lorenzo, Rassegna di Archeologia – Preistoria e Protostoria 24.

Tasca, G. (2019) Analisi de reperti concotti. In G. Steffè and N. Degasperi, N. (eds) *Il villaggio Neolitico di Lugo di Romagna Fornace Gattelli. Strutture Ambiente Culture*, 237–278. Firenze, Origines, Istituto Italiano di Preistoria et Protostoria.

Tichý, R. (2016) The earliest maritime voyaging in the Mediterranean: View from sea. Živá Archeologie – Rea 18, 26–36.

Tinè, V. (2009) Strutture a fossa/e con intonaci. In V. Tiné (ed.) *Favella. Un villaggio neolitico nella Sibaritide, Roma*, 99–172. Roma, Studi di Paletnologia 3.

Toderaş, M., Hansen, S., Reingruber, A. and Wunderlich, J. (2009) Pietrele-Măgura Gorgana: o aşezare eneolitică la Dunărea de Jos între 4500 şi 4250 î.e.n.. *Materiale şi cercetări arheologice* Serie nouă 5 (1), 39–90.

Tozzi, C. and Zamagni, B. (2003) *Gli scavi nel villaggio neolitico di Catignano (1971–1980)*. Firenze, Origines, Istituto Italiano di Preistoria et Protostoria.

Traverse, A. (2007) Palynological laboratory techniques. In A. Traverse (ed.) *Paleopalynology*, 615–813. Cham, Springer.

Tsartsidou, G., Lev-Yadun, S., Albert, R., Rosen, A.M., Efstratiou, N. and Weiner, S. (2007) The phytolith archaeological record: Strengths and weaknesses evaluated based on a quantitative modern reference collection from Greece. *Journal of Archaeological Science* 34, 1262–1275.

Valamoti, S.M., Moniaki, A. and Karathanou, A. (2011) An investigation of processing and consumption of pulses among prehistoric societies: archaeobotanical, experimental and ethnographic evidence from Greece. *Vegetation History and Archaeobotany* 20, 381–396.

Valamoti, S.M., Samuel, D., Baryam, M. and Marinova, E. (2008) Prehistoric cereal foods from Greece and Bulgaria: Investigation of starch microstructure in experimental and archaeological charred remains. *Vegetation History and Archaeobotany* 17, 265–276.

Valamoti, S.M., Petridou, C., Berihuete-Azorín, M., Stika, H.P., Papadopoulou, L. and Mimi, I.A. (2021) Deciphering ancient 'recipes' from charred cereal fragments: An integrated methodological approach using experimental, ethnographic and archaeological evidence. *Journal of Archaeological Science* 128, 105347. [https://doi.org/10.1016/j.jas.2021.105347]

Valamoti, S.M., Marinova, E., Heiss, A.G., Hristova, I., Petridou, C., Popova, T., Michou, S., Chrysostomou, L.P.P., Iliev, P.D.D.G.S., Kotsos, S., Koukouli-Chrysanthaki, C., Leshtakov, K., Malamidou, D., Merousis, N., Nikolov, V., Nikov, K., Panayotova, K., Papanthimou, A., Popov, H., Stefani, L., Tsirtsoni, Z., Ruseva, T.K. (2019) Prehistoric cereal foods of southeastern Europe: An archaeobotanical exploration. *Journal of Archaeological Science* 104, 97–113.

Van Gijn, A. (1989) *The Wear and Tear of Flint. Principles of Functional Analysis Applied to Dutch Neolithic Assemblages. Analecta Praehistorica Leidensia* 22.

Van Gijn, A. (2017) Bead biographies from Neolithic burial contexts: Contributions from the microscope. In D. Bar-Yosef Mayer, C. Bonsall and A.M. Choyke (eds) *Not Just for Show: The archaeology of beads, beadwork and personal ornaments*, 103–114. Oxford, Oxbow Books.

Vanhaeren, M. (2005) Speaking with beads: The evolutionary significance of bead making and use. In d'Errico, F. and Backwell, L. (eds) *From Tools to Symbols from Early Hominids to Modern Humans*, 525–555. Johannesburg, Wits University Press.

Vanhaeren, M., d'Errico, F., Stringer, C., James, S.L., Todd, J.A. and Mienis, H.K. (2006) Middle Palaeolithic shell beads in Israel and Algeria. *Science* 312, 1785–-1788. [https://www.science.org/doi/10.1126/science.1128139]

Vasic, M., Siebrecht, M., Tsoraki, C. and Veropoulidou, R. (2021) Beads and pendants in life and death: Insights into the production, use and deposition of ornamental technologies at Çatalhöyük. In I. Hodder, (ed) *The Matter of Çatalhöyük: Reports from the 2009–2017 seasons. Çatalhöyük Research project 14*, 215–247. Cambridge, British Institute at Ankara.

Vaughan, P. (1985) *Use-wear Analysis of Flaked Stone Tools*. Tucson AZ, University of Arizona Press.

Verhoeven, M. (2011) The birth of a concept and the origins of the Neolithic: A history of prehistoric farmers in the Near East. *Paléorient* 37 (1), 75–87.

Vierra, B.J. and Carvalho, A.F. (2019) The Mesolithic–Neolithic transition: The view from Southwest Europe and the American Southwest. *Quaternary International* 515, 208–224. [https://doi.org/10.1016/j.quaint.2017.09.018]

Vigne, J.D. (1998) Contribution des peuplements de vertébrés insulaires à la connaissance de la navigation préhistorique en Méditerranée. In, *Pour qui la Méditerranée au 21éme siècle? Navigation, échanges et environnement en Méditerranée, Actes du colloque scientifique*: 65–76. Montpellier, Maison de l'environnement de Montpellier.

Vigne, J.D. (2009) Introductions et re ́introduction de mammifères à Chypre aux IXe et VIIIe millénaires av. J.-C. (Néolithique précéramique): indices indirects de l'usage de la voile au Néolithique? In *De Méditerranée et d'ailleurs: mélanges offerts à Jean Guilaine,* 807–820. Toulouse., Archives d'Écologie Préhistorique.

Vigne, J.D. and Desse-Berset, N. (1995) The exploitation of animal in the Mediterranean Islands during the Pre-Neolithic: The example of Corsica. In A. Fischer (ed.) *Man and Sea in the Mesolithic: Coastal settlement and below present sea level*, 309–318. Oxford. Oxbow Monograph 53.

Vigne, J.D., Zazzo, A., Cucchi, T., Carrere, I., Briois, F. and Guilaine, J. (2013) The transportation of mammals to Cyprus sheds light on early voyaging and boats in the Mediterranean sea. In A.J. Ammerman and T. Davis (eds) *Island Archaeology and the Origins of Seafaring In the Eastern Mediterranean*, 157–176. *Eurasian Prehistory* 10, part one (1–2).

Vogt, E. (1951) Das Steinzeitliche Uferdorf von Egolzwil 3 (Kt. Luzern). Bericht über die Ausgrabung 1950. *Zeitschrift für Archäologie und Kunstgeschichte* 12, 193–215.

Vuorela, I. (1973) Relative pollen rain around cultivated fields. *Acta Botanica Fennica* 102, 1–27.

Wagstaff, M. and Cherry, J.F. (1982) Settlement and population change. In C. Renfrew, M. Wagstaff (eds) *An Island Polity: The archaeology of exploitation in Melos*, 136–155. Cambridge, Cambridge University Press.

Wandibba, S. (1988) Prehistoric beads in Kenya. *Kenya Past and Present* 20 (1), 17–20.

Watkins, T. (2008) Supra-regional networks in the Neolithic of Southwest Asia. *Journal of World Prehistory* 21, 139–171. [https://doi.org/10.1007/s10963-008-9013-z]

Wentink, K., Van Gijn, A. and Fontijn, D. (2011) Changing contexts, changing meanings: Flint axes in Middle and late Neolithic communities in the northern Netherlands. In V. Davis and M. Edmonds (eds) *Stone Axe Studies III*, 399–408. Oxford, Oxford Books.

Werker, E. (1988) Botanical identification of worked wood remains. In O. Bar-Yosef and D. Alon (eds) Nahal Hemar Cave, *Atiqot* 18, 73–75.

Whitehouse, R. (2014) The chronology of the Neolithic ditched settlements of the Tavoliere and the Ofanto valley. *Accordia Research Papers* 13, 57–77.

Wyss, R. (1994) *Steinzeitliche Bauern auf der Suche nach neuen Lebensformen. Egolzwil 3 und die Egolzwiler Kultur. Band 1: Die Funde*. Zürich, de Gruyter.

Yerkes, R.W. and Barkai, R. (2013) Tree-felling, woodworking, and changing perceptions of the landscape during the Neolithic and Chalcolithic periods in the Southern Levant source. *Current Anthropology* 54 (2), 222–231.

Zeder, M.A. (2008) Domestication and early agriculture in the Mediterranean Basin: Origins, diffusion, and impact. *Proceedings of the National Academy of Science* 19 (105), 11597–11604. [https://doi.org/10.1073/pnas.0801317105]

Zilhão, J. (2007) The emergence of ornaments and art: An archae ological perspective on the origins of 'Behavioral Modernity'. *Journal of Archaeological Research* 15, 1–54. [http://dx.doi.org/10.1007/s10814-006-9008-1]

Zilhão, J. (2014) Early prehistoric navigation in the Western Mediterranean: Implications for the Neolithic transition in Iberia and the Maghreb. In A.J. Ammerman and T. Davis (eds) *Island Archaeology and the Origins of Seafaring In the Eastern Mediterranean* 11, 185–200.

Zhilin, M. and Savchenko, S. (2020) Fishing in the Mesolithic of the Trans-Urals. *Quaternary International* 541, 4–22.

Zohary, D., Hopf, M. and Weiss, E. (2012) *Domestication of Plants in the Old World* (4th edn). Oxford, Oxford University Press.